Surviving the
Death Railway

Surviving the Death Railway

A PoW's Memoir and Letters from Home

Edited by
Hilary Custance Green

Pen & Sword
MILITARY

First published in Great Britain in 2016 by
PEN & SWORD MILITARY
An imprint of
Pen & Sword Books Ltd
47 Church Street
Barnsley
South Yorkshire
S70 2AS

ISBN 978-1-47387-000-0

A CIP catalogue record for this book is available from the British Library.

Typeset by Concept, Huddersfield, West Yorkshire, HD4 5JL.
Printed and bound in England by CPI Group (UK) Ltd, Croydon CR0 4YY.

Pen & Sword Books Ltd incorporates the imprints of Pen & Sword Archaeology, Atlas, Aviation, Battleground, Discovery, Family History, History, Maritime, Military, Naval, Politics, Railways, Select, Social History, Transport, True Crime, and Claymore Press, Frontline Books, Leo Cooper, Praetorian Press, Remember When, Seaforth Publishing and Wharncliffe.

For a complete list of Pen & Sword titles please contact
PEN & SWORD BOOKS LIMITED
47 Church Street, Barnsley, South Yorkshire, S70 2AS, England
E-mail: enquiries@pen-and-sword.co.uk
Website: www.pen-and-sword.co.uk

If it is of any help my son was a jolly natured chap, with wavy auburn hair and a gap between his front teeth ... (Mrs Woodend)

Although there was nothing outstanding in his appearance, the following might be of help he had a tattoo done on his right forearm, it began at the wrist, and went almost to the elbow. It was the figure of a highlander in full national costume, it was coloured and very unusual and would be the first thing to catch the eye. (Mrs Farrell)

[He] was a great lover of birds and animals ... had a great habit of dressing up in foreign clothes and giving his pals a laugh ... I expect he would speak of 'Bonny Oban Bay'. (Mr Sinclair)

Medium build and fresh complexion, just an ordinary healthy young man ... (Mrs Grant)

Contents

Acknowledgements x

Notes to Reader xii

Preface xiii

Timeline xv

Family Tree xvi

Maps xvii

Part One: Barry, Phyllis and 27 Line Section

 1. Britain: Spring 1937 to Spring 1941 3
After the ball, Barry and Phyllis; Honeymoon and war; 27 Line Section created

Part Two: 6,000 Miles East

 2. Britain to Malaya: July to December 1941 15
Dancing on the docks; Singapore and all's well; Wires across the jungle; First casualty

 3. Britain: Late 1941 32
Phyllis in the White House

 4. Malaya: December 1941 34
Japan and the UK at war

 5. Britain: December 1941 to January 1942 38
Phyllis, Robin and rabbits

 6. Malaya: December 1941 to 15 February 1942 44
Last letters home; War in the city; Singapore falls

Part Three: Wall of Silence

 7. Britain: February to March 1942 55
The silence begins

 8. Singapore: February to August 1942 59
Changi; Early deaths

 9. Britain: March to August 1942 63
Writing to a ghost; False comfort

10. Singapore: September 1942 69
Memorial at Bukit Timah

11. Britain: October 1942 73
News for the lucky few

12. Singapore to Thailand (Siam): November 1942 77
To Siam in cattle trucks; Ban Pong, Siam/Thailand; Moving earth, Tamuang to Wang Lan

13. Britain: Late 1942 86
Dreams and plans; Good news?

14. Thailand: December 1942 to March 1943 91
Making and mending, hungrier and thinner

15. Britain: January to March 1943 94
Postmistress, mother, friend and wife

16. Thailand: April 1943 106
Wampo [Wang Pho] Viaduct

17. Britain: Spring 1943 112
The missing story

18. Thailand: Spring 1943 117
Walking, walking, long time walking; North from Wampo; The end of the road, 211k Camp; Beyond the call of duty

19. Britain: Summer 1943 127
Silent summer

20. Thailand: Summer 1943 130
Chungkai, storyteller and lady almoner

21. Britain: November 1943 to February 1944 134
Down to twenty-five words

22. Thailand: Late 1943 to Early 1944 138
Hospital orderly

23. Britain: Spring to Summer 1944 143
Barry is alive

24. Thailand: 1944 147
Clinging to hope in Chungkai; Kongsi

25. Britain: Autumn1944 152
News of the 'hellships'

26. Thailand: Chungkai 1944 157
Chorus girl

27. Britain: December 1944 to May 1945 164
Phyllis and the War Office; Signalman Potter & Signalman Riley

28. Britain: May to August 1945 180
   Delivering bad news

29. Thailand: Early 1945 186
   Bridge over the River Kwai; Barbed wire at Kanchanaburi (Kanburi) camp;
   The last 200km, Nakhon Nayok

Part Four: Picking up the Pieces

30. Britain: August 1945 193
   Peace at a cost

31. Thailand to India: Freedom 195
   An American paratrooper; Trying to bridge the void

32. Britain: September 1945 204
   The telegram

33. Britain: Autumn 1945 219
   Second honeymoon; Who else came home? The reality of coming home

Part Five: The End of the Story

34. Britain: 1946 to 2009 237
   Phyllis and Barry; 27 Line Section after 1945; The Kongsi; Last days; Postscript

Appendix: The Men of 27 Line Section 243

Bibliography 247

Index 250

Acknowledgements

To my first readers, Maureen Katrak, David King, Jenifer Roberts, Paul Beck, Robin Custance Baker and Toni Battison (later also an eagle-eyed proof-reader), and to Kevin Symonds, for early research, go my first thanks. They gave me the courage to work to bring this story together. To those many others who read, advised or proof-read at different stages: Paul Bacon, Margot Chadwick, Stephen Custance-Baker, Maureen Cottrell, Kate France, Lesley Gore, Tony Goryn, Margaret Hewitson-Brown, Jacquee Mann and Michael Nellis, you all helped keep the project going, thank you so much.

My deep gratitude goes to experts who gave freely of their time and knowledge in this area: Meg Parkes for directing my first research steps, Sears Eldredge for his in-depth theatre research, Midge Gillies and Sara Kinsey for editorial feedback on the story. To David Tett, Jonathan Moffatt, Michael Nellis, Gail Cox, Stephen Walton and Sibylla Jane Flower, thanks for detailed information.

Two towering figures gave me material and advice I could not have found for myself – the late, much-missed Roderick Suddaby of the Imperial War Museum and Terry Manttan of the Thailand–Burma Railway Centre who untangled Barry's chronology and answered my endless questions. To them, and to Rod Beattie for all he does for Far East PoWs on the railway, I send my heartfelt thanks.

I am indebted to the family of Colonel Selby Milner for permission to use extracts from his diary, to Drusilla Goryn for free access to family archives, to Stephen Riley for use of his father's PoW account and to Tim Stankus of the Royal Signals Museum for help and access to documents held there.

My thanks go to Henry Wilson, of Pen & Sword, for having faith in the manuscript and, with Matt Jones, George Chamier and Noel Sadler, for guiding me so skilfully through the publishing process.

To the families of the men of 27 Line Section, Kelley and Craig Ashton, Diane Carter, Reg Hannam, Michael Taylor, Jack Earnshaw and Christine Wood: your encouragement has meant the world to me.

Gratitude goes to my brothers, Robin, Jonathan and Stephen Custance Baker, for trusting me with the task and letting me do it my own way and who, like my daughters, Eleanor and Amy Green, kept cheering me on.

Finally, to my husband, Edwin Green, for doing *all* of the tasks above as well as living with me while I worked on the book, which he read and advised on at all of its stages – my lifetime of thanks.

This is a personal story and not an impartial history. As editor I am haunted by the books on my shelves that I have not yet read, the museums and archives not visited and the endless threads I failed to follow up. There will be mistakes and omissions, and for these I apologize.

Illustrations Acknowledgements
My special thanks to the following for permission to use illustrations:

The Thailand–Burma Railway Centre, Kanchanaburi, Thailand for the C56 on the Wang Pho Viaduct from the Renichi Sugano collection of original wartime photographs and for the photograph of Phi Boon Pong in his shop.

The family of Reginald Hannan for the concert poster *Love Thais*.

Anthony Wilder for William Wilder's drawing of the building of the Wampo Viaduct and David Dewey for the photograph.

Tim Mercer for Jack Chalker's drawings of unloading the sick and dead from river boats, Chungkai 1943, and cleaning ulcers by night.

Kareen Rogers, for permission to use the poster of *Night Must Fall* by her uncle Geoffrey Gee, and to the Imperial War Museum for the image of *Night Must Fall* from the de Wardener papers.

The Royal Signals Museum and Archive for photographs of the men of 27 Line Section in box 'Custance Baker LBH MAJ. 936.5'.

The British Red Cross Museum and Archives for the extract from the *Far East Journal* of September 1945.

The Museon, The Hague, for permission to use the revue poster *Lichten Op*.

My thanks also go to all the relations of the men and women whose photographs fill these pages. I have asked permission from those of you I have found. If I did not find you, I can assure you my intention is to honour your relative.

Notes to Reader

Place names

Siam was renamed Thailand in 1939; both names are current in this account and will be used interchangeably according to the writer's preference. Railway Camp names are written as recorded in the memoirs, with the correct names in brackets. Myanmar will be called Burma throughout.

Letters

These have been transcribed as accurately as possible, but there are bound to be errors due to handwriting and the effects of wear and tear. Minor corrections have been made for clarity's sake. Spelling, grammatical errors and idiosyncrasies of expression remain unless they would create a misunderstanding. Only when a word appears to be a typographical error has [*sic*] been inserted.

Three major correspondents required heavier editing: Barry's split compound nouns (e.g. 'great coat', 'ball cock', 'bull dog') have been corrected and some apostrophes (e.g. in 'I've' or 'they're') have been added. Barry's father, Alan, used full stops reluctantly; some have been added to keep his sentences within bounds. Phyllis's letters contain long passages on the few subjects permitted by the censors; passages in these and other letters have been cut or reduced throughout.

Letters from the relatives of the men under Barry's command are held in the Royal Signals Museum archives. Other letters are currently in the possession of the family.

Memoirs

Selected and edited extracts from Barry's memoirs, written in his eighties, have been used for the missing parts of this story. The war sections, in full, are available to researchers at both the Imperial War Museum and COFEPOW (Children of Far East Prisoners of War) archive.

Preface

In March 2010 I was sitting on the side of a bed in my father's home three months after his death. I opened a box file and one of the first things in my hand was an envelope, much re-used and addressed to my mother in pencil. It contained a rough piece of paper with a print of an elephant, covered with pencilled writing in my father's hand, dated 30 August 1945. It opened as follows:

> Nakhon Nayok Camp, Thailand.
> My darling wife, we have just ten minutes to write before a messenger bag for Bangkok. I am well and strong, have been so since the bad days of '43. Your letters have been arriving about a year late, and only 1 in 4 gets here. I hope for a long leave as soon as we get home. November perhaps, and after I have met my son and my mother and father I want to go right away from everything and everybody with you, and I'll try to make up to you for the years we have lost. I quite agree that Robin needs a sister (or brother) as soon as possible . . .

I continued to leaf through a mass of cards, telegrams and letters, mostly between my parents, Barry and Phyllis. They wrote to each other from October 1941, when Barry was sent as a young Army officer on a posting to the then peaceful Far East, until his return in October 1945 after four years' absence, three and a half of them as a prisoner of war (PoW) of the Japanese. Many of the letters were fragile, torn, stained and threaded together on a piece of string; they had survived the jungle and the building of the Thailand–Burma railroad.

What the box did not contain were some other letters my father used to mention. He would refer to Phyllis as the 'Mother of the Regiment' because during the war she had kept in touch with relatives of the sixty-eight men in his unit – 27 Line Section. It was six months before I finally tracked down and opened a box file in the archives of the Royal Signals Museum to find more than 200 letters. They had been written to Phyllis by relatives of the men in Barry's unit as they waited, many of them in vain, for their men to come home. There was also a simple typed dossier with photos and personal details about most of the missing men.

As well as these two box files Barry left behind his lengthy memoirs, which contain vivid descriptions of life as a prisoner of the Japanese. They were written in his eighties, and sometimes his chronology of those years strayed, but his memory for the tiny, and often positive, details of PoW life was extraordinarily precise.

   The letters, memoirs and dossier provide a unique overview of the parallel lives of these men and women over four years. They were separated by nearly 6,000 sea miles and, for most of that time, by complete silence. They were also separated, for a whole generation, by their contrasting experiences during those crucial years of their lives.

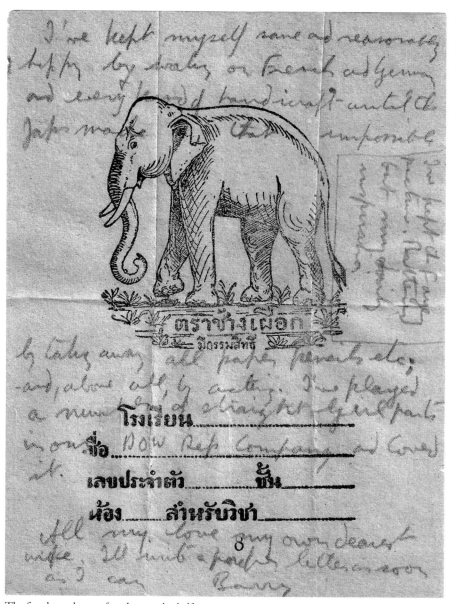

The first letter home after three and a half years.

Timeline

May 1937	Barry and Phyllis meet
July 1939	Barry and Phyllis get married
December 1940	Robin is born
February 1941	27 Line Section is created
July 1941	27 Line Section sail to the Far East
15 February 1942	Fall of Singapore
November 1942	Thailand
December 1942	Wang Lan
April 1943	Wang Pho Viaduct
May 1943	Tha Khanun, Camp 211k
July 1943	Chungkai
Autumn 1943	Barbara & Alan to San Francisco
January 1944	Eden's speech to the House of Commons
September 1944	*Hofuku Maru* sunk
January 1945	Phyllis hands her dossier to the War Office
March 1945	Tamarkan [Tha Makham]
April 1945	Kanchanaburi
August 1945	Nakhon Nayok
6 August 1945	Atom bomb on Hiroshima
9 August 1945	Atom bomb on Nagasaki
15 August 1945	Peace declared
September 1945	Rangoon
October 1945	England

Family Tree

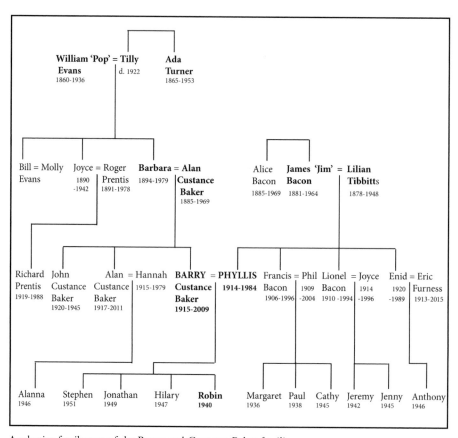

A selective family tree of the Bacon and Custance Baker families.

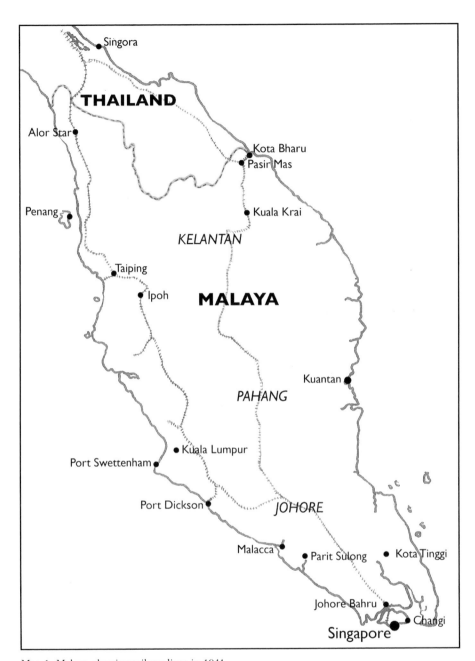

Map 1. Malaya, showing railway lines in 1941.

Map 2. The Pacific Region in 1942.

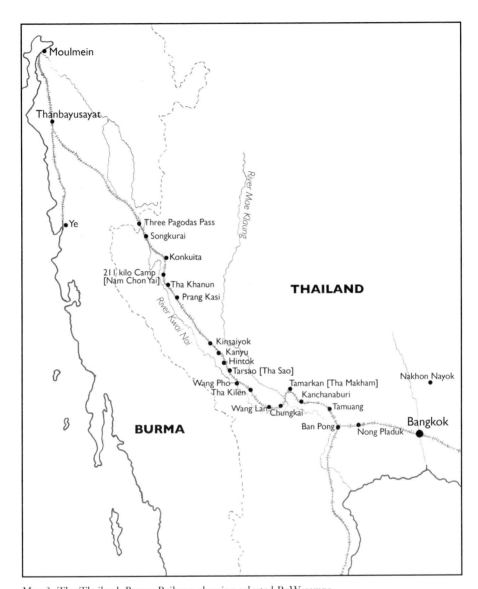

Map 3. The Thailand–Burma Railway, showing selected PoW camps.

Part One

Barry, Phyllis and 27 Line Section

Phyllis Bacon in the City of London, 1937.

Chapter 1

Britain: Spring 1937 to Spring 1941

After the ball, Barry and Phyllis

In 1937 Barry, a 21-year-old student at King's College Cambridge, bought tickets he could not afford for a May Week ball. He left the ball at 6.00am and returned to his rooms feeling a little dispirited. Then, he remembers:

> I went across the road into the Copper Kettle Café for a reviving cup of coffee and allowed myself a little chit-chat with the pretty waitress who served me. The next five minutes changed my whole life.
>
> A young woman in a plain coat and skirt whose face looked faintly familiar came into the café and the waitress, who seemed to be a friend of hers, said 'Phyllis dear, please take this drunk off my hands'. So Phyllis took a cup of coffee and sat down at my table. I soon realised that she was Phyllis Bacon whom I had noticed several times on the stage in plays by the Footlights or the ADC [Theatre] but had never actually met before. We got talking (I was not drunk just rather miserable and very tired). We walked back across to King's and had another coffee in my rooms. She told me that she had just completed her three years at Newnham in English Lit and Lang.

Over the next two years Barry and Phyllis visited each other's homes and Phyllis stayed over at Catterick Camp, where Barry was on the Young Officers training course. They soon became lovers, and Barry's ingenuity was often tested in finding suitable berths without alerting disapproving relatives – not always successfully. They had one favourite stopover, the Wensleydale Heifer, a small pub in West Witton, on their route between London and Catterick.

In 1938, with Barry aged 23 and now a commissioned officer in the Royal Corps of Signals (Royal Signals or RCOS), he and Phyllis became engaged. On 29 July 1939, with war a near certainty, they were married.

Barry (Lancelot Barton Hill Custance Baker, or Barton to his family) was born in Penang, Malaya, in 1915. This, like so many twists in life, was about to have a major impact on his future. He had two younger brothers, Alan and John. His parents, though nearing retirement, were still in the Malayan Civil Service in 1939 and not able to attend his wedding.

From an early age Barry showed an inclination for engineering and enterprise, another factor that was to have an immense impact on the next few years of his life. As a child he created sails for a boat on his great aunt's sewing machine, he constructed his first lathe aged 12 and ran a commercial fudge-making enterprise at school, Marlborough College. At Cambridge he was an indifferent but

Barry and Phyllis at their wedding reception, the Langham Hotel, 1939.

wide-ranging scholar. He studied Natural Sciences, Maths and Physics, then Modern Languages, and finished up with a pass degree in Military Studies.

Phyllis, born in London in 1914, grew up to be passionately interested in the stage, but she was also the daughter of James Bacon, a man of strong Methodist principles. When Phyllis was offered a place at Sadler's Wells drama school, James turned it down without telling her. She was sent to the Institute of Industrial Psychology for career assessment and they advised her to take up a practical subject – ideally Domestic Science. However, Phyllis, a bare 5ft 2in, was cut from the same cloth as her father, with strength of character and a social conscience. In a fit of rebellion she gained a place at Newnham College, Cambridge and completed her degree in English – but spent every spare moment of her student life acting.

Honeymoon and war

In August 1939, Barry and Phyllis set off on a blissful and long-remembered honeymoon in a little *pension* on the Brittany coast near Nantes. War brought this to an abrupt end:

> Near the end of our fortnight honeymoon I received a very peremptory telegram from my CO (Commanding Officer) 'RTU Mob'. So we set out immediately to 'Return to Unit' for Mobilization.

Barry, a fluent French speaker, had been all set to travel with an advance party to France soon after the outbreak of war. However, a young Canadian, driving on the wrong side of the road, ran head-on into Barry on his motorbike. Barry

Phyllis in costume, 1930s.

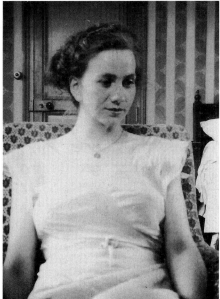
Phyllis on honeymoon in France, August 1939.

suffered a cracked skull and concussion, he was severed from his unit and parked in office jobs over the many months of his recovery.

Meanwhile, in Malaya, Barry's parents, Barbara and Alan, were about to retire from the Residency in Kelantan. Alan had been in the Malayan Civil Service for thirty-two years and British Advisor to the Sultan since 1930. A letter from Barbara gives an insight into pre-war Malayan colonial life in its hectic, multi-cultural late stages. It is also sets the scene for the world into which so many British soldiers were flung eighteen months later:

1 February 1940, from Barbara (Kota Bharu, Malaya) to Phyllis and Barton (Barry)
My darling Phyllis and Barton. We have only one week more before leaving S'Pore and it will be a busy one. Derek came to a very early dinner and we went to an amateur show got up by His Highness's brother for the Malaya Patriotic Fund ... That night His Highness gave us a Farewell dinner at the Balai (orders and decorations). There were about sixty people there and the Sultan made an absolutely sweet speech about Alan and me and then gave Alan a copy on vellum in a silver casket on a silver dish of old Malay silver and to me he gave a most lovely silver dish that is at least a hundred years old. He told me that he had never done this for any other British Advisor. We were deeply touched and Dad made a very good speech in Malay. After dinner we all watched a Mahjong, a sort of Malay play interspersed with Siamese, Javanese & Malay dances, most interesting and the

surroundings were beautiful because at the Balai the crowd (women and children) are allowed to come in and watch and they all wear their gayest clothes. It makes it very hot but lovely to look at. That night we did not get home until 1 o'clock. Next morning we had more music, the Malays came and Truda and Charles played the piano which he does really well and in the afternoon Dad and I had to go to a tea party at the Chinese Chamber of Commerce where more speeches were made and he was presented with an address in a silver frame ... We then hurried home and took Bentley and Truda for a short walk.

Bentley, according to Barry's memoirs, was a Great Dane with a taste for eating the local goats – which was his eventual downfall.

The letter continues:

That evening we had Derek and the three Malay District Officers to dinner and after dinner ten more people came and we gave our final concert ...

On Monday morning all our guests departed, but it was a busy day. I had a St John meeting at 12 to hand over my secretaryship and in the afternoon we went to a farewell tea at Pasir Mas and in the evening ate khuzi with Tengku Sri Akar and many other friends and then went to the pictures, and yester-day we motored to Krai 48 miles up river by launch to lunch with a very old

Barbara and Alan Custance Baker with Great Dane, Bentley.

friend. We got back exhausted for tea. Today we lunch with the Indian community and then go to Krai again for the evening for a Farewell at the club ...

Only a moment now to thank you for your dear letters and say that we will love to stay with you! As to washing up, it is neither here nor there.

No time at all but send our dear love. Mum

Back in Britain, Barry was finally deemed by the army as 'fit for everywhere' but found himself still at a desk. In the June of 1940 he fetched up at Harnham Camp, near Salisbury:

My arrival at Harnham was soon after the retreat of the BEF [British Expeditionary Force] from Dunkirk and everything was in a great muddle. We were then, mid 1940, living under constant threat of invasion. The Air Battle of Britain was happening all around us and the Blitz on London soon started up, but Salisbury and Harnham were not significantly bombed.

Meanwhile, Phyllis, now pregnant, had been living with her parents, James and Lilian, at the White House, Great Missenden, and Barry visited whenever he could. With the London Blitz hotting up, they decided Phyllis would be safer in a cottage in Teignmouth in Devon, which, unlike nearby Plymouth, was never bombed.

During the heavy bombing period of 1940–41 Barry became responsible for the organization of units desperately keeping signals communications going in the hard-hit coastal areas. He would send Line parties or whole sections out:

... to patch up some kind of temporary telephone communications for the Port Installations and the AA guns along the coast. I went to both of the major targets, Portsmouth and Southampton, to see how our linemen were getting on. These towns, after an air raid, showed as much devastation as London docks, yet they carried on with their jobs as Naval Bases and I like to think that our linemen materially helped them to do so. Two of my visits coincided with actual raids, which were very reminiscent of conditions in Singapore a year later though of course I did not realize that at the time.

The linemen had to work on, raids or not, often patching in to an overhead telephone route. If a telephone pole was knocked over, a lineman would climb up one of the still standing poles, joint on a section of field cable to the broken ends of the wires and lead it, either suspended or along the ground, to the next standing pole and reconnect it to the existing open wires – exposed and hair-raising work.

Half way through this period of heavy bombing, on 17 December 1940, Phyllis and Barry's son, Robin, was born in Teignmouth hospital.

27 *Line Section created*

A wartime army has to adapt and change its spots rapidly; it becomes a different beast from the carefully planned establishment of peacetime. In the spring of

1941, Barry was summoned by his CO, Colonel Bury, to discuss a new job. He had studied Barry's file and wanted him to take over a new Line Construction Section that was being formed mainly from members of the Glasgow Post Office Special Reserve Unit (or SR). This was similar to the Territorial Army (TA), but largely made up of technical tradesmen. As they were mostly pre-war reservists they could, apparently, be considered volunteers. It became clear during this interview that the destination for this unit was probably Malaya – Barry's country of birth. The gist of the interview amounted to this:

> Would I like to have the Section and take it wherever? It was larger than a normal Line Section, 72 (later 69) all ranks, a Captain's command, with a Subaltern under him. It sounded ideal but I asked for a day to think it over (and to consult my wife). At that time in the War, the Far East was peaceful and not involved in warfare, wives and families were still with their serving husbands. I confidently believed that Phyllis would probably be allowed to come out later to join me. The decision was not a hard one and we soon agreed that I should accept the offer.
>
> There are certain long established sayings in the Army – never refuse an offer of leave or promotion, it may not come around again, and NEVER volunteer for duty. So next day I went round to the CO's Office and volunteered to take Command of 27 Line Section and go with them to the Far East.

So 27 Line Section, destined for a short life, was cobbled together from groups of Signals men who happened to be available at that precise moment. Apart from the contingent from Glasgow, the new section would also include men who had worked with Barry at Harnham in what was then No. 1 Company, such as his second officer, Second Lieutenant Sutherland Brown. At nearly forty, Sutherland Brown was the doyen of the Section. Like Barry, he was familiar with life in the Far East. Although originally from Scotland, he was, until the war, a Planter Manager in Malaya, where he lived with his wife, Beatrice Winifred.

Other men were regular soldiers, several of them remnants from RCOS 10 Section, originally Londoners, survivors of the Dunkirk evacuation less than a year before who had spent the intervening time rewiring Portsmouth and Southampton during the Blitz. They included Driver Reg Hannam, Signalman Reg Holmes, Corporal Jack Earnshaw, Lance Corporal Harrison, Signalman Lovell and Signalman Murrell. They remained fast friends through all the ordeals ahead.

Others, who came from 39 Line Section, had also served in France and included three more Scotsmen, Lance Corporal Charlie Johnston, Lance Sergeant John Arnott and John 'Scotty' Walls (5ft 5in and with weak eyesight).

Another small group who came together were four boys from Glossop: Signalman Jim Bridge, Signalman George Hobson, Signalman Andy Minshull and Driver Ernest Parker, all from the 4th North Midland Signals.

Ernest Parker in 1941.

Diversity was about all that these men had in common. The baby of the troupe was probably Driver Reginald Albert Walter Hedges, a delivery driver who had enlisted in 1939 aged 17. Signalman Walter Henry Carter, known as Harry, had added five months to his age and ended up at Dunkirk. Signallers spent much of their days driving from pillar to post, so many of the recruits were delivery men, mail van drivers or telephone linemen. There were also waiters, a pantographer in a print works, a telephone exchange operator, apprentice compositor, plumber, shipyard labourer and so on.

The Scottish volunteers were assembled and posted down south with not much more than their Scottish Reserve training. Barry remembers:

> The Glasgow party arrived, bringing most of their own lorries with them, and they seemed to fit in quite easily with the men I knew already at Harnham. We had a few days to sort out duties, stores, transport and drivers and then we were sent on detachment as a whole Section to carry out a most interesting job at Puddletown in Dorset, laying underground cable around an airfield. This was a great bonus as it enabled us, me and the four sergeants, to get to know one another and to get the Glaswegians and the Southerners properly acquainted and working together without the nuisance of Company Parades or CO's inspections. Colonel Bury simply gave us the job and left us to get on with it.

There followed a very busy month, during which the men were housed in the luxurious stable block (comfortable compared to the usual tents) of a very well-to-do vicarage. One of the sergeants, John Arnott, had his wife living in

Barry and Robin in 1941.

Puddletown too, where she got to know the men in the unit. The officers fared even better, with bed and board within the house. As Barry recalled:

> This happy and pleasant interlude at Puddletown is really the last clear memory I have of Southern Command before we set out for our posting to the Far East and stuck very vividly in my mind. The whole job lasted only a few weeks but by the end of it No. 27 Line Section had a firm personality and individuality of its own. Later in Malaya or up country in Siam, if any of our men were asked what Unit they came from they would not answer 'Malaya Command Signals' or 'Attached to 8th Australian Division', or even '2 Group PoW Camp', but simply '27 Line Section'.

After finishing work on the airfield in late Spring 1941, they returned to Harn-ham Camp. Within weeks they received orders for overseas postings and were dispersed on embarkation leave. At least one of the men, Driver John Lyons, got married on this leave. Barry spent his leave with his parents-in-law at the White House, Great Missenden.

In cine films shot on this leave Barry, with Phyllis, baby Robin and his parents-in-law, James and Lilian, are seen in the garden. Barry and Phyllis are proudly showing off their son or sitting in the sunlight, he polishing his tall boots, she sewing baby clothes or mending his equipment.

Not long after this Phyllis went into hospital for an operation. There is a scribbled pencil note from Barry to Phyllis on the back of a pink message form dated 22 July 1941. It is mostly about photos, but Phyllis kept it. It ended:

When will you come out of hospital darling. Not before I go anyhow I expect. I'll try to send you a last minute telegram from here and write to you from the ship.

Those polyphotos [contact prints] create loud laughter whenever they are shown. Yours B.

Part Two

6,000 Miles East

Lieutenant L. B. H. C. Baker in 1940.

Chapter 2

Britain to Malaya:
July 1941 to December 1941

Dancing on the docks

In July 1941, Barry, a bare 26 years old and now a Captain, set off with the men of 27 Line Section to join a troopship for the two-month voyage to the Far East. Barry's parents had given him some serious advice about what to take, for instance a metal-lined trunk to keep out rats and tropical bugs, and '28 sets of shirts and shorts, two a day for a week and the other fourteen in the laundry'.

With all their heavy luggage and military equipment stowed in advance, the men arrived at Liverpool docks with only personal gear:

> Our Unit Quartermaster at Harnham had served in India and knew just what the men should have issued to them, in the way of tropical gear, and the kit bag in which it would be carried. Later on I found that these black canvas kit bags could be retailored into comfortable hardwearing, short trousers. Most of the men carried one or two suitcases as well.
>
> I also had a bedroll or valise. This was a most useful object; a canvas sheet the size of a bed, with flaps, lined with thin blanket, and could be used as a sleeping bag if required. It could also be packed with a quantity of loose clothes, books and so on, and then rolled up tightly and held with two stout straps, joined together with a carrying handle. It made a cylinder about three foot long and a foot thick with a handle in the middle. I took it with me later on into Siam and it became my rucksack and was cannibalised to produce many useful pieces of canvas and cloth for bags and straps.
>
> Our time working together on the Airfield at Puddletown had shaken the Section together and the Glaswegians definitely influenced the rest of the men. We were by now a firmly Scottish unit, and during our long wait on the Station platform at Liverpool Docks the two Scottish Sergeants decided that we should celebrate our departure from Britain with a dance.

They planned eight Eightsome Reels, and after a deal of pushing and shoving the sergeants managed to arrange eight suitable groups on the platform with a few good Scottish dancers in each set. They then did a walk-through of the dance.

> From my nominal roll [list of men] I can say that Sergeant Pawson was the leader, and since we were all soldiers, used to drill, he was easily able to get the sets properly organized. After the walk through we did the whole. The

reel was such a success that it gathered quite an audience of porters, sailors and others, so we did it all through once again. After that came the order to board, so my last memory of Britain for more than four years was dancing on the platform at Liverpool Docks.

After this cheerful send-off they sailed on the *Orontes*, an Orient Liner converted to a troopship. As these ships regularly docked in South Africa, Malaya and India – all still at peace – Barry and the men, used by now to rationed food, were astonished and delighted to receive full-scale peacetime meals.

Keeping men fit and occupied over the two months at sea posed a continuous challenge to the officers. The ships were packed tight and units had to take turns on the deck for exercise and games:

> We of No. 27 practised our technical skills as much as we could. We were all linemen of one sort or another, not telegraphists, and could do no practical work aboard ship, but my Subaltern and I taught the men the Morse alphabet which might come in useful and a few sessions of flag wagging.
>
> Later in the journey, which lasted eight weeks or more, I told the Section that we were going to Malaya, which most of them knew already and I offered voluntary classes in the Malay language, which nearly all of them joined. My own knowledge was only the remains of my childhood speech in Penang, but I knew what it sounded like and with a few simple textbooks we got on quite well. At least they knew how to address Malays and Chinese politely and how to count, how to ask for simple things in the shops, and how to work out values in Straits Dollars. The whole of Malaya was often called 'The Straits'.

Their first stop was Cape Town, where they were able to post letters but not allowed to say in them where they were. Barry, feeling clever, determined to outwit the censor and in his letter to Phyllis included the phrase 'The other day I came across our old friend Dick Grenville'. Since they had no such friend, Phyllis, with her English degree was able to make the connection to the Tennyson poem in which 'At Flores in the Azores Sir Richard Grenville lay'.

> During our stop over at the Cape, we completely neglected the Other Ranks (ORs) of the Section but they seemed to be well taken care of by the local inhabitants, and they had several weeks of pay in their pockets. They had been subjected to lectures from the ship's Medical Officer (MO) about the dangers of infection and were all given packs of prophylactics before going ashore, and I pointed out to them that by incurring a venereal infection while in HM service, they would in fact be guilty of damaging government property, a chargeable offence! I cannot remember that any of them did become infected but in Wartime it was a constant anxiety for Section and Company commanders. When we came aboard again they all seemed to have had a good time and to be much refreshed by their run ashore. At least

one of them, a Glaswegian, had tangled with the local police but was none the worse for his adventure.

Singapore and all's well

After a diversion to India with a brief stop in Bombay, Barry with the men of 27 Line Section arrived at Singapore in September 1941. They were reunited with their kit and enjoyed a short stay near the city.

Barry's first surviving letter started with a prescient Malay *pantun*, a traditional poetic form:

4 October 1941, from Barry to Phyllis

Dari mana hĕndak ka-mana?   [Whence are you and where away?]
Tinggi rumput dari padi.   [Grass is taller than the grain.]
Tahun mana bulan yang mana?   [When will be the year and day?]
Hĕndak kita berjumpa lagi?   [That we two shall meet again?]

Here we are at last, Darling, and all's well. I shall have cabled by the time you get this and so will uncle Roger also I may write clipper mail.

The censorship rules are still in force in that we may not disclose our exact location nor describe our journey here.

I had dinner with Joycie [his aunt – thus giving Phyllis his exact location] and Roger two days ago and I'm going to a play with them tonite [*sic*]. They are looking very well indeed and incredibly young. J. has just recovered from a nasty illness. Tumours of the breast, operation for almost complete removal of both breasts. She now wears a slightly padded brassière and looks about 35. She's much fitter and well looking than before. Runs a War Market, gives about $3,000 per mensem [month] to charities.

Roger's [rubber] business almost gone …

We're lucky in our camp. About 3 miles w of town an attap [palm fronds] roofed hutted camp. Plenty of room cool and comfortable. Background of red sand covered with grass trees pineapples etc. Also a Chinese cemetery. Separate rooms. Cold showers but no baths. Cheap messing. But S'pore prices high. We have to take a taxi whenever we go shopping or whatnot to S'pore. $1 in, same out. I can make myself understood to the Chinese boys in the mess but my Malay is still very patchy …

I'll stop now poppet so that I can get it off this pm. All's well here. Send me all news from home, and snaps.

Your Barry

The Singapore population of that period was mainly European and Chinese, with some Malays and Indians and a considerable mix of Eurasians, many of old Portuguese stock. The Europeans were mostly civil servants like Barry's father and grandfather, who administered and helped to govern the country, merchant bankers and brokers who dealt in rubber and tin like his aunt's husband, Roger Prentis, or managers of tin mines or rubber plantations like his mother's brother,

Roger and Joyce Prentis in
Singapore, 1937.

Uncle Bill Evans. The Chinese were also bankers and shopkeepers; many were
second- or third-generation, born in Singapore.

From the time he left Britain until February 1942 Barry wrote frequently,
though irregularly, to Phyllis, and many of his letters survive. Phyllis also wrote
to Barry, but almost all of her letters for this period are missing.

Mail from Britain was a lifeline for men stationed so far from home and in
what, for the majority, were alien surroundings. However, news from home going
by the long sea route was out of date by the time it arrived. This led Barry to
develop a crucial arrangement because, as he later explained:

> Letters home went by sea for the equivalent of a few pence, but letters from
> Malaya took five weeks or ten weeks for a letter and reply. There was a newly
> established Air Mail service which would make the journey in four or five
> days, but letters were restricted to half ounce (14 grams) and cost 5 shillings,
> worth now about £5 or £10, far beyond the reach of most soldiers. This
> caused considerable discontent in the Section and with the help of my wife
> we devised a scheme to please everyone.

This fast airmail service, originally run by flying-boat, was called Clipper Mail after the Tea Clipper ships that used to trade between America and the Far East. Barry sold half or even quarter sheets to the men for the same price as stamps for the slow sea mail. Then he would fill each envelope up to the half-ounce limit and post it to Phyllis in Britain:

> Each sheet or part sheet had the name and address for delivery and Phyllis posted them on at her own expense. My father-in-law James Bacon may have helped out with the considerable cost of the postage. It enabled Phyllis to build up a list of all the next of kin of the Section and their addresses, which later on proved to be very valuable to us all.

Wires across the jungle

Barry, having been born and spent several childhood years in Malaya, regarded the country and the people with much affection. From his letters it is clear he was enjoying rediscovering his childhood home and relished the work he and his men had to do. In his memoirs he wrote:

> We spent a few weeks only on The Island (Singapore), building a new over-head telegraph and telephone route to the Naval Base. This work enabled me to make useful contacts with the Post Office engineers and with the Chinese contractors whom we employed to dig the postholes. Englishmen doing manual labour in public would have been very unacceptable. We paid one Straits Dollar per hole, which I had been told was the going rate and at nine dollars to the pound this was a fair bargain. Our Glasgow Post Office sergeants inspected the first few holes very critically but found that the Chinese could dig a hole just as well as they could and much faster too, so everyone was satisfied. The arming and furnishing of the poles and the fittings and regulating of the wires was, of course, carried out by our own linemen. At first we all wore pith helmets against the dangers of sunstroke. Later the men were permitted Aussie hats.
>
> When this job was finished, in autumn 1941, we were detached from Malaya Command and sent up into Johore in mainland Malaya. As No. 27 had a somewhat individualistic outlook about the rest of the Army this proposed detachment suited us well.

The whole of the Malayan peninsula was covered in jungle, except the coastal strips and hill country, and rubber plantations were carved out of the jungle wherever a suitable spot presented itself. Barry and his men were stationed a few miles north of the town of Kota Tinggi, billeted at a rubber plantation.

Driver Percy Shaw sent a photo of some of the men from 27 Line Section in Kota Tinggi to his mother. They are all looking extremely relaxed and cheery. On the back it reads (top row, from the left): 'Reg Holmes, Earnshaw, Me, Lyons, Cowboy Ted Taylor, Lew Jackson'. (Front row) 'Charlie Wilson, Larry Whitton, Dawson and Jim Bridge fra' Glossop. (Kota Tinggi 1941, 27 Line Sec)'.

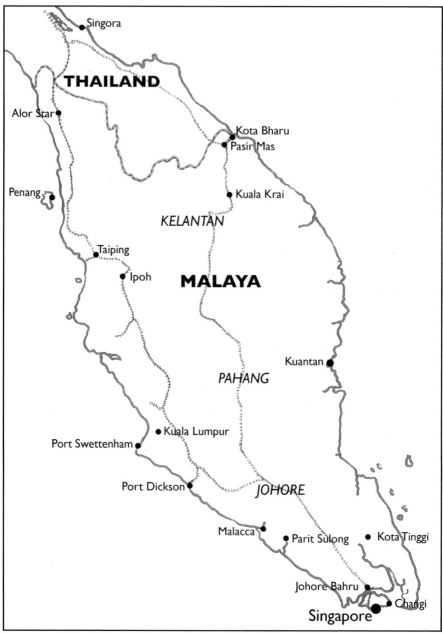

Malaya, showing railway lines in 1941.

Members of 27 Line Section in Kota Tinggi, 1941.

At the bottom someone (Percy's mother?) has added later 'Percy Shaw, Driver 2340027 3rd on top row'.

For Lieutenant Sutherland Brown, Barry's second in command and a rubber plantation manager, this must have felt like home. He may well have been meeting up with friends and even with his wife Beatrice, as they travelled about. Their third officer, Lieutenant Bob Garrod, an architectural surveyor in civilian life, was new to the country. Barry recalled:

> We three officers fed with the Manager in the fashion that I remembered from my childhood in Penang. Very early wake up with tea and a slice of bread and butter, called 'chota hazri' or little breakfast; a few hours work before the heat of the day, then proper breakfast followed by inspections and office work. This was followed by a late lunch ('tiffin') and siesta until teatime, then a visit to the Club for swimming and tennis. This was the Manager's day but we soldiers had to do without the siesta and go on with whatever job was on hand.
>
> Our jobs were vaguely warlike. We were building the telephone routes to various temporary airstrips that had been set up in the jungle in Johore, and the area to the north. We were working very hard, mostly in small parties, and there was a definite feeling that something dramatic was due to happen

quite soon. The jungle cover on the Malay Peninsula was so dense that it was thought that no army could ever penetrate it. The Japanese invasion was only a few weeks away but no one was willing to believe that such a thing could really happen in Malaya.

Europeans living and working in Malaya, like Barry's uncle and aunt, believed that the Japanese had no tanks, or if they had that they were made of bamboo and paper, like their aeroplanes; also that the Japanese all wore spectacles and would be too short-sighted to fly planes anyway.

Barry continued to write to Phyllis both by sea mail and by the new Clipper airmail. He also enclosed tiny makeweight scraps of tissue from himself with the mail from the men in his Section. The prevailing tone of these letters is light, even domestic. In spite of the war raging in other parts of the globe, there is little in them to suggest foreboding of the future. Of course, censorship limited some subjects, and it is possible that in part this bright tone was a kind of courage; it would have been considered 'good form' to carry on as usual. Sometimes, however, perhaps as a response to news from home, the tone slips and his homesickness escapes onto the page:

8 November 1941, from Barry to Phyllis
Phyllis Darling, only one sheet from me, mostly to say that I have had two letters from you at last. One written in hospital and one from Wye on Aug 20th. Terribly glad to hear that all well and you sound so happy. Please write just like that all about the things you do and the things you think the shoes you buy and what our one and only [Robin] does and says and looks like.

　　Thank heavens for the pictures of you and him. With them and your letters you both seem much closer to me.

Phyllis took this plea to heart. Throughout the war, the letters she and other relatives wrote were full of these undramatic and familiar details that their homesick men craved, as Barry's letter makes clear:

You have been feeling rather far away lately but your letters make all the difference in the world. They should be arriving regularly now thank the Lord. You said that Mum and Dad had one from the ship. I wrote to you as well, naturally, dated 28th July but some unmentionable dingbat indescribable horror, for some unknown reason must have scratched out the address. I got it back today with your other two letters marked 'Adress [sic] mutilated.' I'll send it off again with my next sea mail [if this letter ever arrived, it is not preserved]. I've now bought a very old very cheap but good Kodak so I can send you snaps. I've taken groups of all my spread-out army in its various little jungle corners. The work here at K is rather light just now so I may move over to M for a week or two as there are some interesting jobs up there. That teaching diploma sounds an excellent idea if you can find the time to do it. When this war is over and we are scratching in the muck for pennies and crusts of bread a wife who can earn even a pittance will be a Godsend. Teaching diplomas will always get a job somewhere and coupled with a Cambridge Honours degree, almost anywhere.

Phyllis, later in life a legend for her extreme busyness, was already filling every moment. She was clearly feeling a need to accomplish something in preparation for a life together in which she would contribute financially. Barry continued:

Please remember to send a recent snap of the child. The ones I have are much admired by the local ladies, three of them, so I want more. Use a fast film and … [Barry includes detailed instructions]. Sorry to be so long winded but I do want lots of pictures of you both.

You can keep an a/c of the stamps you use on my charitable 'Mother of the section idea', and much good may it do you.

All my love my own dear wife.

Your Barry

The following day, he wrote again:

9 November 1941, from Barry to Phyllis

My Dear, here is some more mail for the section. If you could find out about a return service you could put in a chit with each letter to say you will send out Air Mail Clipper to me at so much per sheet.

Several of the blokes have asked if you could fix this. You'll find that several of the letters in the other packets refer to you. I know because I have to censor them. The local Tamil ladies are most immodest. They wear a loose scarf over one shoulder tucked into their belts, but it never seems to fit. They are however quite untroubled. I am untroubled too as they have red or black teeth, rings in their noses and anyhow I prefer my wife. There is one very wicked lady in the town but as one of the Aussies who visited her is now in hospital I think my lads will keep clear.

Barry notes in his memoirs: 'I managed without the comfort of a bedmate. In fact from the time of leaving home in summer 1941 until my return to the bosom of my (small) family in October 1945, I took part in no sexual activity at all, the longest period of deprivation in my whole adult life until old age caught up with me.' The letter continues:

In a week or so I prepare to go up to a Junglies station where more work is. We are going to build a line by a method never yet used. I shall take pictures and write an essay for *The Wire*. My working parties all go out with one armed anti tiger and bear man. But all they have seen so far are monkeys snakes and skeeters. I'm beginning to believe there aren't any tigers but one lonely post of 2 men in the Ulu [jungle] say they hear roaring at night and one found tiger prints by their cookhouse.

Don't forget to send me beautiful pictures of you and the Robin. Goodbye dear heart, never forget that somebody loves you and concentrate on bringing him back.

Your Barry

There were other dangerous forms of wildlife, as Barry remembers:

In late 1941, we were building telephone lines between the many small headquarters – unmanned but established 'Just in Case' – and the small airstrips in Johore and Pahang. I don't remember much in detail of this period just before the invasion but one incident vividly comes to mind. I was with a small party building a two-pair route in fairly heavy jungle, using trees instead of telephone poles. I had surveyed the route in advance and marked the trees which were to be used for the route. We had a light van to carry our ladders and all the other kit and, of course, our packed lunches and drinks. Two members of the working party went ahead with a ladder and a hand auger to bore the four holes required, in the marked trees. The next group climbed up and screwed the L shaped bolts into the holes and fitted the insulators on to them.

Everything went on smoothly except for the odd leech. We were used to them and a touch from the hot end of a cigarette caused them to drop off quite easily. Then one of the forward party came rushing back to the van waving his arms and shouting 'hornets'. He was followed by a cloud of very angry hornets eagerly seeking targets. We had no shelter except for the van which fortunately had an enclosed cab into which we all scrambled, about eight of us, a very tight fit but this discomfort was much preferable to being stung by a jungle hornet.

These hornets, about 2.5 to 3cm long, have a reputation for very aggressive behaviour and deliver a sting several times as powerful as a wasp's. One of the party had climbed the ladder to make the necessary holes in the selected tree, had heard a buzzing noise and realized that it was a hollow tree with a hornet's nest in it. He was stung once as he climbed down and ran back to the van as fast as possible.

So we sat or stood in the cab on top of one another for an hour or more with the hornets buzzing around looking for a way to get at us, but the windscreen and the windows were a good fit and a thoughtful signalman had stuffed bits of paper or rags around the holes in the floor of the cab where the pedals came in. When the hornets eventually gave up we drove a circular course around their tree and continued our route building on the next section, taking great care to avoid any hollow trees. A day or two later we returned to the area and built a wide curve around the hornet tree. When I told the Manager about the incident he said that we had been lucky as three or four stings from jungle hornets could be fatal.

Barry does not seem to have relayed the story of the hornets in his letters to Phyllis, though not all his letters arrived. Of course, the more likely reason is that it was part of the spirit of the time to protect your family from worrisome news of any sort. It is difficult to convey how much communication, though slow and unreliable, mattered.

In Britain, Phyllis took her role of postmistress very seriously and collected the addresses of relatives to whom she posted on letters. She also sent out a covering typewritten letter to each new addressee. We have a later example, in which it becomes clear how much work was involved in this postal service.

(15 December 1941) from Phyllis to the relatives of the men in 27 Line Section
Dear _____, In case the enclosed letter does not say how I came to receive it, here is the explanation.

The Clipper service costs 5/- per half ounce letter, but is very rapid (this letter [from your relative] left [Malaya] on Nov. 28th). As this is too expensive for most people, my husband, Capt. Custance Baker, is selling to his section notepaper at 10d per sheet, and sending me envelopes containing 6 sheets each to pass on to their addressees. This morning I received eight Clipper letters, containing 48 letters of 1 sheet each, for redistribution.

I am running a 'return service', and send, on the first and fifteenth of each month, all the letters I receive by that date. If the correct paper is used (try to be sure 6 sheets and an envelope do not exceed ½oz.), 6 letters can go in each envelope. That works out at 10d per sheet. Of course you can send me as many sheets as you like, but please enclose 10d in stamps for each one.

In Malaya, Barry would put together letters from his men until they were up to the weight limit. Even if he wasn't including a letter for Phyllis in the envelope he usually managed to add a tiny note for her.

17 November 1941, from Barry to Phyllis
My Good Woman, can just squeeze one sheet in this packet but the other letter has only got a tiny piece of tissue paper in it from me, one of the blokes used a sheet of rather thick paper.

I'm still living in my little bungalow on the estate and very comfortable too. I've just taken a very beautiful (I hope) head photo of me sitting at my desk. Taken in the mirror. I looked upwards and arranged a very soulful smile on my face.

Have I told you about Agatha? I think not. She is a Tamil woman who cuts the trees round the bungalow, and she hates being snapped [photographed] so naturally we do it. The Aussie got away with a cursing but when I tried she rushed at me with a rubber knife and threw one of the pots in my direction. I caught her with knife upraised coming towards me, so it may be a very guilty picture. My snaps are coming out quite well but films are very difficult here. I went all the way to E. recently on learning there were films there. I had to go anyway to pay my detachment there. There was only one film of

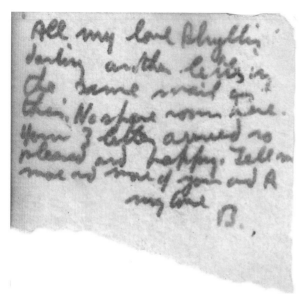

Makeweight scrap of tissue paper
added to a clipper letter in
November 1941.

the right size but not on the right spools so he rewound it for me in his darkroom. It cost me $1.50 so I hope to goodness it comes out properly.

I had dinner y'day with a young married couple named Dick, planters. They have two smalls [babies] 3 and 0 which I was allowed to see. It was quite heartbreaking, darling, to look at and admire someone else's babies when I have a so much better one myself but couldn't produce it for inspection. Still Mrs D. has seen my snaps so she knows how beautiful he is.

We were talking about politeness to Native servants. I complained that so many Europeans here, particularly soldiers and other newcomers were very ill-mannered to Chinese boys. I said that I always tried to be very polite to them. Mrs D. said, I think you'd be polite to anyone! Which was rather nice wasn't it. Your husband is appreciated here.

Bridge going very well. Another $2.70 last Saturday. I really did learn quite a lot on that ship. We played nearly every day.

I've had three letters from you so far my dear, 1 in hosp. 1 hospital & Wye, 1 Wye. I'm so glad you had a happy time there. There or thereabouts is where young R will spend most of his school holidays so it's fortunate it's such a lovely neighbourhood.

. . . All my love dearest wife and I do wish you could share this nice little home and nice big bed with me.

Your Barry.

First casualty

On 21 November 1941 the Unit had its first serious setback. One of the Glasgow men, Signalman H. Nairn, died of a fever. Barry believed this was leptospirosis, which was also known as *Tsu-tsu-gamushi*, or Japanese river fever. At 34, Nairn was one of the older unit members.

[21/22] November 1941, from Barry to Phyllis on a small undated enclosure with airmail
Phylly Darling, You'll see my letter to Mrs Nairn in this lot. Will you write to her too and say how sorry you are and can you do anything to help.

I think he held a good position in civvy life so financially they should be OK.

Has 3 children. Really was one of my best men in the section. V. sorry to lose him.

Will write another letter [missing] with this mail.

Love, All my love my darling. B.

24 November 1941, from Barry to Phyllis in red and blue ink, headed Ulu
Darling, here's a picture of me taken with my new (very old) camera. I've made several good pictures this isn't one of them ... This ink is govt supply. They've run out of blue in my unit and sent me some red ink powder, so I'm trying it out.

Trip with my new Aussie officer y'day. 14 miles jungle line. Half way we suddenly came on a small Chinese village. Just a square with a doz houses. No roads to or from. Fifty near-naked infants and one elderly Malay very reserved and uninterested. We stopped for a bottle of beer at the shop and drank, the centre of admiration (or interest anyhow) of the whole village. The Malay however continued to contemplate the top of a coconut tree. I passed the time of day with him and he informed me that I had a long way to go and would need more beer before I arrived. We did. It rained soon after that and in two minutes we were soaked to the skin. I always wear slacks in the jungle as it keeps the leeches out. But one managed to find a way in spite of that.

Our casualty had a fine funeral. Firing party and bearers provided by Dad's old regiment and they certainly did a good job for us. I'm going to get a snap of the grave for Mrs Nairn.

I had an airmail from Mum today enclosing two of [brother] Alan's letters. He seemed to think you and Robin were all well and happy which is prime. Brother seems to be getting along very smartly acting Captain last May and Hon Bimbashi. I wish I could sign letters BCB Bimb. It looks beautiful.

Another dinner out last week. Played piquet and had the pants taken off me. Had roast beef and onion for b'fst this am which always sets me back a trifle but otherwise am fit and well. Always waiting and longing for news of you and R. He'll be just about 1 when you get this. Kiss him happy b'day from Daddy.

All love dear. Your Barry.

Barry's younger brother Alan had followed him into the Royal Signals. After taking part in the ill-managed foray into Norway and a spell in Glasgow that threatened his liver, he volunteered for service in the Middle East. He was posted to Egypt, then in 1941 joined the Abyssinian campaign and was seconded to the Turkish army – hence 'Bimbashi', the equivalent of captain.

? November 1941, from Barry to Phyllis, undated note
Darling, ... I'm wondering if these airmails are straining your finances a bit. Let me know and I'll turn it off. But the blokes really do appreciate it tremendously. Also it lets me write to you oftener than I could otherwise as $2 is rather a lump.

It's rained here for two days solid. The rubber trees are growing in a little lake and our septic tank is full so the pull and let go doesn't work any more.

Our cook has gone sick so late last night I had to phone a doctor at U, many miles away where there is an amateur cook. He arrived this morning so all went off smoothly.

I have also located a good Malay teacher and he is going to open up negotiations very soon. An elderly planter called Dato Bin Mahood.

I'm going to try and send Robin a cable at Christmas but if it doesn't come wish him a very happy birthday [17th Dec] and Xmas from his daddy and for you too my darling. You've done so well in the last year and I'm so extra pleased with you.

Your husband, B.

29 November 1941, from Barry to Phyllis, ink on writing paper, headed 'My Wife and Ulu'
Darling, this letter is all for you this time even tho it is mostly photos. I think they're good. The head only was taken in a mirror, pressing the button myself. No more snaps for a bit until you or my Aussie friend rally round with films ...

Barry was still in an area not at war and had very little idea of conditions in Britain. Although food supplies had been restricted when he left, by now many commodities, such as petrol and photographic film, were becoming extremely difficult to obtain.

I've written quite a long letter to Dad in Malay and sent one of the photos too. I had a delightful airmail from Mum with two of Bro Alan's letters inside.

No letters from you since the first batch of three. But I expect they are on the way. It is just about 3 weeks now to the little's birthday, the only first birthday he'll ever have. I do wish I was there to wish him many happy returns. Perhaps he'll get them anyhow, give him something very belch-making on his dad's behalf.

I've been making myself sick too. I ate some Durian (Dad will explain) which disagreed. I gave most of it away to my teacher, E–Mahood bin Naam. I am also eating Rambutans which are a great favourite of mine.

Barry would have encountered the notorious durian as a child; these fruits are exceedingly smelly, but apparently delicious. Rambutans resemble peeled lychees and taste more like grapes.

> Just called away to the phone for some very good news. We are to stay up here for some time and to build a big route of very many miles, which will delight the lads.
>
> I've been having some interesting talks with the Aussie officers about after the war. If everything goes quite smoothly and there is no great crash we might carry on soldiering. But as an alternative, schoolmastering in Australia might be a go …
>
> This new job needs a lot of phoning now and I must do it. All my very best love my darling. You may kiss my picture good night: I do yours.
>
> Your own. Barry

From the rather sad passage about mails – only three letters from Phyllis between July and November, and Robin's missed birthday – it becomes clear just how precious letters were. Although Phyllis is now organizing letters to go from England by fast Clipper Mail, this has not yet happened. What is missing from his letters is any sense of impending danger; yet in his memoirs he writes:

> Looking back on this period I realize that the threat of a possible invasion was at last being recognised. We were continually being called on for more and more lines in the jungle to connect up new temporary gun positions and provisional Brigade and Divisional Headquarters in Johore and in the next state of Pahang. These HQs were, however, all situated near the one and only North/South road in the peninsula, or close to the East Coast where coastal shipping could provide transport. There were several other Line Sections at work around here but we had little contact with them or with our own Regimental HQ, which was on The Island (Singapore) in the Changi area which was where most of the Military were concentrated. Singapore Town remained very firmly a civilian business centre and the harbour was very busy handling rubber and tin exports and Chinese trading junks.
>
> The Japanese army had already been fighting for several years in mainland China. We had heard of the atrocities in Nanking and elsewhere but had not taken much account of them. They were even now busily conquering Siam and Indo-China.

Everyone still assumed the Japanese would never dare to attack Malaya, and even if they did it would be by sea and their ships would be blown out of the water by the big guns of the naval base.

At last, on 5 December, Barry received letters that were now three months old. Although his reply shows an awareness of threat at last, it is still relatively light-hearted:

5 December 1941, from Barry to Phyllis

Wife darling, two more letters from you yesterday dated 5th and 15th September. Very comforting. Also letter from Wye and telegram from you. I expect that was in answer to one of my earlier letters from here where I was complaining about not having heard from you for so long. Your letters are arriving now. We've had two mails since we landed. The last was a fine big one and it's not all sorted out yet; it arrives in dribs and drabs daily . . . Malay letter enclosed for Dad. I hope he can understand it.

Rain here remains very heavy. You are sitting in bright sun on the verandah, possibly sleeping, with a stengah (whiskey and soda water) in your hand (studying for the staff college is the military term for these quiet moments) when there is a distant roar in the jungle. A faint noise like a rushing wind in the distance and in about ten slow seconds it hits you. Sun goes out, noise on the roof which means shouting to be heard. Garden becomes a pond in half an hour. I walked or rather ran twenty yards from my car to the mess last week when it was raining. Soaked to the skin. Underpants even and my shoes full of water. Still it stays warm.

I've a new detachment out now, further still and I had a great round on Wednesday inspecting everybody, 260 miles. We get up early and start immediately after bkfst. I take a mouth organ, some French plays and my Malay pantuns (poems) to pass the time. The first thirty miles are good roads with several plantations. Then it turns to a red earth road (laterite) with jungle on both sides. It's very tall and hangs over our poor little poles quite dwarfing them. Like this.

The trees do almost meet. Sometimes they fall down and bang go our poor wires. About sixty miles away, tucked into the jungle is our post at U. Two men relieved weekly in case they go mad. I've had to put six more men there as we've got a new job on, building open wire route for the PO. Right up our street.

The local post office (Post and Telegraph Co, P & T) are doing rather less than half and we have the rest. Naturally we want to finish first although they started before us. So far we are well up to schedule. The men love it. It feels like real work. They're permitted Aussie hats instead of topees, and they're all as brown as Malays.

We go on past U. up through tin mine country and one or two villages up to E. Then round the back and way off into the blue ...

Road seems to get smaller and smaller, trees bigger and bigger and as for the poor little telegraph poles they look like undergrowth. Always rumours of tigers from the P & T Malay linemen ... One told me that he was up a pole one evening when a tiger walked over and upset his bicycle which was leaning at the bottom of the pole. It then trampled on the machine and tried to climb the pole after him. Fortunately he had gone up without a ladder using his bare feet and the tiger's claws slipped on the concrete pole. He lived to tell the tale. I'm sure it was a lie but it was a very artistic one to cover damage to a P & T bicycle which was really its only purpose. He told it in Malay to quite a crowd of us so I may have missed many of the finer points, but his gestures and expression were enough to tell the story.

After a bit the jungle clears out giving way to more villages, plantations, sawmills, fruit farms and so forth, until we come to quite a large centre. Looked at my people there and then called on the local P&T man, Kandiah by name. He offered me some coils of heavy copper wire which are hard to come by as a reward for nothing in particular but I expect he will want my good offices for some purpose in the future. Then down South again passing quite near Dad's stamping ground of about ten years back and so home. A very interesting trip.

Your two delightful letters, such fun hearing about the child. I can't have too much of that. He seems to have made a capture of his Wye G'parents too. Dad had many sweet things to say of him and of you too dear. How brave you were about your operation all in all.

He's very nearly one year old now and I shan't see him probably until he's two or three. Such a shame ...

We have been on our toes a bit lately with the Japanese trouble. I still can't make a guess which way she will jump but it seems a safe bet that we can, between us all here, take care of any little troubles which may arise. The expression 'to liquidate the Japan incident' is quite current here, as an answer to the Japanese 'China incident'.

Good bye sweet heart until we meet again next Mail.

Your Barry

Chapter 3

Britain: Late 1941

Phyllis in the White House

During all this time Phyllis and baby Robin were living with her parents James and Lilian, at the White House, Great Missenden, Bucks. Her two older brothers, Francis and Lionel, had married and left home, and her younger sister, Enid, was at Cambridge. Living at home was secure, but never easy. James was not prepared to relax his strict time-keeping just because there was a war on, and Lilian, although often in precarious health, insisted on maintaining high standards in the home.

When Barry was posted to the Far East, Phyllis expected to join him in the near future. By late 1941, with the news of disturbing events there, she must have been realizing that this was unlikely to happen. Naturally she was concerned, yet she was still writing cheerfully to Barry and hoping all would turn out well. A letter from her on non-airmail paper (the first in terms of date that survives), though faded, does not look as though it was with him during his imprisonment. It was probably among those returned to her or delivered after liberation.

James Bacon, Phyllis's father.

7 December 1941 from Phyllis (the White House) to Barry

Darling one, I've sent you off a P.C. yesterday by airmail. I'm going to try to cable you today. I'm trying not to worry about you, & have my own ideas on your present position, if it's anywhere near where you were when I last wrote. All the same, I'd like a little more news of you soon.

Robin keeps me too busy to have much time for worrying. He is developing into a fierce, tough, small boy. His energy is terrific & almost inexhaustible ... Yesterday he was in his playpen in Enid's room, & Mother was ironing there. She heard him making noises at her & turned round. He took from his mouth & offered her part of a napthalene [moth] ball! Mother removed some more, but he probably ate some. He then succeeded, through the bars, in opening the door of the little cupboard by Enid's bed, & proceeded to remove and examine the contents. He can hurt me when he hugs me now, but very seldom lets anyone else 'love' him – he is so fierce that Mother can't hold him ... The other day he dropped some cake overboard at tea-time. I said 'no' & picked it up. He dropped it again, so I lightly smacked his hand, & told him 'no' again. He dropped it again, his eyes, full of mischief, on me, & I smacked him harder. So we went on, till I smacked him hard enough to hurt & he winced and gave a little cry. Then, his eyes on me, he very deliberately dropped the cake & quickly held out his hand to be smacked, & screwed up his face in anticipation. What can one do to that?

He is now up in his cot, bouncing up and down, with gurgles and growls and other queer noises. He seems very well, is as sturdy as they make 'em, & has the most terrific calves for a baby. He stands with his legs well apart, feet firmly planted, when I put him in his bath, & laughs at me in the wickedest fashion when I try to make him sit down – a feat which can only be accomplished by guile, & not by force. He & Daddy get on very well together, & when [brother] Lionel was here last week, Robin called him Ded-dee. He does need his Daddy, without a doubt, & he is so very sweet & lovable at present, that I am afraid of spoiling him. He's so full of impish mischief & so funny!

Enid is going to post this in Aylesbury, & is leaving in five minutes, so I must stop.

Oh! Daddy is taking me to see 'Jack and the Beanstalk' at the Coliseum tomorrow – I'm very much looking forward to it.

As always, all my love, my dearest husband. Your wife, Phyllis

The day after posting this letter, on 8 December 1941, Phyllis and all the other wives and mothers of the men in 27 Line Section woke up to confirmation of the news of the Japanese attack on the American Pacific base at Pearl Harbor. While the entry of the US into the war brought enormous relief to the Allies, Phyllis and other relatives of the men in the Far East faced the realization that their men were now in the fighting line.

Chapter 4

Malaya: December 1941

Japan and the UK at war

In Malaya on 8 December, Barry and the men of 27 Line Section heard, in quick
succession, that the Japanese had bombed Singapore, that a small Japanese force
had landed near Kota Bharu but had been repulsed and driven back out to sea,
that there had been a second landing further down the coast, that Pearl Harbor
had been wiped out and that Japan and the UK were now at war.

On that day Barry wrote from Malaya:

8 December 1941, from Barry to Phyllis, on a small scrap of paper
Darling Wife, very darling wife just now. War declared this am. You will
have read all about it in the papers. Bombs on S'pore, landing in Kelantan.
All safe so far. Dad will explain the position to you. He has a very thorough
knowledge of the strategical positions in the country and probably has a
good idea where I am. Only time (and weight!) for this scrap to say I love
well [?], always have and always will love you. I came here for a quiet war and
I'm not going to let any nasty little Jap interfere.

All the love I have my darling. Your Barry

Then, as Barry's memoirs recall:

The news of the Japanese bombing at Pearl Harbour on Hawaii was fairly
accurately reported, and we learnt then that the greater part of the US
Pacific fleet had been destroyed. A few days later two of our biggest and
strongest battleships, the *Prince of Wales* (a new battleship) and the *Repulse*
(an old 1914–18 Battle Cruiser), steamed out from the naval base, up the
East Coast of the Peninsula to destroy any further Japanese attempted landings and the first any of us heard of this bold naval strategy was that both
ships had been sunk by Japanese torpedo bombers.

All these disasters happening within a few days of one another must have
made us realize that Fortress Singapore might not after all be quite as
impregnable as we had been taught to believe.

At the time, though, Barry and his men believed what they were told. In fact, the
report of the first landings being repulsed was untrue; the Japanese had landed,
established a good bridgehead and captured the strategic airfield at Kota Bharu.
The ships seen hurrying back out to sea were empty, having landed their troops,
and were going back to fetch more. There was still a belief that the impenetrable
jungle would prevent any actual invasion. And yet, Barry's parents, Barbara and

Barbara and Alan on a trip in the Malayan jungle, 1930s.

Alan, had made several well-organized trips through this supposedly impenetrable jungle and had said that it was not impossible; but no one believed them.

From here on, events moved swiftly. The Japanese navy carried out a landing
on the island of Penang (Barry's birthplace). The island and its capital Georgetown were very quickly captured, with much bloodshed. This invasion, even
more than the landings on the east coast, came as a very sudden shock to the men,
as it indicated that the Japanese now had control of the sea all around Malaya.
The fighter aircraft sent in to defend Malaya were Brewster Buffaloes, poorly
armed machines and much slower than the German-designed Japanese fighters,
which quickly shot most of them out of the sky. Meanwhile, the big guns at the
naval base on Singapore Island pointed out into the South China Sea and waited
for the naval attack that never came.

Barry, now in a maelstrom of action, tries to write a cheerful letter to Phyllis.

10 December 1941, from Barry to Phyllis in blue and red ink
My very dear Phyllis, if you've had the tiny slip I put into my last Clipper
packet to you you will know that this is written just after the declaration of
war on Japan. It has not touched us very closely here yet, but Wars and
Rumours of Wars are close at hand. There is work to do. A great deal of
work. So far this is a rapidly moving war and in any such battle Signals are on

the job day and night. Don't be worried if you have no news for some time. I may be too busy to write, and the Clipper service will probably be suspended or at least delayed. One of the airports in the Pacific which the Pan American Clippers use has been bombed but we've not yet heard how seriously it is damaged. Above all don't worry. Bad news always goes home by telegram and I promise you'll hear soon enough if anything goes wrong. But, as I've so often said, I came here for a pleasure cruise and a quiet and peaceful end to the War, and I'll have no Jap interfering with my plans.

14 December (same letter)

This was not finished as the Clipper service was stopped. It is now going again but it may not get through so this may or may not reach you. No war here just yet and I don't think it will reach us. But it may. These Japs seem to do a lot of unexpected things. I told my cobber here about the sinking of those two ships a day before it happened. By name and by time, accurately, which was astonishing. I've had no other premonitions yet. Perhaps I'll get news in time to get out of the way when it's my turn. But I don't expect it ever will be.

I can't write you a newsy letter now my darling. Just remember how much I love you and how much I am looking forward to a long life with you and our large family. I shall look after myself very carefully.

All my love my dear. Your Barry

Over Christmas 1941, 27 Line Section was still in mainland Malaya, based in Johore and Pahang, building lines for anyone who asked for one. Meanwhile, the war was being run from the relative isolation of Singapore Island by a War Council consisting of the Governor, Sir Shenton Thomas (once boss to Barry's father, Alan), the Military Commander in Chief, Sir Robert Brooke-Popham, an old man who tended to fall asleep during meetings, and Lieutenant-General Percival. Alan had not thought much of Sir Shenton, who had resolutely refused to believe in the danger of a Japanese invasion.

Barry remembers that period:

While we were beavering away in Johore, troops were continually passing through on their way North to join the fighting against the invading Japanese army, but the reports we heard were all about confusion and muddle. Basically there was no front line where our soldiers could form up into a defensive position, but rather a series of raids on our flanks and rear from Jap soldiers who seemed able to work their way through the jungle wherever they wished. We had several tales of a regiment taking up a chosen position across the road, siting their machine guns, digging trenches, arranging for Artillery support, and then learning that their Regimental or even Brigade HQ, many miles to the rear, had already been overrun and captured by Japanese patrols.

There were some apocryphal tales of a signalman laying a few miles of field cable, connecting a telephone to it to test the circuit and getting an answer in Japanese.

Much has been written about that period between Pearl Harbor and the fall of Singapore. What emerges is that the old guard and the new shared little common ground and that none of the people in charge had a realistic appreciation of Japanese intentions and capabilities. With hindsight one can admit that the Japanese were better fighting soldiers than the British regulars. They had been at war in China for four or five years, were used to harsh conditions and could live on a little rice with not much else. While there was a very considerable British army in Malaya at this time, they were either well prepared for the wrong kind of warfare or altogether unprepared for fighting. They were used to three hot meals a day, a comfortable bed in a barrack room, motor transport if required to move any great distance and attention from a medical officer whenever it was needed. Perhaps even more importantly, they lacked any experience of actually encountering an enemy and killing him, something to which the Japanese soldiers were thoroughly accustomed.

Chapter 5

Britain: December 1941 to January 1942

Phyllis, Robin and rabbits

In Britain at that period genuine information was extremely hard to come by. When Phyllis heard on 8 December the news that Japan was at war with Britain, she started a letter straight away but did not get very far, partly, no doubt, because she, like everyone else, was waiting and hoping for further news. She finished it on 15 December and sent it just before the post ceased to operate. This letter did reach Barry and survived the war, but it is heavily damaged and partially missing. This is the first of the letters that Barry gathered and kept on a piece of string with a tiny bamboo toggle and the last letter he received for over a year.

> *8 December 1941, from Phyllis to Barry (received, no date)*
> in bed 11.45pm My dearest one. It is December 8th 1941, and all day I have been thinking, hoping, wondering about you. Are you still safely in your up country job or back in Singapore? Will you ever have to become part of a fighting unit? Oh, darling, I'd so much rather you were safe than glorious. Your poor parents must be feeling this bitterly – I'm sure part of Alan must long to be back in Kota Bharu, directing those defences he planned and organised. Dear darling, if anything happened to you, life would be so very empty and lonely – and to live for Robin alone, so very bad for him. What it all means is, I love you dearly, & pray God to keep you safe. He must try sweetheart for your son needs you. Already I feel he would be better for your presence, for he is very strong willed, though sunny tempered, and so very very sweet ... This last weekend he has discovered how to pull himself up in his playpen and lower himself again without bumping. He also claps his hands in time if you recite 'Pat a cake, pat a cake' to him. He knows a few names such as Mummy, Grandad, Nanny & Roy [black Labrador] (particularly quick on Roy)! He has seven very sharp teeth, & weighs between 19–20lbs. I'll continue the list of his accomplishments tomorrow. I've come over very, very tired. It's now 12 midnight, so goodnight my dearest husband. I hope you may dream of that day (night) when I lie in your arms again – at peace.

Phyllis, always practical and busy, kept chickens and bred Blue Beveren rabbits ('my blues'); they provided food, gloves and mufflers for everyone. The rabbits were a big part of Robin's life at the White House as he was growing up. Later in the war, Robin remembered his grandfather James – who went with his trilby and umbrella to his City office every weekday – coming in from the garden with fur on his hands from the butchery of rabbits.

Monday, 15 December (same letter)
A whole week & I've written no more! It has been such a week – making Xmas puddings, killing bunnies, making Robin's cake etc & of course the climax was last Saturday, when we celebrated, a bit previously, Robin's 1st birthday. It was a perfect party for he loved every bit of it & we all adored him! He wore a white woolly suit I made him, with a square yoke to set off his sturdy little figure. Such a lovely little figure – very like it was at six months but stronger, squarer & so beautifully straight. Mother and daddy gave him a birthday cum Xmas present, which I chose – a lovely horse on wheels, a solid animal, such as, as Barbara says, one could grow up with. A back broad enough to sit on comfortably for rides, & a handle affair behind to teach him to walk. And he did a few steps with it right away. (He walks round his playpen now, holding on.) Then, when he had duly admired that, he was given a coloured ball, from [his cousins] Paul and Margaret. Again much appreciated. Then came your parents pile of gifts. First an envelope with a Savings Cert in it. Then a ... [?], then a box with screws, & then the thing he dived for and wouldn't leave a little coloured book. He loves books, & turning over the leaves ... [the next couple of lines are in a torn fold and have been damaged by water] ... dining room & Enid opened the double doors with a flourish. The table was gay with bonbons and cakes. His whole face lit up, he held out both arms to the table, and cooed! It was lovely. He was too excited to eat but loved it when we pulled the crackers and put on paper hats, and sang 'happy birthday to you'. There was only Dad, Mother, Barbara, Alan, Enid & of course Kathleen [the young paid help], who sends you her fond regards. Barbara says that she doesn't think he'll ever enjoy a birthday more for he loved all of it. And there were no strangers to distract or upset him.

   ... This morning I received 8 section letters [from relatives of Barry's men] together. I have phoned the P. O. & they have had no notification about the Clipper Service, so I am sending and hoping. I have to send on spec here, as they won't say when the Clippers go. I'm so sorry about Mrs Nairn. Of course I'll write to her ... Thank you for the snap – I love it. I'm afraid I can't send film – they're almost unobtainable, & anyway, I wouldn't be allowed to seal them. Also, dearheart, snaps of Robin are out of the question in this weather ...

At this point there is half a page missing. With each line stopping half way, it is impossible to make sense of what is left.

   On the day she finished this letter, Phyllis, concerned about her duties as post-mistress, sent out the information about how to use the Clipper Mail again but with the following additional paragraphs:

15 December 1941, from Phyllis to 27 Line Section relatives, extract from circular letter
The Post Office tells me that they have received no notification that the Clipper service is suspended, though the letters may have to go overland in places, and so take longer.

My father-in-law, the late Resident British Adviser of Kelantan, is sure, from references in my husband's letters, that our men are north of Singapore, but 400 miles south of the Kota Baharu area where the Japanese are attacking, so that we have no cause for undue worry as yet.

Yours sincerely

On this same day Phyllis started her second letter to Barry.

15 December 1941, from Phyllis to Barry (never sent, or received after liberation)
Dear darling, I sent off 2 Clipper letters this pm. But find I have omitted one note [from a relative of one of Barry's men], so I'm going to send it tomorrow, with any other late letters & this note from me. I have worked out my system, & have an index notebook for addresses and dates of receiving and sending mail. I shan't be much out of pocket, dear one, as Mother and Daddy are paying for stamps for re-addressing. My only expenses, in fact, were in getting the book, & a supply of stamps and envelopes.

Our bobbity boy was so funny tonight. He was sitting on Mother's lap, facing her, in his fluffy yellow dressing gown, & she was singing 'Hark the herald angels sing' to him. He tried to follow her, about an octave lower, till she went up very high. He followed, giving a cross between a squeak and a shriek, and deciding this was fun, continued loud and long on the same note! ... The other night I came up as usual to bed & started to remove the spare covers and pillow, and tiptoed gently to put them down by the desk. Suddenly I was startled by a wicked little chuckle, & there was Bobbin, sitting in the middle of his cot and laughing at me, highly tickled by my antics. How long he'd been watching I don't know! I find him in the weirdest attitudes, usually lying on top of the covers facing the wrong end of the cot, & face down, or all in a ball, or behind well in the air.

My darling, Robin is pure joy to me, & I can never be sufficiently thankful that we have him; but it grieves me greatly that you are missing his lovely baby days. Each day he does something new & exciting or funny. He goes to sleep in his pram in a blue Kanella sleeping bag, with a big yellow bunny on it (added by me). This morning he received a dear monkey from [your aunt] Molly; an old favourite of the children's scrubbed up, & 'better than a cheap new toy' as Molly says ...

Now I'll say goodnight and try to dream I am sharing that small bungalow and big bed with you. All day I want my husband and Robin's Daddy home again, but now I want a lover back, and those times when you read bits of Bilitis, or Song of Songs to me before we once again translated their subtle, delicate, sensuous imaginings to glorious reality. My body lacks the vigorous, healthful stimulus of your presence, beloved, almost as much as my mind the perfect peace & relaxation of our fulfilled love. I can keep myself busy during the day, but at night I ache for you, body and soul. Remember, won't you, your love means my whole life, darling.

In bed. Nearly midnight (same letter)
I'm very sleepy & it's late, so this bit is just to recall that it's December 17th, 1941 and our bundle is one year old. This time last year I was sleeping the sleep of the very very weary, but oh! So happy. You had not long left me. And now ... you are in the other half of the globe, & I am less tired, but less peaceful. My darling, I pray that before the Dec 17th next, you may have shared with me some of the great joy and happiness that Robin means.
    Goodnight husband dearest.

Phyllis had planned to send this letter on 16 December, but she continues to add to it all through Christmas – postal services to the Far East were probably suspended over this period.

26 December 00.15am (same letter)
Well, darling, thank God this Christmas farce is over for another year. We've all been dreading it here, but with Robin to keep Aunt Alice fairly cheerful, it's not been too bad – just us & A. A. When we rang Wye up after lunch, I found that Aunt Ada was in a Nursing Home – if only she'd gone sooner then your parents could have come here & we would have been really cheerful and moderately happy.

Aunt Ada's name runs through these letters like a thread of steel. A formidable woman, once a hospital matron, who, with Barry's grandfather, ran the house that the four boys, Barry, his brothers (young) Alan and John and their cousin Richard, called home for most of their childhood. It was normal practice to send school-age children born in the Far East back to England to live with relatives, and Great Aunt Ada had dominated Barry's childhood but was clearly finding 'retirement' and old age difficult. Her wishes, instructions and welfare clearly had to be taken into account at all times by all members of the family. Phyllis writes more about Robin then continues:

There's lots more to say, but I'm far too sleepy to go on now. So goodnight, dear darling husband. I love you rather a lot.

Sunday, 28 December 3.15 (same letter)
Dear heart, they are just playing 'one fine day' & Ruth Naylor is singing, on the wireless. I am attempting to round up some of my stray correspondence – this will have to go via Africa, and most of the letters, as you will see, were sent to me to send by Clipper. I'll send regularly once a week by the Africa air-mail.
    About our finances, dear one. They're not too good at present! ...

Barry's Great Aunt Ada in the 1920s.

Monday p.m. (continuation of above letter)
Confusion all round! [Brother] Lionel arrived, unexpectedly, about 1.20. (I had to go down to meet him) & now all electricity cut off at the main till 4pm.

Quite a lot of letters [from relatives of men in Barry's unit] arrived this am for Malaya – hoping they'd go by Clipper. Just off to the village with Lionel to post these.

Very much love, darling,
Your own wife, Phyllis

Apart from a postcard about mails sent on 1 January 1942, the letter above is the last one that Phyllis wrote thinking that Barry was alive and free; but as it shows no signs of wear and was not attached to Barry's string of letters, it was probably among those returned to her or received after liberation.

Just after Christmas she heard from Mrs Nairn, the widow of the signalman who had died of a fever in November 1941. The following letter is a foretaste of the difficulties widows with children would encounter.

January 1942, from Mrs Nairn (Glasgow), wife of Signalman H. Nairn, to Phyllis
Dear Mrs Baker, As I am at present staying in Glasgow I have only just received your letter enclosing Captain Baker's. I am very grateful indeed for your kind letter of sympathy, and for Captain Baker's kindness in writing to me.

I am writing to Captain Baker direct, and have told him I would be very pleased to receive a photograph of my husband's grave.

The Record Office have sent me a list of the Signals Associations, and I have written asking them if they can help me in placing my three children in a boarding school in a safe area near Glasgow, as it will now be necessary for me to return permanently to town to find employment They have replied saying their local agent will call on me. Should they be unable to help me I will be very glad to avail myself of your kindness, as perhaps you may be able to advise me in this connection.

Meanwhile I can only express my thanks once more. So much has happened in Malaya since my husband's death, I know how anxious you must be. I hope though, that Captain Baker, and my husband's comrades and other officers, may come through safely, and victory soon be ours.

Yours Sincerely, Ellen Nairn

Widows were possibly the least regarded victims of the Second World War. Pensions were still very low, especially for Other Ranks. They could be denied for a variety of reasons, such as that the man died of natural causes or even that the widow was not 'deserving' due to moral failings. An assortment of charity funds were available as back-up, though these were run by volunteers at a local level and decisions were often arbitrary. However, there are no other letters in the file for Mrs Nairn, so hopefully she received the assistance she needed.

There are two more letters from Barry before the Japanese overran the Malayan Peninsula and the long silence began.

Chapter 6

Malaya: December 1941 to 15 February 1942

Last letters home

30 December 1941, from Barry to Phyllis
The day before New Year's Eve. There's no getting away from it my dear. The only real hardship out here so far is being so far away from you. About 15,000 miles by sea or 3½ months by letter. Either way is impossibly far. I can go on imagining you for a bit but after a time there's nothing else will do but I must see you and I can't. I make love to you by letter as I could when we were just naughty young bachelors but that's not what I most want of you. Someone I can come home to and tell my troubles too. I've no real troubles to tell but oh darling I do so want you here.

This letter must be making you think I am unhappy. I'm not really. Just very lonely. I don't suppose I shall write to mum and dad this mail. Give them and all your families my love and best wishes, and any news you think might interest them. SEND ME A PICTURE OF MY SON.

Can you remember how much I love you?

I wish you were here to be told. Barry

21 January 1942, from Barry to Phyllis, first half in pencil
My Own Darling, Hospital again! But a mild one this time. I've been in a week and I'll be on duty again in a few days time, with only a little scar on my forehead to show for it. Motor smash again. I was passenger in an Australian car with a very young (17) Aussie driver. He misjudged the width of a Chinese pedestrian and then to avoid him had to make a head on collision with a big lorry. Cut forehead, cut nose, cut cheek cut chin for me. Driver unhurt. My cuts have healed, very neatly stitched up but I have a very stiff and tender neck that will straighten up in a day or two, I hope. Very comfy hospital in xxxxxx (censored by me). Real female women nurses and sisters. Many of them evacuees from further up country. The other patients are mostly gunshot wounds from rifle and Tommy gun and I am quite surprised how little a bullet wound seems to bother them. The war is getting nearer but it is some way off yet. I am pleased to note that Command Signals seems to be keeping up its reputation as a pretty safe billet.

It's a long time since I have written to you and simply ages since I had a letter from you. Last one still dated Sep 41. We've been rather busy for letter writing lately. I've shifted the section to another part of the country where we are busily taking over the civil lines and altering them to suit our own requirements. I wish I could tell you more about operations here. But that is obviously not possible. The papers are full of howls of mismanagement and there have undoubtedly been mistakes, but none of them as grave as they may appear on the surface. There appears to be a perfectly sound basic policy, which, as Army Signals, we must know something of, and so far everything is working to the proper end. But like having babies, 'you've got to be much worse before you're better'.

As I still have headaches the Doc tells me I may have to stay here a week or two longer which will be boring just when things are boiling up nicely.

My batman [Driver Reginald Hedges] came in after I arrived here with some clothes and my big picture (of you). It's had some pretty queer adventures already that picture. It's been with me everywhere … There is proper drill for it now. As soon as my charpoy bed is made down and the net slung, the picture is unpacked and set up nearby. Driver Hedges knows that my picture my cash and my penknife are my most treasured possessions. Not counting my family that is. xx …

31 January 1942 (same letter, in blue ink)
(Convalescent Depot) I've had 2 letters from you and one from Mum! Letter dated Aug 41 telling of your last few days at Wye and the two presents Mum gave you. I'm so, so glad about that. It means that you are now irretrievably one of the family. Almost more so than we boys. Mum really is such a darling. I don't think she can really regret the decision she made. Dad is a good husband. He's certainly a bloody good father. And also a p.c. by air dated 1 Jan 42 from you and one from Mum. Yours to say all well and you're sending out mail by S Africa …

I will of course send my own mail by S Africa. I'd no idea it was fast.

I hear that since I left them my lads have finished their job and returned to HQ camp. It is a comforting thought that in what has been, I suppose, the hardest and most dangerous part of this whole campaign, there have been no casualties at all in my whole unit from enemy action. We have had bombs fairly near and even machine guns but no harm done yet.

I think it's a safe job. I'll try to send a Number Cable tomorrow but we're not very near to a PO I hope to be back on duty any day now. Neat scar on forehead [sketch of face with scars]. Little ones on nose cheek and chin, v slight.

Keep happy and brave my darling. We're all safe here and hope you'll keep yourself safe for me at home.

Your own (very own) B.

As Barry was writing this letter the Japanese were steadily advancing down the Peninsula, dealing fiercely with any opposition. One extremely unlucky person was Alan's successor as British Advisor to the Sultan of Kelantan, George Kidd. He was among the men killed by the Japanese on 23 January 1942 at Parit Sulong in Johore.

War in the city, Singapore

Barry and his (now) sixty-seven men of 27 Line Section, a complete functioning unit of the Royal Signals, were deployed wherever they were needed. They had already been attached to and detached from other forces. Some time in January 1942 they withdrew to Singapore and were attached to the 8th Australian Division, whose newly arrived reinforcements were short of Signals units.

Barry notes in his memoirs:

> These troops had been hastily recruited, mainly in Perth, many of them ex-prisoners or from magistrate Courts. They were thoroughly disaffected and saw no reason to fight for these snooty Pommie Merchants who in turn treated them with disdain. We lived with one of the regiments for a short time and immediately formed a very poor impression of them. At this time other Australian troops in the Desert were fighting very bravely and success-fully in Tobruk and in other desert battles, under Wavell and Montgomery.

Life with the Australians was not without its lighter moments. In a 1944 letter written to Phyllis, Verdi Earnshaw described an incident from this period when his son, Corporal Jack Earnshaw, was attached to the Australians: 'One day when he had gone on duty, the Chinese laundry man arrived to collect the laundry, and ... the Australians in a joke handed his bag over and told this Chinese that it belonged to One Long Man (he is tall ...) and of course when the laundry came back, they were all shouting for One Long Man, he [Jack] did not take any notice until they drew his attention that it must be his.' (See photograph on p. 21)

At the end of January 1942, 27 Line Section was again detached and sent out of Singapore City to build an overhead route in the north-east part of the Island, to replace an underground cable which had been bombed.

> It was, as usual, a matter of extreme urgency, life or death, finish by yester-day, so I decided to employ local labour to supplement our own men. Stores, poles, arms, bolts, insulators, wires, etc were available from Post Office stores where they had not been bombed out, and the slowest part was digging the post holes, seven every quarter mile. I hired a Chinese contractor and, as before, found that Chinese coolies on piecework could dig holes far faster and better than we could. This route which ended somewhere in the Changi neighbourhood was finished in a few days, but as far as I know was never connected to anything.

About this time the last British troops, the Argyll and Sutherland Highlanders, completed the retreat down the Peninsula and crossed the quarter-mile causeway that joins Singapore Island to the coast of Johore. The Royal Engineers then blew a gap in the causeway.

> 27 Line Section then retired towards the town of Singapore where we found ourselves a suitable section HQ in an empty bombed building. Here we spent the rest of this short and nasty War (the period of actual fighting)

working with what was left of the Post Office organisation, generally under the guidance of the PO Engineers, trying to repair and replace damaged telephone lines and cables as best we could, to provide some sort of communication. My Company Commander and the CO, Lieutenant Colonel Pargeter, must have been somewhere around but I cannot remember any contact with them.

With the Japanese now in complete control of the Peninsula they were able to line up their Field Artillery on the southern shore of Johore and shoot at targets of their choice all over the Island. They had complete air superiority and regularly bombed the town and harbour of Singapore, as well as various military targets in the north-east corner of the Island. In late January a flight or perhaps a squadron of Spitfires was flown in from India and operated from an airfield on the Island. They had considerable success at first, flying continuous patrols.

A pilot, one of the few who survived, told me later that it was a continuous series of fill the tanks, load 1,200 rounds of .303 in eight machine guns, look for bombers, shoot for 12 seconds then return to base. A fresh pilot then took over and the aircraft tanks were re-filled and the guns ammunitioned and set out immediately on another patrol. They were one by one either shot down by Zero fighters or Japanese AA guns or became worn out and unflyable from lack of spares and maintenance, though in this brief active period they managed to shoot down a large number of Jap bombers.

It was during this period that 27 Line Section suffered its one and only active wartime casualty. A new circuit was required on the airfield so I sent a small detachment of linemen to install a field cable, not an overhead route. Their visit happened to coincide with one of the frequent bombing raids on the airfield and one of the party, R. S. Holmes, was hit by an anti-personnel bomb.

Holmes had set off in a truck with the equipment, while his friend, Hannam, who was usually with him, took a motorbike dispatch in another direction. Holmes, at 21, was among the youngest of the men. He was wounded and later, on 13 February, died, but Hannam, who survived, never forgot him.

To no one's surprise the Japanese successfully crossed the Johore Strait on 9 or 10 February and advanced rapidly to set up a strong line on both sides of the Bukit Timah road, which runs north and south from Singapore Town to the causeway. The big guns of the naval base were facing in a direction almost exactly opposite to the Japanese invading forces.

Barry remembers:

The bombing and shelling had now increased and, since the range had been shortened, Infantry mortars joined in and caused the few minor wounds which members of the Section (including me) received during the last few days of the invasion. One of their targets now was the Reservoir that provided most of the water for the town. This reservoir was supplied by a

Reg Holmes in 1941.   Reg Hannam in 1946.

pipeline across the Straits from various sources in Johore and that pipeline
had already been cut.

The Army alone, properly led and with a few tanks and aircraft, might just have
held out long enough to wait for a relieving force, but none was available, and
Singapore was most emphatically not a military unit. The army were mixed in
with a civilian population of Chinese, Malays and Indians of over a million. The
Japanese brought up more heavy artillery and the Allies' field gun positions were
blanketed by continuous dive-bombing and quickly put out of action.

Japanese soldiers in civilian clothes then started very successfully to infiltrate
the British positions. There were many Japanese already in the City, most of
them photographers or hairdressers, who later proved to have been Japanese
agents.

Barry recalls:

In our Section HQ we had become aware of occasional rifle shots nearby,
presumably from a Japanese sniper. One of my sergeants and I set out at
night to try to find him with our Thompson sub-machine guns. Crates of
these guns, popular with American gangsters of the twenties and thirties, had
reached the Island a few days earlier from an American cargo ship and had
been issued to anyone who wanted one. There was no instruction manual
with them and we had to find out by trial and error how to load and fire
them. We had ours working well however and the sergeant and I set out in
the general direction from which we heard the shots.

We located him quite easily perched in the branches of a tree and silhouetted against a moonlit sky. At a range of about twenty yards we each gave him a short burst from the Tommy gun and he fell out of his tree, an ordinary looking native man in cotton trousers and shirt with a rifle and a bandolier of cartridges slung over his shoulder. I heard later that such snipers had been found scattered all over the town, some local residents and some infiltrators.

As the situation became very grim indeed, ships were busily carrying away evacuees, mostly women and children and a few government officials and senior officers. Lieutenant General Percival stayed on. Barry became involved with this evacuation:

> One of my most disagreeable jobs happened at this time, when I was ordered to mount an armed picket at the gangway of one of the evacuation ships to keep off unauthorised people who thought that they had a right to a place. The few men who were selected for evacuation had been notified individually but the whole population of [expat] women and children had to queue up for many hours at one of the offices set up temporarily to allot places to the most deserving. Among the many unauthorised people who tried to board there were, regrettably, a number of Australian soldiers who were quite convinced that this War had nothing to do with them and they just wanted to get back to Oz.

Beatrice, the wife of Barry's Lieutenant Sutherland Brown, got a place on one ship and was evacuated to South Africa. Barry's uncle Roger also obtained a place for his wife, Joyce Prentis, now in her late fifties, on the SS *Kuala*. While they were queuing on the dockside to go aboard, the docks were bombed and a few women and children were killed or wounded, but Joyce survived and got aboard on 13 February 1942. However, on 14 February the SS *Kuala* was bombed by a flight of nine planes while at anchor off the Island of Pompong. Joyce was among those killed.

Singapore falls, 15 February 1942

The city environment in the last few days before capitulation became, if possible, even grimmer. Massive oil stores in the northern part of the Island near the Navy base were set on fire and the whole north-western view was clouded by dense columns of black smoke, an obvious sign that the base would serve no further useful purpose. Dumps of raw latex rubber in several different parts of the Island were also set on fire and added to the smoke and smell.

> 27 was busily trying to patch up the damaged telephone lines in Singapore Town, as the Higher Command concentrated on destroying anything that might be of use to the invaders. Several buildings in Singapore Town and on the docks were also on fire and it became obvious that we would soon have to

'Harry' Carter in about 1940.

give up any further resistance. Columns of black smoke all along the northern horizon are a vivid memory of the last days of Singapore.

Fighting actually stopped on 15 February 1942, but the formal capitulation may have been a day or two later. I remember it very clearly as I was up the top of a telephone pole trying to regulate and terminate a new section of open wire, while meantime a brief air raid was going on at ground level. This consisted of the usual small high explosive fragmentation bombs, which killed people and broke shop windows but did little heavy damage except for holes in the road. The bombing and shelling suddenly stopped and one of my NCOs on the ground shouted, 'I think the war is over'. And so it was.

This moment is clearly one of those flashlight memories that remain all through life. One of Barry's signalmen, Harry Carter, told his daughter Diane, many years later, that when Singapore fell he was with his mates playing the piano in the bar of Raffles Hotel and 'pissed as a newt'.

We, of No. 27, made our way back to our temporary HQ in the bombed out building and a head count assured me that no one was missing or seriously damaged, so Reg Holmes was our only active wartime casualty. While we were sorting ourselves out a small Japanese patrol armed with rifles and fixed bayonets came up to us; they were commanded by an officer wearing a sword. I called the Section out of the billet, lined them up on parade and saluted the Officer. He saluted and bowed which I returned copying his actions as closely as I could, the first of many such bows over the next few years. On my order the men then 'piled' their arms in the neat cones as laid down in the drill books. The Jap patrol then heaped our rifles into a waiting van, and the Officer accepted my pistol and our two or three Tommy guns. More bows and saluting and the patrol then drove off. Our next duty was, of course, to find my Company Commander and the CO at Regimental HQ, which we did after much useless searching around the bombed streets of the town.

We were left free to wander for a day or two and became aware immediately of the vigorous actions of the occupying Army. A considerable number of Chinese nationals whom the Japanese had listed as spies or of particularly anti-Japanese sympathies were arrested, summarily tried, then tied together in pairs, back to back and thrown into the harbour, where they drowned or were eaten. To discourage looting from the windowless shops anyone caught by the Japanese Special Police, the Kempi Tai [Kempeitai], was immediately beheaded. The heads were then displayed on small bamboo stands at street corners in the city, each head being guarded by a Japanese sentry with a fixed bayonet. Each stand also had a small notice in English and in Chinese characters describing the man's crime. The Japanese policy, as we later learned, was to be generally very anti European and pro Asiatic, this being part of the 'Greater Co-Prosperity Sphere'.

Part Three

Wall of Silence

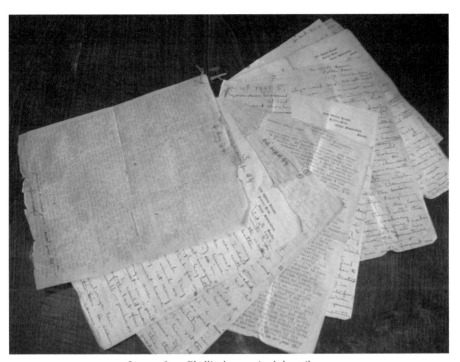

Letters from Phyllis that survived the railway.

Chapter 7

Britain: February to March 1942

The silence begins

With the fall of Singapore postal communications, indeed all communications, ceased. From then on Phyllis and the other relatives wrote into the blue, always hoping, always trying to believe, that one day they would be reunited with their men. By Byzantine routes some of these letters *were* delivered, though they often took a year or more to arrive. Miraculously, some letters even survived the jungle and though blotched, faded and creased are readable today. Alongside them are the letters, stoical or desperate, written to Phyllis by relatives of the men with Barry.

Barry kept his letters in two sheaves, one from Phyllis and the other from his parents, Barbara and Alan. Each sheaf is gathered on a scrap of string, the sheets pierced in one corner and threaded with a small sliver of bamboo as a toggle. On some the ink has seeped in damp conditions, yet apart from a few words on a crease and a missing half sheet on the bottom-most letter from Phyllis (8 December 1941, p. 38 above), all are still legible. Thousands of undelivered letters also survived and were handed, unopened, to survivors or to grieving families at the end of the war.

For the mothers, wives, grandparents, fiancées and friends in Great Britain, 1942 started and continued as a year of enormous stress and frustration, with complete silence from the men in the Far East and little help from the Royal Signals Records Office or the War Office. Those at home had only the newspapers and radio to tell them what might be happening to their men. Clipper Mail posted late on (including Phyllis's letters of 7 and 15 December) was returned about now. Phyllis sent out a circular letter (which we do not have), probably in mid-February 1942, to all the relatives of men in Barry's Unit for whom she had addresses. Tina Douglas, wife of Driver Gilbert 'Gibby' Douglas, who later plays a significant part in Barry's life, wrote:

26 February 1942, from Tina Douglas (Glasgow), wife of Driver Gibby Douglas, to Phyllis
Dear Mrs Baker, Many thanks for your kind letter, which has given me new heart at a time when I have nearly made myself ill with anxiety. You have been a great friend to me, and I find it difficult to express my gratitude to you, but I'd like you to know that I'll never forget you for it. I've enquired at several places here, for news of the men, but I've been told it might be weeks or months before I hear anything . . .

Not many people would take the trouble you have taken, in advising and giving comfort when things go wrong, and when your own heart must be heavy.

Somehow, you make me ashamed of myself, letting my fears and worries get the better of me, when you too are suffering the same pangs of suspense, but are keeping your spirits up and hoping for the best ...

Yours sincerely Mrs G. B. Douglas

Similar letters came from the fiancée of Lance Sergeant Cyril George, from the wife of Signalman Jack Taylor and the mother of Lance Corporal Peter Sampson.

27 February 1942, from Mrs Sampson (Glasgow), mother of Lance Corporal Peter Sampson to Phyllis

Dear Mrs Custance Baker. It was so kind of you to send me that message, giving me hope that my son may be safe and well and that you will send me word if you get any further news. It is a trying time for you also, as well as for me and all those other mothers and wives of our soldiers. You tell us to keep high hearted & hope for the best & so I shall.

Thanking you for your kindness.

Yrs Sincerely, Margaret Sampson

The families of the men under Barry's command came from all walks of life and they were writing to Phyllis during this most stressful times of their lives. Their letters are transcribed here as they appeared at the time, with no attempt to correct idiosyncrasies of spelling, grammar and punctuation.

Although a few of the relatives had been in touch with Phyllis in the past, the way 27 Line Section, and no doubt other wartime units, were put together, meant

Peter Sampson in about 1940.

that up to this point most of the relatives were isolated from each other. A letter to Phyllis, arriving in March 1942 from a Mrs Queenie Garrod, wife of Barry's Lieutenant, Bob Garrod, made it clear that, like Barry and Phyllis, he and his wife also ran the Clipper Mail service and kept in touch with the relatives of men in the section. She writes:

18 March 1942, from Queenie Garrod (London), wife of Lieutenant Bob Garrod, to Phyllis, typed and unsigned, but one of several from Mrs Garrod's address
Dear Mrs Baker, I sincerely hope you do not mind my writing to you, but I am very anxious to get some news of my husband.

He is an officer in the Royal Corps of Signals, and went to Malaya with your husband.

My husband has often written to me about Barry, whom I believe is your husband. They both went to Singapore together to visit some relations of yours. I wondered if you had any news from them at all. As my last cable was sent on the 1st Feb. from Singapore, and the last lot of 'Clipper' letters was sent on December 2nd 1941 which I send to various relations of the men.

I have had many enquiries from relations of some of the men that was in my husband's section, about their husbands and sons. But unfortunately I have been unable to give them very little news.

This week I have had many letters, telling me that various people have had letters from the Records Office stating that they must count their people as missing.

Mrs. McCarthy wrote to me, and I visited her on Monday, she has had one of these letters. I believe she has told you as well. I asked her for your address and that is how I came to write to you.

I have made enquiries through the War Office and the Red Cross, and they have no news from Malaya or Singapore yet.

I sincerely hope you will have good news very soon, and should I get any news at all I will write and let you know.

Yours Sincerely, [Queenie Garrod]

This is a month after the fall of Singapore, but not even those in charge have much idea of what has happened. The following is a copy of one of the letters described by Queenie and sent by the Royal Signals Records Office to the wife of one of the men in Barry's section.

13 March 1942, from Royal Signals Records Office to Mrs Grierson, wife of Signalman J. A. Grierson
Dear Madam,

               2327032 Sigmn. J. A. Greierson [sic]

According to information received your husband was serving in Malaya when the garrison of Singapore capitulated on 15th February, 1942. Every endeavour is being made through diplomatic and other channels to obtain information concerning him, and it is hoped that he is safe although he may be a prisoner of war. Immediately any further information is obtained, it will be sent to you from this office, but in the meantime it is regretted that it is necessary to post him as 'missing'.

Should you yourself receive any further information from any source regarding your husband dated later than February 15th, I will be most grateful if you will inform me at once stating full particulars.

Queenie's letter to Phyllis (above) was the start of a correspondence which clearly included phone calls and later joint visits to the War Office. Her next letter read:

26 March 1942, from Queenie Garrod (London), wife of Lieutenant Bob Garrod, to Phyllis
Dear Mrs Baker, Thank you very much for your letter, very sorry I have not replied before.

No I have not had a missing notice yet. It seems to me that they must know something about the men, not to have sent a notice ... When I enquired at the War Office a fortnight ago they gave me an address were [*sic*] to enquire about Officers only, but I have had no reply to my letter yet. The address is:- Officers Section (B), Blue Coat School, Church Road, Wavertree, Liverpool 15.

I would like to know how we do stand once we've had the notice, if you have the time to spare.

I am afraid I am not on the telephone at home, as I am with my mother, and have to continue at the office owing to my age (22) being in the conscription age ...

I have enclosed a list of relatives of the men that I write to. Should there be any that duplicate, would you please let me know.

Needless to say, if I get any news, I'll contact you at once by the telephone.

Yours Sincerely, Queenie L. Garrod

For the families at home there were some practical problems to be faced. There was a difference in income between the wife of a serving soldier, of a prisoner, of a 'missing' soldier and a soldier's widow. The army had systems in place for coping with the allowances and pensions granted to wives of servicemen. However, these were based on the assumption that if a man was missing and if, after a reasonable period, no word arrived of his capture and imprisonment, then he was presumed dead, allowances ceased and a meagre pension (around £1 per week plus about 6 shillings per child) was paid instead. However, the enormous number of men captured in Singapore and then not heard of again created a new situation.

Behind the scenes the authorities were paddling furiously. David Tett's comprehensive study, *A Postal History of the Prisoners of War and Civilian Internees in East Asia during the Second World War*, documents the many efforts involved in attempting to persuade the Japanese to release names of PoWs, and in trying to find some route to communicate with them through neutral territories such as Argentina and Switzerland.

Chapter 8

Singapore: February to August 1942

Changi

Meanwhile, the Japanese began sending their unexpectedly vast number of prisoners to a complex of camps at Changi in the north-east of Singapore Island.

Once we were all reassembled in our proper Units and under Command of our COs the order came that the whole garrison was to march out of Singapore Town to the north east or military corner of the Island, around the Changi district.

The English and Scottish regiments that marched out to Changi were about 50,000 strong, though that is a very vague figure. There were barrack blocks and married quarters available for perhaps four or five regiments, say 4,000 men and we filled up every room available, contriving double- or treble-decker bunks where we could. At least everyone had a roof of some kind, which is very important in Singapore owing to the recurring daily rainfall.

The regular Japanese Army quickly moved on to invade and conquer Java and Sumatra. This left their prisoners almost unattended for some time, as the Japanese had not been prepared for the scale of this capitulation, and it was a few weeks before sufficient guards, many of them Koreans rather than Japanese, arrived and took over full control of all the prisoners. Most men were still fully organized into army units of different nationalities, with medical support and the service corps who provided food from the garrison's emergency stock.

This appeared to be mostly cans of corned beef and hard bread. The Japs supplied us with sacks of rice, requisitioned from local stores which the army cooks boiled up as rice pudding since they were unused to cooking rice as a vegetable or substitute for bread and potatoes.

Meanwhile, 27 Line Section, once again part of Malaya Command Signals, tried to keep up normal peacetime army routines with morning parades and inspection followed by detailed working parties trying to improve accommodation for ten men in areas intended for one. They had enough roofs to cover everyone and field kitchens to supplement the cookhouses in the barrack blocks, but the latrines were very inadequate for the number of men needing to use them.

The Royal Engineers dug latrine trenches in any spare piece of land available but they soon became filled up and had to be earthed over and new ones dug.

This led to a rather scary adventure that happened to me during those early days at Changi.

I put the suggestion to our CO that I should try to rig up an earth boring kit to produce an experimental borehole latrine and he agreed, as this was at the time our most troublesome shortage. I took a small party to the nearest Post Office stores which had not yet been looted by the Japs and found a selection of auger bits of various sizes including a few, seldom used, of the largest, around 15 or 16 inches diameter (over 45cms). As we planned to go quite deep, by fitting extra lengths onto the rods, we had to build a tall set of sheer legs fitted with a block and tackle to pull the auger out of its hole and then swing it aside to dump the earth.

The CO and the MO chose a suitable spot for our first experiment. The first hole went well, about 15 feet deep, say 4 metres. One of our carpenter-and-joiners built a seat with a cover, very civilized. We set up a second team of bore hole makers and made several holes within our Unit's area and a few for other regiments, until one day when we were at work the sergeant in charge of the other party came to me to announce a disaster. The head had fallen off the end into the shaft and they could not fish it out. They had tried hooks on ropes, or tied onto long bamboos but could not get a purchase. The hole fortunately was only about half way down, say eight or nine foot. I went and had a look but could not see any way round our difficulty.

Sometime later two of the sergeants came to tell me that they had a solution. Someone must be lowered upside down into the hole, using the existing block and tackle and must grip the auger bit and then be heaved up again. Since I was the officer I would, according to the sergeant, naturally volunteer for the job, especially as I was probably the thinnest and lightest man in the section. So I volunteered.

My ankles were tied onto the rope and I was heaved up and then lowered into the hole with my arms stretched out like a diver. I just fitted, but only just. When I reached the bit I found that there was luckily only a little earth in it and I was able to loosen it and get a good grip on it. At my word the team pulled me gently up again and swung me aside onto the spoil heap, untied me and then untied the bit. We found that the fastening bolt was too thin and had sheered [sic] under the strain, so we fitted a stouter bolt and restarted the work. I warned them that if it happened again someone else would have to go down. It is not an adventure that I recall with any pleasure.

Early deaths

Within weeks of capitulation, the crowding and lack of sanitation in Changi resulted in sickness. Dysentery was rife and without appropriate medication it was a killer. Two of Barry's Section died on the same day, 27 April 1942. One was Second Lieutenant Sutherland Brown, who had been an NCO and had received his first commission only that January. Lance Sergeant Cyril George, who had had dysentery for some time, finally died too. Tropical diseases also took their

Gordon Hunt in about 1940.

toll. Sergeant Gordon Leo Hunt, highly regarded, died of cerebral malaria on 3 May. In those few days, therefore, Barry and 27 line Section lost three of their most experienced and senior men.

The relative freedom of those early days of captivity changed, and by mid-summer their camp was run by second-line Japanese troops, Korean guards, Kempeitai and Indian PoWs recruited to the Indian National Army and hoping, by siding with the Japanese, to free themselves from colonial rule. All the senior officers, including Lieutenant-General Percival, were sent to Japan, leaving lieutenant colonels (of very variable calibre) in charge of the regular formations. This was, apparently, to prevent the organization of uprisings or escape attempts – a very real concern to the Japanese, given the sheer number of prisoners. However, as Barry recalls, the general spirit of the PoWs was in fact very sad and pessimistic, with no serious thoughts of revolt or even of escaping. In the European war, once out of prison camp a man might well pass for a native of the country, but in Asia any European is immediately recognizable.

Barry mentions one moment of hope:

While we were still in the Changi camps in summer 1942 there had been quite a number of secret radios, forbidden by the Japs of course, but with so much of our army gear still available there were always ways and means. We heard much false propaganda, which even then seemed untrue, but once, quite unexpectedly, I heard the recognisable voice of Winston Churchill. It made a lasting impression as he was quoting a poem by Arthur Hugh Clough which we had used as a hymn at [my school] Marlborough College. I had never considered the words of this hymn to have any particular significance, but in the Changi camp they suddenly took on a whole special meaning. The war was going very badly for the Brits. We were out of Europe with not much prospect of getting back again. Rommel was winning all his battles in the desert against Wavell, the Russians were falling back on Moscow overpowered by the Nazi armour, our Fortress Singapore had fallen, our two biggest battleships had been sunk and the US Pacific Fleet almost destroyed at Pearl Harbor. So Winston quoted:

> Say not the struggle naught availeth,
> The labour and the wounds are vain,
> The enemy faints not, nor faileth,
> And as things have been they remain.
>
> If hopes were dupes, fears may be liars;
> It may be, in yon smoke concealed,
> Your comrades chase e'en now the fliers
> And, but for you, possess the Field.
>
> For while the tired waves, vainly breaking,
> Seem here no painful inch to gain,
> Far back, through creeks and inlet making,
> Comes silent, flooding in, the Main.
>
> And not by Eastern windows only,
> When daylight comes, comes in the light;
> In front the sun climbs slow, how slowly!
> But westward, look, the land is bright!

This was obvious reference to the fact that the USA was now at war and on our side.

Chapter 9

Britain: March to August 1942

Writing to a ghost

Anxious relatives waiting in England for news after the fall of Singapore hung on the radio and scanned the papers. As the weeks dragged on they were unable to believe that the authorities knew little more than they did. Yet hard news from the Far East remained difficult to come by and what got through to relatives was, naturally, censored. They had no way of knowing whether their husbands, sons or brothers were alive or dead, prisoners or free men in hiding. The news they hoped to hear was that they were prisoners and could be reached and sent comfort parcels by post, as were PoWs of the Germans.

Phyllis and other relatives continued to write, hoping every day to be given an address for Far East PoW letters. The following is the first surviving letter from Phyllis to Barry since the one she began on 15 December 1941.

1 March 1942, from Phyllis to Barry (received, no date)
In bed 11.40pm Dear Love, I haven't written for a fortnight hoping each day may bring me good news from you. Now I am weary of waiting, but can do nothing about it. I feel sure you are as alright as can be under the circum-stances. I have been hoping you might have been evacuated, but now I am not so sure! Java seems rather uncomfortable at the moment. Bother – I meant this to be such a nice cheerful newsy letter, & I've begun badly & my pen isn't going right. So I'll say goodnight and try to do better tomorrow.

It is now Thursday March 12th, & exactly one month since we received uncle Roger's last cable. One weary, weary month, & news seems further off than ever. I have kept very very busy, & written you dozens of letters in my mind, but usually at night have been too dead tired to write – I could have written, but only dead letters, if you know what I mean.

Oh my darling, I'm sure you are alive, but I am appalled to think of the horrors you may have seen & endured. May they leave you, not embittered, but determined to work wholeheartedly to see a better world is built for our Robin and his brothers and sisters. Oh my dear, our Robin is so lovely – he is so fittingly the living witness of our love, the small part of you left with me, for my love and care. And now I live for the day when we can say his favourite word 'Dad-dee' & get the response 'Yes, my son' instead of 'no dear, that's Grandad' – or Dolly or Monkey or whatever it is.

He is full of the most endearing little tricks, & is an imp of mischief. If he is not sure about something he has done, he looks you square in the eye, his own alight with fun, but a solemn face, & slowly shakes his head, but if he can detect the faintest twinkle in your eye he slowly smiles, then giggles, then squeals with laughter, so infectiously that everyone who is in the room has to laugh too. The other day he tried to stir the sugar about, with some lumps in it on Mother's tea tray. She found a very small lump & cut it in two, & put one half back in the bowl, & one on the tray in front of him. He picked it up, started to put it in his mouth, then suddenly put it back in the bowl, seized a large lump, & popped it into his mouth. Mother's 'Robin!' made him realise he had done the wrong thing, so he hastily spat it out & put it back in the bowl!

This letter starts in March, but was not signed off. Phyllis put it aside, and although she wrote and posted further letters, the one above was not posted for another six months.

On 29 April 1942 the War Office finally published a leaflet to say that the Japanese had promised names of those captured but not yet delivered them; that plans to supply food and clothing to the Far East had been set up but not yet agreed to by the Japanese; that a route for mail through the USSR had been negotiated, but the Japanese had not yet supplied an address for correspondence. So it concluded, 'At present it would only raise false expectations to invite the posting of letters to prisoners in the Far East.'

On 17 June the British Postmaster General announced that, while waiting for a formal agreement from the Japanese about mail, relatives should write and post mail in ordinary mailboxes, but unstamped and headed 'Prisoner of War Post, Service des prisonniers de guerre'. Relatives could now attempt to communicate. However, from now until the end of the war, as far as I can ascertain, no letter to a Far East PoW was *ever* answered, so it took massive devotion and faith to continue writing.

The trickle of letters that did eventually reach the men bore no relationship to the order in which they were sent, and took anything up to two years to arrive. The first letter to reach Barry in captivity was from his mother and was on the string of letters he kept from his parents.

24 June 1942, from Barbara to Barry, much damaged (received 26 March 1943)
My very darling Barton, It is so long since we have written to you or had any news of you, even now we do not know if this letter will reach you. Every day and night you are in our thoughts. You first, then Roger & our many friends. We wonder if you have heard that Joyce is dead. We were told that she died of exhaustion on reaching a small island after the ship she was on had been bombed & set on fire. It is hard to believe that Joy, so full of life and happiness is lost: we are very sad. But that news may have reached Roger through Richard [his son] & perhaps you too.

The rest of us are all well though it seems a long time since we heard from (young) Alan who was still in the same place when we last heard. John is training as a Navigator [a crease has obliterated the next few words] ... Phyllis, she remains wonderfully brave & is well. She and Robin are at present looking after a friend's household while the friend has a baby . . . We are asked to send short letters so I will not go in for details. News of the treatment of prisoners in Japan and Singapore has given us great comfort; but oh dear we would so love to have a letter from you. We are having strawberries from the garden and the chickens are laying well.

Relatives assumed that, if their men were prisoners, their treatment would be similar to that of PoWs in Germany, and this is supported by articles such as the one on pages 67–8 below. It is not until early 1944 that it becomes clear that conditions for the majority of Japanese PoWs are utterly different. The letter concludes:

Dad has a full time job on Farm Surveys. I cook, Red Cross, & one morning a week in hospital. God be with you always dearest.

We love you and send you our love, ever your loving mother Barbara.

Throughout the war Phyllis depended for her sanity on Helen Smijth-Windham and two other close (and lifelong) friends – fellow undergraduates Yvonne Patterson and Marjorie Ewing. Helen's husband, William 'Smidge', was also in the army and her home provided Phyllis with a much needed relief from the old-fashioned restrictions of life with her parents. She was staying there in May 1942 when she started the following letter.

10 May & 28 June 1942, from Phyllis to Barry, pencil and ink (received 26 March 1944)
Dear Darling it's now 12.30am (11.5.42) & I am as near happy as I've been since Feb 15th for this is the culminating point of a week of Helen's company, during which I have been able to talk about you to a woman who can enter fully into my feelings, in the interval of her talking about Smidge! We've both loved it, for it's been so refreshing, though not good for us to do it too much.

<u>28.6.42</u> I have begun many letters, as above, but felt too discouraged to get far. Dear Love, at last it really looks as if it's worthwhile writing to you. It is going to be like a miracle to be in touch with you again, dear one. But until I get something from you, I'm not going to send photographs. But I'm having them taken, & collecting quite a lot for you. Also, Daddy takes film of Robin periodically so that you can fill in the gap a bit when you come home.

You have one of the brightest, most adorable babies you could wish for. At his present stage he says quite a lot of words but no sentences . . . He climbs up anything that he can get a foothold on . . . He runs all over the place, full of fun, & with the wickedest grin a baby ever produced. Just at this present time he is not very well, & I am very tired out. For Marjorie Ewing has just had another baby (boy, and I'm godmother) & I took Robin over to her wee bungalow at Watford, and looked after baby Sally and husband John . . . John is a dear, and very good with her, but had to leave at 7.40am, & did not get home for his (hot) supper till anytime between 9.30 and 10pm. Robin and

Sally were apt to upset each other, but got quite good later on. But they flatly (& oh so loudly) refused to sleep in the same room. All very difficult.

When I've sent this letter off, I'm going to begin a sort of diary letter, and send it off each week. Also, I'll send the letters which have been returned to me and were sent from Dec 1st [1941] onwards.

Dearheart, we are both flourishing and as happy as we could be without you. Robin hopefully tries out 'Daddy' on all new men he meets; he really needs you now – at times he's too much for me …

How much I miss you. I could never really tell you, only you are so necessary to me, that I think of you continually … One thing I know. That with your brains & patience, my determined help, & the inspiration of providing the best for Robin, you'll make good at whatever you choose to do. Are you learning Japanese, by the way? …

Oh! [brother] Lionel & Joyce have a son – born May 15th. Jeremy Charles [who has a tiny part to play later in this story], and he is just like Lionel, according to Joyce – ie, a fair, blue eyed baby.

<u>Morning</u> I had to stop to 'pot' Robin, and then fill in our new ration book forms. Dear one, as soon as I can hear anything definite, I'll keep up a flow of letters to you, & as many parcels as they'll let us send, this is only one a quarter.

Robin sits beside me now, cheerfully playing with his 'hammer pegs'. He has lots of lovely toys – some of them special 'modern' ones, given by Paul and Margaret. Not new, of course, but unbuyable just now.

Needless to say, here we live on the fat of the land [from their own garden]. Veg. and fruit ad lib, eggs ditto & I have 29 rabbits at the moment …

Now I must stop as I want Daddy to post this in the village. Remember, won't you, that all you can do is keep healthy in body and mind as a contribution to the happy future of our darling Robin (& my other unborn children) …

All my love, my darling husband. Your wife Phyllis

In July Phyllis went to stay with Barry's parents, Barbara and Alan, in the village of Wye in Kent. Their house, stretching over four floors with tall windows, was filled with intricately carved wood, Chinese vases, paintings and tapestries. It smelled of the Far East and Barbara's Turkish cigarettes. There was a large walled garden and a mulberry tree, and the social rules here were easy-going compared to the rigid timetables of the White House. Barbara was also one of the most open-minded and gentle of beings.

2 July 1942, from Phyllis (at Glenthorne, Wye, Kent) to Barry (received 26 March 1944)
Dearest One, Here I am, having my annual rest-cure and loving it, as I always do here. The place is so full of you, and Barbara the one person I am not afraid of tiring by talking of you. Tonight we have been listening to a

Tchaikovsky Concerto, and I have been reading her latest poems … Mrs Cole was here today (Do you remember – lovely – with two children; the loveliest young married in Wye, you once told me) and brought back so vividly that 2nd Wye ball, when I made that lilac frock, and we were late. Here, where life seems so comparatively leisurely, I want to write down all I think, plan and hope. And I will try, for I might make a story of it one day – our lovely dream house & eight children (I think I could do it on £3,000 p.a.!!). Meanwhile Robin grows in beauty, impishness and size, & can recognise 'Daddy' on the ciné films. Your mother sends her love, you have all mine already.

Your loving wife. Phyllis.

Finally, on 13 July 1942, the Postmaster General announced that arrangements for Far East PoW mail had now been established and gave out an address.

20 July 1942, from Barbara to Barry, much damaged (received August 1943)
My dearest Barton, We have been to Great Missenden [the White House] and can give you good news of your Phyllis and the precious Robin. Phyllis is very well, quite recovered from a most hectic time spent in looking after a friend's baby, house + husband whilst the friend had another baby. From the description of the house the new baby will have to be kept in the garden. Robin … will obviously be a mountaineer, he already climbs with agility. Oh darling he is so ridiculously like you were when we were at Crowmarsh during the last war, perhaps because of that this gap in knowing each other won't matter. You need only think back to what you were like & needed & I'm sure that will suit your son. We've had no news of (young) Alan since my last letter to you. John may get leave on the 24th when I imagine he will have finished the 2nd part of his training as an Observer. He loves flying. We are both well and busy, I've made about 40lbs of jam! Ada has fixed up to live with a family quite near her own house, she is happy. We are asked to write short letters. Our dearest love to you, God be with you.

Your loving mother, Barbara.

False comfort

With no direct news of Barry, Phyllis, like other relatives, must have been listening to the radio and scouring the papers, currently full of the European or the Middle Eastern theatres of war. Among Phyllis's letters is a newspaper cutting from the *Daily Telegraph* in 1942 headed:

JAPAN'S UNEASY HOLD ON MALAYA
ESCAPED BRITON'S BELIEF THAT THE PENINSULA COULD
EASILY BE RE-CONQUERED

Early in the piece it reports: 'Little has been heard about conditions in Malaya since the invaders, in the first flush of success, streamed down it and into

Singapore. Now, however, the mystery has been relieved.' The piece contains an account of the escape from Malaya in June, and subsequent return to London, of a British mining engineer who was interned briefly at the fall of Singapore and then allowed, like many other civilians in the early days, to wander off. His cheerful account suggests lax surveillance of prisoners, general Japanese incompetence and pro-British local people. Prisoners' food rations, he believed, were reasonably satisfactory: 'The "Aussies" have the good fortune to have Australian mutton, supplied by an arrangement between Australia and Tokyo. Other prisoners have goat or mutton from stock raised on the spot, as well as rice, fish and fruit.' This heartening report, though misleading in the extreme, no doubt gave Phyllis and all the other relatives considerable comfort.

Around this time there were also new instructions from the GPO (General Post Office) to keep letters short. These were among a series of directives over the course of the war that progressively limited communications.

The next letter by date is from Barry's father, Alan. It becomes clear from this and subsequent letters that they imagine Barry locked up in a conventional prison and suffering under-stimulation and boredom.

8 August 1942, from Alan to Barry (received 26 March 1944)

Dear Barton, I do not know when, where or how this letter will reach you but it brings to you our love and hope that one day we will see you again and that you will see for yourself how splendidly Phyllis has looked after Robin and what a fine boy he has grown up to be, determined good tempered and full of interest in life as he sees it. Phyllis has been staying with us, and we have a reasonable hope that we will soon have news of you. I know that you will understand how important it is in spite of the many difficulties of being a prisoner to try and keep fit in mind and body. I hope you will try and find some special interest. You have a real gift for languages try if possible to keep up your French and Malay to learn to write in Arabic characters, and if possible also to learn to speak Japanese. Also learning good verse will be a help and writing and composing yourself. Also if possible work with your hands. I'm afraid that as yet we cannot send you any parcels but perhaps you can get some books in Singapore. I am a very old friend of the Catholic Archbishop Devals [Bishop Adrien Pierre Devals was Archbishop of Singapore from 1934 to his death in 1945] perhaps you may be able to meet him or some of his priests ...

I will say no more except to send you all our love and our hopes for happier days. Mother keeps fit and very busy in spite of our sorrow and anxiety. Dad

Between this letter of 8 August and the next of 12 October there are no surviving letters from the family. Some have almost certainly vanished, but relatives were still waiting daily to hear if their men were prisoners and if so where. They may have been advised to wait until they received further instructions.

Chapter 10

Singapore: September 1942

Memorial at Bukit Timah, September 1942

In Singapore, during these months, Barry and the men were experiencing their first taste of labour as captives:

> From Changi we were now called on to provide working parties to move stores or unload ships in the harbour and this was done quite smoothly by detaching a platoon or a whole Company still under their own Officers and the NCOs. The Japs never specified the members of a party but simply called on the British Commandant of any particular group to supply so many men.

At this stage there were two major areas of disagreement between the PoWs and their captors. Firstly, the Japanese saw no reason why officers as well as Other Ranks should not work. Secondly, they were becoming incensed, after several escape attempts, by the refusal of the PoWs to sign 'no escape' agreements. The latter issue led to a sudden clash, a very unpleasant affair at the end of August known as the Selarang Incident. Thousands of prisoners from Changi, both sick and well, were squeezed into barracks and a square designed for 800 men, with no prospect of release until they signed. Several senior officers were forced to witness the botched execution of four escapees. After four days, with epidemic sickness becoming hourly more likely, PoWs were instructed by their commanders to sign the forms, under duress.

Soon after the Selarang Incident, in early September, part of Barry's unit, including 27 Line Section, was detached and sent as a working party to Bukit Timah. This was a small hill in the middle of the Island of Singapore where the Japanese had decided to create a memorial to the gallant soldiers on both sides who had been killed during the invasion. It was now accepted in most regiments that officers should stay as much as possible with their own commands and that junior officers would work with the men. Barry and the rest of No. 27 had always worked together and only adhered lightly to the Officer/Other Ranks divisions, but this was not true of all Army units. When conditions became more severe some (particularly British) officers hung on grimly to their traditional privileges and this became a source of discontent and even a matter of life and death.

> No. 27 still a complete formed body, marched quite a long way from Changi to some temporary huts near the new job and on the march I played to them on my mouth organ. I never really mastered this instrument and I don't

think the men enjoyed my efforts but they accepted them as being the best I could offer. We had no transport and by now were carrying everything we owned. I had made shoulder straps for my valise bedroll and carried it on my back with odd spare clothes, the picture of Phyllis and my copy of *Le Théatre Complet de Racine*. During this and subsequent marches, we all wore our ankle boots and best (and only) uniform which were all put away on arrival.

We were by now down to basic rations of rice and whatever might be available to flavour it. The commonest extra was dried fish or dried vegetables, which could be made up into a soup or stew and a spoonful or so poured over a mess tin of rice. We all kept a pair of mess tins, spoon and fork and a mug.

As our party, No. 27 and the rest of No. 1 Company, arrived at the site, one of the PoWs already working there whispered to our CO 'Just keep the tools moving. Make a noise. Don't stand still.' We noted guards standing around the site all with fixed bayonets and each of them carrying a stout bamboo rod to encourage the laggards. We had not met this situation before as none of us had yet experienced the sensation of working directly under the eyes of a Jap guard.

Our job of digging and shifting earth together with removing stones, rocks, trees and bushes was much of our life for the next few years. Every working group of 200–500 men had a pair of PoWs named as tea-men. It was their duty to carry a 60 gallon kerosene drum to the working site, set it up on a small hearth of stones, fill it with water and keep a fire going under it. When it boiled they threw in a few handfuls of tea, which was the day's ration and once an hour came round the working site with buckets of tea. We all had a mess tin and a mug with us, so we had a five-minute tea break and then got on with digging. The tea-men kept the drum full of boiling water, which on this site at Bukit Timah was readily available from a tap. But we all knew that water must be boiled and preferably boiled for twenty minutes to avoid many water borne diseases with which it was always infected. Our rice, which came round in buckets at midday, was of course also boiled, but somehow dirty spoons or pans or hands managed to carry infection and dysentery was a continuous hazard.

We worked in teams of four men, the officers with the ORs, and tried to give an appearance of busyness all the time. Our tools were chenghols, pronounced 'chungkl', and shovels. The chenghol is a heavy mattock used all over the east where we would use a spade. It was useful to get hold of an extra tool so that chunghkter, shoveller and stretcher men, could all appear to be at work at the same time. Some of my Glasgow men had inevitably been in prison at some time in their careers and we had good advice from them. 'Keep your head down, do not be noticed. Do what you are told to do and never give the slightest hint of reluctance. If you are hurt or very tired carry on with every appearance of bravery and co-operation and perhaps a guard will take pity and give you a rest.' I found this kind of behaviour fairly easy to follow and managed to avoid any serious confrontation with the guards myself, but any hint of reluctance, idleness or insubordination earned an immediate beating, and some men, especially the Australians, seemed quite unable to grasp the fact that their very survival depended on their maintaining a very humble appearance, obeying orders, combined with eagerness to please our masters. A sour look, a shrug, a turned away shoulder or any such gesture earned an immediate swipe, accompanied by loud shouts of encouragement in some kind of mixed up language which we learnt to recognize if not to understand.

Unintentional disobedience was cracked down on equally brutally. Driver Reg Hannam told his son that on one occasion he was driving along a dusty track and failed to notice a Jap staff car behind him. When it finally passed him it stopped, and the Jap officer gave him a thorough beating for failing to pull over and causing the staff car to be covered in dust.

Work on the monument at Bukit Timah went forward steadily in what we later realised were comparatively comfortable conditions. Our camp was quite near the working site and we were surrounded by villagers with something to sell, and a few Chinese shops for anyone with any money left. Duck eggs were often available at 10c each, and a hardboiled duck egg added to one's rice bowl made a very agreeable meal. As we later learnt duck eggs are a good source of vitamin B, lack of which causes beriberi, one of the earliest of the deficiency diseases to appear among us.

I had just about run out of my hoarded dollars and cents when an unexpected windfall came my way. From using my local knowledge to help with a jewellery transaction, I was the happy beneficiary of a percentage, which I was able to turn into cash. We had been hearing rumours of radio broadcasts, which made it appear that the Japs were on the point of being beaten and the War would soon be over. All untrue propaganda, but it encouraged me to share my wealth with some of my friends. I kept half for myself and cashed cheques with the other half.

Barry recorded these transactions on the blank and advertising endpapers of his book of Racine's plays.

After the war some of the cheques I had cashed for others were honoured, some were dead, and one, an Australian who had survived, refused to pay on the grounds that it would be absurd to pay a debt, which I probably would not be able to enforce.

The entries have various notes or letters marked against them whose meaning I have forgotten; paid up, lost or dead, I suppose.

With my new money I bought duck eggs or peanuts whenever I could find any for sale and continued to do this for the rest of my time as a PoW as long as the money lasted, and this may have been the reason that I did not suffer

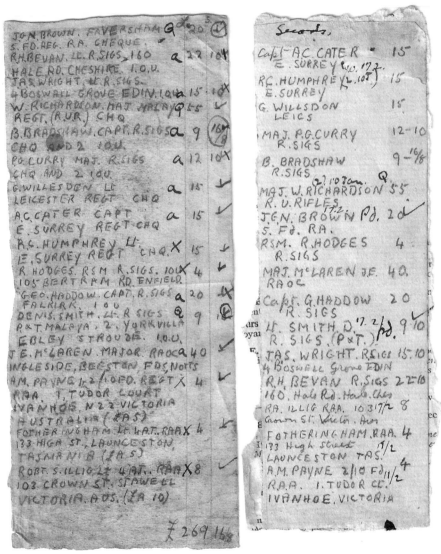

List of loans written into the endpapers of *Théatre Complet de J. Racine*.

from any of the usual deficiency diseases (except starvation). We often discussed our various appetites for sex, tobacco or food. On our very meagre diet of rice with virtually no meat, the sexual libido soon faded although reminiscing about our various sexual exploits remained a continued entertainment and pleasure. Tobacco was still available on the Island but hard to get and most smokers gave up almost immediately as I did. Most of us came down to food as our only remaining chief interest.

Chapter 11

Britain: October 1942

News for the lucky few
Back in Britain, in October 1942 Barbara wrote the first letter we have since the one dated 8 August. Her tone suggests that she, at least, never stopped writing but the intervening letters simply never arrived. Alan wrote soon afterwards.

12 October 1942, from Barbara to Barry, with fold damage (received November 1943)
My dearest Barton, we are still without news of you or Roger and the time seems very very long. If only you are getting letters from us &, even more important, from your Phyllis, it would not matter so much. Being a prisoner must make you feel so cut off from everything of home; if only our thoughts could reach you you would know, as I expect you do, how great a part you take in our daily lives, how terrifically we love you & long to see or hear of you. There is not much news, I'll tell it quickly as letters must be short. We have not heard from (young) Alan for a long time & then only a cable as I told you before. John writes regularly … Flying seems to suit him but on the ground he still gets a bit of asthma …

Aunt Ada is well and living at Hythe as a paying guest … We are both very well & will go to the White House, Great Missenden for Christmas, I haven't heard from Phyllis lately but she was much better, indeed I think well, last time we 'phoned. Robin was splendid … How quickly a page fills up darling. We love you and think of you continually.

God be with you always. Mother.

PS Phyllis rang up just after I had closed this letter. She and Robin were both very well.

13 October 1942, from Alan to Barry, with fold damage (received November 1943)
Dear Barton,
… Mother [Barbara] goes on with the Red Cross work and has been nursing at Millesboro hospital. I am still very busy with the Farm Survey. We have had a wonderful harvest and all the county has been very lovely. I hope that one day you will see all its beauty again. I am very sorry that we cannot send you any parcels or books yet do let us know as soon as you are allowed to receive any …

[He then talks about the death of Joyce, Barbara's sister.] It is life that is important and death only the last and least important incident in our life.

We will look forward patiently to seeing you again when [that] may be and will do all we can to safeguard Phyllis and Robin.
Love from Dad.

Some time early in October 1942 Phyllis received information which made the hope of reaching Barry by post more likely. At this point she hastily added a note to her old unsent/returned letter of 1 March (p. 63 above). In the top left hand corner she scribbled:

18 October 1942, continuation of letter 1 March from Phyllis to Barry (received, no date)
I have just been horrified to discover I could have been writing often. I can only pray you haven't been worried about us because of not hearing. We are all well.

At the bottom she added another paragraph:

October 18th Now, my darling one, I am going to post this at last, for I really believe it may reach you one day. Mrs McCarthy has heard that her son is a prisoner of war, but no one else that I know of from your section. Are you with your men? What do you do all day, what do you want me to send you in the way of books (I can send them once parcels are allowed from an accredited bookshop). Your very loving wife. Phyllis

She posted this and began another letter immediately, using a number, which she explains.

18 October 1942, from Phyllis to Barry (received, no date). Letter 1
Dearheart, I have had a nasty shock. I have just discovered that I could have been writing to you all this time – and I dread to think how you must feel when other men get letters and you don't. But from now on, I'll be sending regularly, of course, – & I'll number each letter, so that you will know if any are missing or in the wrong order.

Where to begin! The trouble is, that it isn't like writing to you in the usual sense, because it feels like writing into space. I don't know how you are, what conditions you are living under, what you think and feel about things. All our respective families are reasonably well, I think. I'm only half alive, but it's a very pleasant half – in other words I couldn't be dull with Robin around, but I'm only functioning properly where he is concerned. For the rest, time goes by somehow, but no events seem to leave any impression on me, & I can't even remember clearly things that happened last week. A dream world, in which you and I are together again, is just as real to me, and so much more lovely. Each day is one day nearer to our re-union, is my most comforting thought …

Our darling Robin is the joy of my life, &, I think, Mother's … Dearest, here is the end of the paper and it's a very stiff letter, I fear. I've forgotten

Daniel McCarthy in about 1940.

how to put my thoughts and love on paper. But you know how I feel don't you.

God bless you dear love, Phyllis

As Phyllis mentioned, around 18 October 1942 she heard of the letter sent to Mrs McCarthy, mother of Signalman Daniel McCarthy of 27 Line Section, from the Royal Signals Records Office. This is a duplicated letter suggesting that the Records Office have had other letters/cards by this route. Mrs McCarthy sent Phyllis this copy:

Undated 1942, from Royal Signals Records Office to Mrs McCarthy, mother of Signalman D. D. McCarthy
Dear Madam,
               2345594 Sigmn McCarthy D. D. Royal Signals.
I have to inform you that although no official Prisoner of War report has been received from the Japanese Government a post card believed to be from Shanghai written by the above named is now in transit to you by post from Lorenco Marques [*sic*], Portuguese East Africa. On the evidence of this post card you [*sic*] ..son.. has been recorded as a Prisoner of War. Confirmation from official sources is still awaited. Pending further instructions letters to the Prisoner of War should continue to be addressed as directed in the recent Post Office pamphlet P.2327 B., obtainable at any Post Office.

Yours faithfully, Lieut. [no signature] for O i/c R. Signals Records.

25 October 1942, from Phyllis to Barry (received, no date). Letter 2
Dearheart, It is now a week and a half since I wrote to you, – I cannot get used to the idea that it is worthwhile trying to reach you, & just forget about writing, it's so long since I wrote regularly.

Now first of all we are both well and fairly happy – Robin would be quite so if it weren't for his second back double teeth … His vocabulary is always astonishing me, and he never misses anything said or done. We all have to watch ourselves carefully now. Today when I called him a 'silly-billy' he said, 'No, si'ee Bobbitty'. He rarely says Robin, but has found Bob-er-tee easy to say. He seems to understand what I say, & I can send him to fetch things upstairs, or reason with him now. One of his favourite games is to get into bed beside 'Nanny' (Mother, who has been unwell for a week now) with a 'Woman's Journal' & work through it. All the babies in the advertisements are either laughing or crying, & he imitates them. If they have their mouths open he 'feeds' them with the cake and foods illustrated in the cookery section. We also get portions of pies, cakes and 'matoes. He can say the names of all his own clothes, the foods we have, the furniture, & all his toys. Such small sentences as 'I find it' 'I fetch it' 'Here y'are' are in frequent use. He can count up to ten, but leaves out seven & repeat the alphabet after you very clearly. But all his words are very clear, & he doesn't talk gibberish. And, my darling, he is very tidy. He knows where things belong, and likes to see they are kept there. If you go down the garden in wellingtons, leaving your slippers by the door, they are quite likely gone when you come back, because Robin has put them away. And he always shuts any door he finds open … One of his most embarrassing tricks is never to miss an unfortunate noise or tummy rumble, to look severely at the delinquent, and then point and say 'Pot' very firmly. His vocabulary includes such words as naughty, barking, hic-cup and finished. In fact, my darling, you have a remarkable son, who kisses his Daddy's photograph whenever he can get hold of it & is the joy of his mother's heart.

Dear darling one, till I know if letters are reaching you, I find it difficult to be intimate on paper. But it's 'come rainy, come fine' alright for me. I think of you, dream of you, all day, & meanwhile try to do all I can for you through the care of our son. As soon as possible, dearheart, I'll get books sent to you. Meanwhile, keep up your heart, & I trust you are getting some of the strength and & comfort I pray for you every night, dear one. Yes, I do, nowadays.

Your own as always, Phyllis.

While his family still clearly imagine Barry coping with confinement and idleness, he is at the start of the most testing year of his life.

Chapter 12

Singapore to Thailand (Siam): November 1942

To Siam in cattle trucks

Over the course of 1942 the Japanese detached large working parties of men from the body of prisoners at Changi. Many were sent to labour in dockyards, mines or on building projects all over Japanese-occupied territories in the Far East and in Japan itself. In October eight of Barry's men, Lance Sergeant Arnott, Signalman W. Stanley Blackburn, Lance Corporal Andrew S. Graham, Signalman Dennis Lovell, Driver John Lyons, Signalman Arthur Newton, Signalman H. P. O'Donnel and Signalman David Tomkinson, were detached and sent to Java. Only two ever came home.

A large proportion of the British PoWs were allocated to Group 2, under Lieutenant Colonel Swinton, and sent north to Thailand (Siam) and Burma to work on the notorious railway. Barry remembers:

> In late autumn of 1942 we were told of a new delight to come. We were to be moved north into Siam where we would be engaged in light healthy labour

Andrew S. Graham, from a postcard with two friends in France, 1940.

John Lyons in 1941.

with good food and pleasant sunny weather, housed in well-built camps in open country. We couldn't wait for this promised treat.

Our promised holiday trip to Siam started badly. We were organized into working groups of 500 more or less under our own Commanding Officers, I still had most of No. 27 with me.

The unit now numbered fifty-three men, since as well as deaths and the absence of the Java party, three others, Signalman Charlie Knee, Corporal Lewis Jackson and Signalman Horace Randle, were left behind in hospital in Changi.

On 4 November 1942 Colonel Scott's 'N Party', which included Barry and the remaining men of 27 Line Section, now under Lieutenant Colonel Selby Milner, marched to Singapore station carrying everything they possessed. There they entrained in metal-sided cattle trucks. These became scalding during the day and exceedingly cold at night. Water was in short supply for the whole journey. With about thirty men per truck, there was no way to be comfortable. A senior officer controlled the seating and standing arrangements:

[Otherwise] it would soon have developed into an ugly scramble, as everyone preferred a place near the outer shell with something to lean on. We took it in turns to sit in the better places and arranged our packs in rows so that we could sit on them with our legs pointing towards the middle of the truck. This system was agreed, as it seemed to make the best of the space available. The wide sliding door on the side was not fastened and we kept it open most of the time to create a draught as these metal trucks became unbearably hot.

There were no latrine arrangements at all, not even a bucket. One could pee through the open sliding door and the train stopped twice a day at some

Lewis Jackson in 1941.

point well away from a village so that we could get out and ease ourselves squatting over a ditch or under a hedge. As many of us were already suffering from dysentery, these two stops were not nearly enough and we got over the problem by rigging a rope across the doorway at a convenient height so that one could hang on with both hands, bottom outwards and shit on to the track.

There were food stops twice a day at stations where buckets of rice and stew were ready for us. Two men from each coach ran to collect the rations for their coach and we then held out our mess tins and mugs to receive our share. There were as usual a great crowd of native stallholders and hucksters offering fruit and other goodies for sale to anyone with dollars, and more pressingly trying to buy watches, rings, cigarette cases or any other valuables which a PoW might still own. Most of such goods had already been taken by our Jap guards, so we had little left to barter.

The scenery was monotonous: rubber plantations almost all the way and the heat became very trying and uncomfortable. From Singapore to the Siam frontier is about 400 miles and we then covered another 800 in Siam to reach our destination, the town of Ban Pong.

Ban Pong, Siam/Thailand

Up to the moment when the prisoners, now filthy, dishevelled, hungry and very thirsty after four days in a scalding metal box, disembarked at Ban Pong, the idea of the railroad was just a rumour. They soon learned that this was a base camp for the wildly ambitious Japanese project of building a railroad from scratch in sixteen months through Thailand and Burma. The aim was to transport goods and troops safely across their conquered territories, avoiding the dangers of the sea route. Technically the new railway started 5km further east of Ban Pong at Nong Pladuk on the existing railway line to the capital Bangkok. This part of the peninsula is narrow, divided down the middle by a range of hills which forms a frontier between a thin strip of Burma to the west and Thailand to the east.

The Thai section of the new railway up to the Burmese frontier would be about 300km and the Burma section about 135km, so it would be something over 400km altogether. The route chosen was along the eastern side of the river Nam Kwai Noi, which rises in the hills on the Thailand/Burma frontier and flows south-south-east down to the Gulf of Siam, joining the Mae Klaung and passing Ban Pong on its way. This river route, which was navigable to barges up to Tha Khanun, was chosen to provide a temporary line of communication for stores and other supplies during the construction of the railway.

The majority of British PoWs found themselves building the Thailand section from Ban Pong to the Three Pagodas Pass alongside some Australian, Dutch and Malay Volunteer groups. Meanwhile, a combination of Australians, Java Dutch and some British started from an existing railway at Thanbyuzayet in Burma and continued south over the Burma/Thailand border.

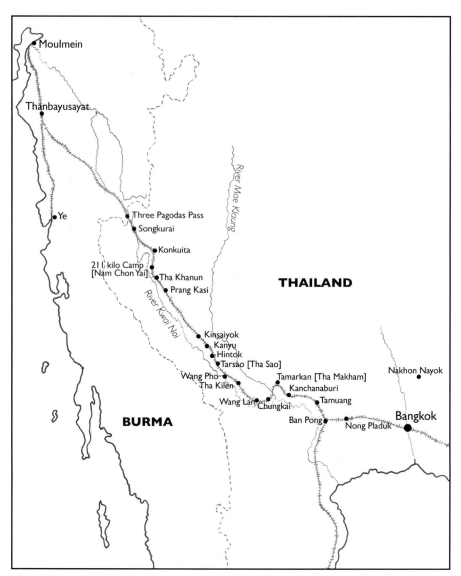

The Thailand–Burma Railway, showing selected PoW camps.

By the time 27 Line Section and the rest of N party arrived, the route of the railway had been selected and surveyed. Some working camps had been partially built and supplies collected.

We arrived at Ban Pong, all 800 of us soon after the start of the rainy season. Ban Pong was a substantial small town of about 5,000 and the camp was a very disgusting place. As it was a transit camp, there was no senior British officer in command who could see that the place was kept in order. Each Unit came and went in a few days and the actual daily running of the camp was in the hands of a particularly idle and brutal Japanese major who deputed everything to his second in command who was equally idle.

The Camp, occupied by several thousand PoWs, was almost underwater, the latrine trenches full and overflowing, so that the general surface was a layer of wet mud mixed with excrement. The local Siamese buzzed around trying to sell eggs, peanuts, bananas, and to buy or steal anything the PoWs still had. Some PoWs unwisely bought a complete 'hand' of cheap bananas for a few cents and ate them all. They were in fact unripe wild jungle bananas that gave a feeling of bulky food to their purchasers' empty stomachs, but soon brought on very violent attacks of dysentery. With the overflowing state of the latrines this simply added to the general misery and filth.

Ban Pong was the first of innumerable camps reached by lorry, barge or, more often than not, on foot. Camps of all sizes were created or abandoned according to need as the railway inched through Thailand/Siam towards Burma. A great many of these camps, like the railway itself, were built by the prisoners out of raw terrain with a few simple tools. Their size could vary – anything from a couple of hundred men to several thousand – and they might last for two months or for the duration. As the war went on, bigger camps lower down the river became more settled in terms of buildings – though monsoon flooding could wipe out sections of a camp within hours. Large numbers of men and officers were moved in and out on a daily basis.

On any one day, as the war progressed, PoWs died. Mostly they died of disease, malnutrition or starvation, though beatings, overwork, accidents and outright sadistic torture also took a steady toll.

Nationalities abounded, and there were cultural fault lines between Australians, British, Dutch, Eurasian, Malay Volunteer Forces and (a few) Americans.

James Stewart in 1941.

Japanese commanders and Korean guards varied enormously in character and were moved about too. So, while every element of each PoW's experience was shared with thousands of other men, each one's account is unique.

As Lieutenant Colonel Selby Milner's group of about 400 men prepared to leave Ban Pong, 27 Line Section now numbered forty-nine. According to a list Barry made of the last time he saw each man, Corporal Bobby McWhirter, Peter Sampson, James Stewart and Signalman C. Wakeling were too sick to travel further, though some may have rejoined the unit at a later stage. Movements over the next few months were confusing, but thankfully Selby Milner kept a meticulous diary. Individual movements are also recorded on the liberation questionnaires (lodged at the National Archives at Kew) filled in by those men who returned.

Moving earth, Tamuang to Wang Lan
Barry recalls:

> After a few days we marched out of the pigsty of Ban Pong and on to our first working camp. This was Tamuang, near to a friendly native village. We were now wholly under the command of Milner. Each working camp dealt with a stretch of embankment, about 5 or 6km long, and then we packed up and moved on to a new camp and a new piece of railway.
>
> Every morning every working camp on the railway began in the same way with the roll call, or tenko. We had suffered many such roll calls in Changi and at Bukit Timah and knew the drill fairly well. Our own CO and Company Commander marshalled the working party in files ten deep with an interval every ten, a total of anywhere between 300 and 800. The Japanese officer then called 'attention' which in Japanese is approximately 'Kyotzge', and bowed to us. We all bowed while he slowly turned his glance from left to right. When he had completed his survey he raised his head, which we copied. Another order followed which I cannot remember which meant 'Number'. We then counted off from right to left in Japanese, 'Ichi, nee, san, see etc ... ju (ten), ju-ichi, ju-nee, etc'. The smallest mistake in numbering earned an immediate slap or swipe with a bamboo cane.

The guards had a passion for counting the men and a paranoia about getting the right number. Tenko could be called again and again at any time of day and, if the numbers failed to tally, could last for hours in baking sun or monsoon rain.

When they had finished the job at Tamuang they marched about 25km further upriver to what Milner, in his diary, describes as an 'even filthier staging camp, Kanchanaburi'. Lance Corporal Daniel McNicholl and Lance Corporal C. Hann were left behind there.

> From Kanchanaburi we marched up past the working party at Tamarkan [Tha Makham] who were building the bridge [the famous 'Bridge over the River Kwai'] across a substantial tributary of the Kwai Mae Klaung. This

bridge was by no means complete, but there was sufficient roadway to march across it. It was made almost entirely of bamboo.

Our next working camp was at Chungkai, 60km. This was a passing visit of a few weeks while we built one more stretch of the embankment. We had hitherto been working in fairly open country, of scrub and bamboo clumps, which had of course all to be cleared from the line of the railway before the embankment was made.

These moves were made between 4 November and 4 December 1942. Milner records an incident on 4 December. The working day started and finished in the dark and involved a three and a half mile trek to the site. One work group returned late to camp; a staff sergeant had thrown down his shovel after they had been given an extra task at knocking off time and then another one. The punishment was that these men should stand all night. They were shirtless after work and so tormented by mosquitoes; they had neither food nor water. Milner, assisted by Barry and two other officers, spent the night bargaining with the guards for small alleviations of this punishment. At 1.00am the men were allowed to sit for short periods. At 4.30am they were allowed shirts (the pockets had eggs and cigarettes in them). Milner wrote: 'At 5am they were each allowed a blanket, so I told Baker (Barry), Bygrave and Brown, who were doing good work in these matters, to send out a bucket of tea as well, as a try-on. The men were allowed to drink it and then to lie down – until daylight when they had to stand up again . . .' After thirteen and a half hours an apology over the shovel incident was finally accepted by the Japanese.

Daniel McNicholl in about 1939.

Soon after this, Barry, the dwindling number of men in 27 Line Section and the rest of the group under Milner marched on and fetched up for a longer stay at a new camp, Wang Lan.

Here the sleeping huts had already been built but nothing else. The building of the latrines and cookhouse were left to us, as was the general administration and organisation of the camp. The Japs provided a guard detail of a junior officer and twenty or so guards and engineers, they doled out our daily ration of rice and sacks of dried cabbage and dried fish, but we did the rest. The cookhouse provision was a stack of qualis, the local basic cook pot. They were very large shallow cast iron circular pots, nearly a yard wide but no more than 8 or 10 inches deep in which water could very quickly be brought to the boil – in fact, simply a big wok.

We were provided with a heap of bamboo poles of various sizes, a stack of attaps (palm fronds used for both roofs and walls) and bundles of rattan binders from which we quickly set up a lean-to shelter for the cooking fires.

Another party was urgently digging trench latrines. We had soon learned that latrines should not be sited in some dark and secret corner, like WCs, but rather in the highest, openest and windiest part of the camp. Owing to the illnesses from which we were nearly all suffering, the efficiency and convenient location of the latrines was one of the most important parts of a good camp. We had by now learned to perform while squatting without the need for a seat and the latrine trenches generally had a bamboo rail on each side, to hold on to if you needed the support.

As this camp was quite new and everything had to be made by us, the guards allowed a small detail to stay back from the railway working party to complete the buildings and accommodation in the camp. Most of our later camps had already been built and we as newcomers, merely had to repair and maintain them. Our first meal, of rice with a watery fish soup and tea, was ready by about bedtime.

The work at this camp was a pattern for what we did for the next year or so with few exceptions. The (very) small camp maintenance party was left behind; the rest of us divided into smaller working groups collected our tools and walked out to the already surveyed line of the railway. These groups, each with its own guard, were small enough for the guard to count without the need for a formal tenko. At the site, one or two Japanese army engineers would have the shape of the work marked out with bamboo poles and we would then proceed to dig earth from a selected borrow pit and carry it on stretchers to tip it on the marked space where the embankment was to be formed.

Sometimes the earth was taken from alongside the track to form a ditch and this was easier as it meant not so far to carry the very heavy stretchers. The guards, with their bamboo poles and fixed bayonets, were simply there to ensure that everyone kept at work. The engineers stood by the embankment to direct where the earth was to be tipped. The basic task was one cubic metre per man per day. This is no great effort for a chenghol or shovel man, but it all has to be loaded and carried so that, in a working group of four, the digger has to shift four cubic metres, which the others must then shovel and carry.

The day's task was marked out on the embankment by one of the engineers and it was the unhappy duty of the Senior British Officer (SBO) to protest (but not too much) if the task set appeared to be unreasonably long. A more vigorous protest by the SBO earned him a slap or swipe. His other duty was, quietly and unnoticeably, to control our working rate so that the job was completed not too early and not too late. We knew by the sun, (few of us had watches by then) about when we might expect the welcome order 'Yasme' meaning rest, followed by 'Orr men go housu'.

We were amused at the Japs clumsy attempts to speak English but their ability was far ahead of ours to speak Japanese. We picked up a few useful words as well as the numbers, but never enough to carry out any sort of discussion. I am told that conditions were better in those camps or groups, which were lucky enough to have a fluent Japanese interpreter, but they were very rare.

During the day the two tea men would have carried out the required water, boiled up their 60-gallon drum and brewed up. Once an hour the tea buckets came round and the guards allowed us time to sit and drink it, perhaps five minutes, then a series of angry shouts put us back to work.

In those early days while we were still in the populated southern part of Siam, rice was quite plentiful and we would have three meals a day, with a half hour break at noon to eat hot rice carried out from our cookhouse. In one of the camps our midday rice even came out on a lorry, but this was rare. There was nearly enough to eat, though endlessly dull and tasteless and we were simply hungry but not starving. Unfortunately, the rations fell far short of what was required to keep us in good shape and everyone gradually or quickly became much thinner.

No average-sized European can carry out heavy labour on a diet of less than 2,000Kcal per day and European stomachs are not used to digesting such large quantities of rice even if it were available. So the Japanese plans for rationing the labour force on the railway fell woefully short of the minimum needed – and that was even before we left the rice-bowl of Siam.

Chapter 13

Britain: Late 1942

Dreams and plans

While the men of 27 Line Section were enduring their train journey through Malaya to Thailand in cattle trucks, Phyllis started her third letter since she began numbering them. She mentions a newspaper cutting – perhaps the one about the escaped mining engineer quoted above (p. 67).

11 November 1942, from Phyllis to Barry (received 20 April 1944). Letter 3
My darling, as always now I find it difficult to sit down and write to you. But yesterday Alan sent me a letter with a cutting on Malaya which gave me a clearer & better picture of possible conditions than any I have seen before. It isn't that I don't think of you! Day and night you are with me in spirit, but always in the past, with its lovely memories (and we have some very good ones, haven't we?) or in the future. The present I cannot imagine, & is just a time to be got through by both of us as best we can. I pray that for us both it may leave no bad mark. My darling, come back to me as much as you can like you went away. At any rate, not embittered. You must have plenty of time to think things over, so you'll probably be a communist in spirit if not in party. I wish I could know that the brighter outlook of the last few days [military success in the Middle East] is known to you as well – perhaps it is.

Your son continues to enlarge his vocabulary & field of activities. He seems to know all the things he ever comes in contact with by name, & is now putting correct adjectives to them (e.g blancmange, horrid; shoes, brown; wool, soft; flowers, pretty etc). Oh, he's worth working for!

I long to know what plans, if any, you have for after the war. Would farming on a large, and entirely scientific style, appeal to you ... Or have you still a longing for the East? My chief concern is for you to be working where you are happiest – only, I hate the idea of parting from the Bobbin & 7 other little Custance Bakers (!?) I'm collecting all the snaps I can of Robin for you, but films are difficult now. Everyone here is convinced that wherever you are, you're making the best of it, & learning all you can in the language line.

Dearest darling husband – all my love, Your wife Phyllis.

In those days most children with parents working abroad were sent back to live in Britain when they reached school age.

30 November 1942, from Alan to Barry, with fold damage (received November 1943)

Dear Barton, we have been writing regularly but have not yet had any news of you and do not even know whether you are a prisoner. We have had good news of (young) Alan who is still in the same service and also of John who has got over his asthma and has been doing a lot of flying. Ada is with us for a stay near her 78th birthday.

We are going to spend Christmas with Phyllis and Robin and do hope we may have news of you by then. I sent Robin some coupons recently to buy himself some nice warm winter pants, we hear he is growing in grace and beauty.

Mother has just started a girls club for the 15–17 year olds. 18 turned up in a rowdy group so the drawing room was nearly as full as for your sherry party. I was not allowed in but I could hear gusts of laughter and giggles. They are taking a club room at the New Flying Horse which seems a good address for a girls club …

In many ways Robin is very like you. He has that alert interested way of looking at the world. I hope that there will be much happiness for you both together again.

Love from Dad.

9 December 1942, from Phyllis to Barry (received, no date). Letter 4

My dear one, I'm writing you a letter, because it is some weeks since I last wrote & so I feel I ought to. But it is difficult to feel personal about it. Everyday I feel – surely today something may happen. And I know one day it really will. Meantime I go on existing, with half of me asleep, & dreaming of you as I knew you, & the future as it may possibly be, when I wake up again & begin to live fully. What women without children do, I can't think.

But Robin takes such a lot of loving, I can keep going on that. He seems fully to understand now that there is Grandad, & Daddy whose picture he kisses goodnight every night, & of whom he tells people 'Daddy gone away to Singapore'. He says Singapore so sweetly – Sing-ga-paw – but can't manage Malaya. He also loves playing with 'Daddy's ties' which hang in my wardrobe. He is so full of vitality & original sin, that every day I feel how much he needs you, & find it harder to be father & mother too. He is too concentrated on me, too, I think. Daddy (Grandad) is very sweet with him, & while he never interferes, he occasionally takes him in hand when I'm getting desperate …

Oh my dear husband – it grieves me that never can I give you even a second hand joy in our Robin. It's a real thrill to watch his rapid development. Oh dear, he's nearly 2, & I feel it's time we started another now. We won't have to waste any time when you do come.

Darling, when things seem most 'bloody' remember you have a wife who just counts the time till your return, and a son who she is trying to teach to

Robin in 1942.

love you, and who is most assuredly worth the very best that is in you – &
after all, he is, thank God, part of you.

I want you so badly, my darling – your Phyllis.

Good news?

For their relatives in Britain the greatest fear was that men had died or been
wounded in the fighting before the fall of Singapore. The best news they could
hope to hear was that they were prisoners. They knew they might be ill-treated,
sick, poorly fed or bored, and that Other Ranks might be made to work, but they
assumed they would be safe from violent death until the end of the war. In
addition, they could be sent comforts, they would be able to communicate with
them (when the authorities had sorted a route out) and all would eventually be
well.

Ten months after Barry's disappearance, Phyllis has news:

14 December 1942, from Phyllis to Barry on a slip of paper (received, no date).
Letter 5
My own dear husband, At last that blessed news has come to me – the
assurance that you are a prisoner of war. I am awaiting the letter from the
war office now with further details. The relief has left me a little lightheaded,
I think. Dear darling, I fear my letters have been dreadful lately – but it was
like holding a telephone conversation with a deaf & dumb person. Things
have become real again now, & <u>worth while</u>.

I've just found one of my 'returned' letters – so I'm sending it off, & then
at next weekend I'll send you an account of his second birthday. I shall give

him a book on both birthday and Christmas from 'Daddy'. He knows now that 'Daddy come home to Mummy and 'Obin, one day'. I've taught him about you, but never dared carry it too far, just in case ... Now he has added to his list of names for himself. He says he's Bobbity, 'Obin, Nanny's Pet, Mummy's sweetheart, & Daddy's boy. He suddenly remarked yesterday 'Daddy's 'Obin'. You'll have a high reputation to live up to by the time you get home!

My darling it's nearly Xmas again. What Christmases we're going to give our children, when Daddy is home again – & we must make it children as soon as possible.

Dear one, very very dear one – I love you so much. Phyllis.

26 December 1942, from Phyllis to Barry (received 2 July 1944). Letter 6
Dearheart, It is Boxing Day, 1942. Yesterday we all drank a toast to you in Sherry which cost 35/- [shillings] for the bottle! And I felt I wanted to creep away and cry. Do you remember Enid's friend Grace? She and her husband are here, as well as your parents. Jack is most romantic looking – handsome, lean & 'fine drawn' & oh! he makes me feel so much wanting you. Grace is 23 and Jack nearly that – & I'm feeling elderly and on the shelf, without any man to love me. Jack has just been trying to mend the wireless, & and he reminds me of you in so many ways ...

At this point I was interrupted & it is now 12.30am. I've just left Grace and Jack upstairs in the bed in my room, & come down to write this by the remains of the wood fire in the lounge. My own dear darling, how long, how very, very long will it be before you and I are in that bed together again? I feel that once I can just lay my head on your shoulder & know that if I go to sleep you'll still be there when I wake up, then I'll find a few years leaving me – for I feel such years older than when you went away. And you? Will you be much changed, I wonder? So long as you still love me, my darling, my world will stand alright. I'm saying things all wrong, somehow, but I cannot convey in words that dreary ache for you which sometimes, as just now, gets a little out of control. How are you dear love – mentally & physically? What are you doing, thinking about, reading, eating – & above all, writing? Are you writing to me, is my constant watching of the post in vain or not? How is your head?

Phyllis is remembering that in Barry's last letter to her before the long silence he had been in hospital after a car accident. Then comes a rare moment when she allows her frustration and the build-up of anxious questions about his fate to get into a letter:

Are you in an officer's camp or with your Unit? (Were there any casualties in 27 Line Section)? Have you had sufficient time to think things out deeply, & to decide what our part must be in the struggle for a better world? While I had no news of you, I made so many wild glorious plans. Now I know you are officially a P. of W. I have stopped – for all I care about is to have you home again, & we'll make our plans with your head on my breast & my arms around you dear one, in a reunion which I hope will make this interim period seem like a nightmare – so real now, so soon to fade away in the light of heart and soul that will come back to me with you.

Our darling son is now 2. His birthday was marked by a party given to the children of the people we employ (6 children) & only remarkable for Robin's good behaviour. Oh! and his enthusiastic reception of his Teddy Bear (from Mother and Daddy). I gave him also a nursery rhyme book from you and wooden beads for threading from me. Toys are difficult to get and <u>very</u> expensive now, but Robin has done very well indeed.

Monday evening (same letter)
Mother & Enid are both here now. Mother sends her dearest love (Enid says 'well so do I!') & cannot tell you how overjoyed they were to hear that you were safe. They are not writing because only next-of-kin should write to make the transit better … My belovèd, I don't believe I attempted to tell you just what that news meant to me, & I won't now, because I can't. It's just made life full of meaning again that's all & that's everything, too …

Darling one, I must stop or the censor will throw this out as too long to wade through. I look forward to the new year with renewed hope and purpose, and that prayer that it may bring us together again.

You know you have all my love, dear husband, Phyllis

Chapter 14

Thailand: December 1942 to March 1943

Making and mending, hungrier and thinner

Back in Siam/Thailand the prisoners were suffering regular brutal treatment from their captors, working conditions were harsh beyond imagining and their health was at all times parlous. Yet, in a strange parallel to their relatives in Britain, Barry and his men were surviving by attending closely to basic and essential day-to-day needs and supporting each other.

In Wang Lan on 12 December 1942 Barry's commanding officer, Milner, noted in his diary, 'Baker [Barry] yesterday made 3 pairs of bamboo crutches'. By now all Barry's practical problem-solving skills were in demand and his child-hood inclination to make anything he needed became essential to his and others' survival. He remembers:

> One of my most successful and valuable artefacts was my mug. Mess tin, mug and spoon were your most valued possessions as without them one did not eat or drink. Somewhere, when we were in one of the up-river jungle camps my mug was missing, stolen or lost and there were no spares. One could not share a friend's mug for fear of passing on one of the many infectious diseases from which we all tended to suffer. I found a discarded tin can in the refuse heap behind the Guard's hut and got by with that for a day or two but then decided to make myself a new one. I found a piece of very thick, 4″ (10cm) bamboo, old and dry, and cut out a piece next to a knot, which would be the base of my mug. I cut a section about 6″ (15cm) above the notch and smoothed the edges which gave me a capacious and useful mug.
>
> A knowledgeable friend warned me that the mug would soon crack if not reinforced. I got hold of a piece of copper wire, telephone wire probably, and chipped out a shallow notch near the rim of the mug. The wire was then middled with one whole turn around this notch and the ends twisted tightly together. I continued this twist for two or three inches and then twisted the two tails around another notch near the bottom of the mug. This gave me a capacious drinking vessel with a twisted copper handle and two strong bands to hold it together. It lasted the rest of my time as a PoW and being slightly porous it absorbed the flavour of tea to such an extent that you could fill it with plain boiling water and then drink a weak infusion of tea-tasting liquid from it.
>
> On our marches from camp to camp we wore our best strong ankle boots and long trousers and shirts – if we still had them. For work, however, we

improvised our own working kit. Most PoWs got hold of pieces of motor car tyres from rubbish dumps near the villages and used them as a base for a pair of sandals with short pieces of army webbing equipment as a toe strap. Several of us, however, tried to make wooden clogs of the type worn by all the Chinese and many of the Siamese too.

The odd thing is that I clearly remember carving these wooden clogs with my own parang [machete], which had been made for me at Kota Tinggi. I kept it with me at Changi where our kit was not closely inspected and I believe I left it there when we were working at Bukit Timah, yet I have this clear recollection of using it on the wooden clogs, and on similar jobs at later camps. The Japanese guards could not possibly have allowed me to keep such a dangerous weapon and I am not brave enough to have risked trying to conceal it. Perhaps the guard who took it from me originally, may have lent it back when I wanted to make clogs. I can think of no other explanation of this bothersome but very clear recollection. The clogs felt better than the rubber tyre sandals, but several of us began to work bare foot when the ground was smooth enough.

Barry may have been braver than he remembers. One of the men who knew him in the camps was rescued in late 1944 from a torpedoed transport ship. He reported back to Phyllis that in mid-1944 Barry still had his picture of her and his precious knife (though perhaps this was a smaller penknife).

At this time too we began to copy the Japanese soldiers' underwear, a garment that we called a 'Jap happy'. It is a plain strip of white cotton, torn from a sheet, about 8 inches by 2½ foot long, (say 20cm × 80cm) with tapes at one of the short ends. The tapes are tied round your waist with the strip of cloth hanging down behind. The cloth is then pulled forward between the legs and drawn through the tape in front. The excess length then hangs down in front like a sporran. This garment is obviously very convenient for performing any of the necessary functions and can be washed in the river and hung out to dry while bathing. By mid 1943 almost everyone wore a Jap happy except for the unlucky few whose skins could not accept sun tanning and who had to go on wearing the tattered remains of uniform shirts and trousers. We soon found that hats were quite unnecessary and we gave up wearing them.

At no time did the Japanese issue any kind of clothing or bedding during the three and a half years of our imprisonment. We made do with what we had and begged or borrowed surplus kit from later parties coming up from Changi. Regular deaths ensured that there was spare kit to be found.

By now we were getting hungrier and thinner. Nearly all of us had intermittent attacks of diarrhoea or actual infection of dysentery, amoebic or bacillary. This meant ten, fifteen or twenty visits to the latrine trenches daily and increasing dehydration and soreness. There were no drugs to treat the condition and we just carried on in the hope that it would get better. Our efforts were always to try to avoid infection. River water, our only source, was always boiled before we drank it, cooking gear, mugs, mess tins, were all dipped in boiling water, a bucket of disinfectant stood by the latrines to dip hands after performing, but the infections got into the food somehow. In addition to camp latrines we now had to dig extra trenches near the working site.

Between Christmas 1942 and March 1943 they led an unsettled life, marching and working up and down the railway, finishing up at Tha Kilen camp. Many men, even at this stage, tried to maintain a semblance of civilization and continued to strive to improve their minds – easier for the more senior officers whose role was difficult but usually less physically exhausting. On 21 March 1943 Milner noted, 'Am still practicing [*sic*] [French] conversation with Eddington (Sgt.), Baker and Forester-Walker. I read Racine's plays, of which Baker has a complete copy.' (see below pp. 119, 147).

Chapter 15

Britain: January to March 1943

Postmistress, mother, friend & wife

Over the period of Christmas and New Year 1942/3 Phyllis wrote another circular letter to the friends and relatives of the men in 27 Line Section for whom she had addresses. To write to them all was a major undertaking. She typed these letters and made carbon copies, but only a few copies were possible at a time and she needed to retype the letter many times.

Again we have no copy of this letter, but it rejoiced with the relatives in the news she received late in 1942 that Barry was a prisoner of war (and therefore alive). There were many replies.

5 January 1943, from Mrs Hilda Povey (Walton-on-Thames), wife of Signalman Nobby Povey, to Phyllis

Dear Mrs Baker, Thank you very much for writing to me, I thought it very kind of you, and I am also very pleased to know you have received the good news of your husband, although I already knew he was a prisoner, as I have been scanning the papers each day, for news of the prisoners and saw his name, but it did not say whether he was in Malaya or Singapore.

I have had no official news of my husband, but a friend of his, serving in the Middle East, sent me an airgraph, telling me my husband was a prisoner, he wrote as though I had already heard the news, so each day I hope the good news will arrive, and as soon as it does I will let you know. I have been very tempted to write to you again but I did not want to be another worry to you.

The army has informed me that my allowance is to continue for another six months, so I am very pleased about that, and as I am working at the local fuel office, I have one big worry off my mind. My mother takes care of my baby for me so that is a big help. I called her a baby, but she is nearly three now, and when my husband sees her again he will be surprised, for she could neither walk or talk when he last saw her, but I am always talking about 'daddy' and she kisses his photograph, every night before going to bed, it is very pathetic to see her, war's are terribly cruel, aren't they, but I do hope this New Year will bring the end and our husbands back again, so I wish you all one can for 1943.

Yours Sincerely, Hilda Povey

6 January 1943, from Mrs Canning (Glasgow), wife of Driver Hugh Canning, to Phyllis

Dear Mrs Baker, I received your letter I am sorry to hear that your husband is a prisoner of war, but it is good news to know that he is alive, I had no

Hugh Canning in about 1940.

word of my husband yet but still hoping for the best. I thank you very much for sending me the news of your husband as it gave me hope that my husband may be alive and safe.

Yours Sincerely Mrs Canning

There are fourteen similar letters from mothers, wives, sisters and girlfriends of the men in 27 Line Section. They have been scanning the papers during the weary months of 1942, desperate to hear anything. It seems that at this stage only a few families, the majority of these being officers', have had confirmation that their men are prisoners of war of the Japanese.

One letter, however, dated 6 January 1943 from Edith McCarthy confirms what Phyllis had heard (and referred to above) from other sources. As far as we know, Mrs McCarthy was the only one in the Section to hear directly from her son in 1942. She writes:

6 January 1943, from Edith McCarthy (London), mother of Signalman Daniel McCarthy to Phyllis
Dear Mrs Baker, I am awfully glad to hear that you at long last have had the good news that your husband is a prisoner and I hope you will soon hear from him.

I had a card from my son [October 1942] he just says he is being well looked after, that there is no need to worry. Will let you know if I hear more.

Yours Sincerely Edith McCarthy

In January 1943 Phyllis wrote again to Barry. She was following the new rules issued by the Japanese for PoW correspondence – letters must be either typed or written in block capitals. This one is numbered 8; number 7 is missing.

11 January 1943, from Phyllis to Barry (received, no date). Letter 8
My dear Darling, You have been badly neglected this last week – I have been up in Birmingham, inspecting the latest member of the family. As the directions now say I must write to you in block capitals, if I cannot type, I decided to leave this letter until I got back, which I did last night. Jeremy Charles Bacon is a darling ... He has auburn hair and the corresponding complexion. As he is very energetic, he normally looks the colour of a ripe tomato. His eyes are bright blue, and have somewhat the same devilish twinkle as Robin's have. I was so pleased with my reception from Robin last night, after having been away for five days – he was obviously just thrilled to see me, but did not get upset or almost hysterical ... I often tell him that 'Daddy come home to Mummy and Robin, one day'. When I got up to Mother's room last night (Robin had been watching me come up the drive through the window) she said 'Well, Robin, Mummy has come home to you now', and he at once rushed back to the window, crying 'Daddy, Daddy. Daddy coming too, Mummy?'

I have written to the next-of-kin of the men in your section as far as I was able, and they all seem overjoyed to hear of your safety, and to be convinced that the men are still with you. I wish I felt so sure. I'm afraid that now they will be bitterly disappointed if they don't hear soon. You can have little idea of what a difference it has made to me, to know for certain you are alive. I've never really doubted it, but it was so very depressing getting no word, as the months went by. I still comfort myself that at least you will not be worried about us as regards material comfort and safety. At present we are trying to make arrangements to go and stay at Wye for several weeks ...

Phyllis's parents are well-to-do and, in spite of shortages and rationing, are able to live comfortably on their own vegetables and livestock.

12 January (same letter)
I can't remember if I told you about Robin's first [Christmas] party. There were only four guests, but the room was gay with paper hangings etc and there was a tree with fairy lights and small presents and coloured balls. The room was almost clear of furniture, and there were two big cupboards full of toys, which were wide open, for the children to ransack at will. There were no organised games, and they all enjoyed themselves thoroughly in their own way. Enid took Robin, as I had to go to the village, and I went along about 6 o'clock to fetch them home. I didn't realise at first that the red-cheeked, big-eyed creature that hurled itself at me was Robin. He was excited! ...

Last night I had put him into bed, and put the screen round him so that he couldn't see me. He said something to me which I didn't catch at first, but when he repeated it, it was 'What doing, Mummy?'. Now before all his questions have been in the form of a statement with a query in his voice. This is, so far as I know, the first time he has put a question directly like that. I was thinking of this, and not replying to him, when he said 'Little pots?'

(his usual way of putting things). He meant was I at my case of Innoxa things [face creams]. I was!

Every day now I hope perhaps I may get a word from you. That <u>will</u> be a wonderful day, if only the news you give me is good. What I now want to hear of more than anything else except your own well being, is that the men in 27 line section are all safe and well. These women who write to me seem to think that you will be looking after their menfolk personally, and almost make me feel responsible for their safety too! ...

Darling, typing as I am doing, in the midst of the family, is not conducive to an intimate style, and I'm getting near the end of my allowance space without telling you much about how I am thinking and feeling – about you, of course. But I think you are already assured that you are the most important thing in my life, bar none, and that being so, you can have no doubts about my love or fidelity. Robin I always regard as part of you, left in my care. Indeed, he is very like you in many ways (and in looks). I am trying to take a realist attitude to the question of when we will be together again, but I can't help hoping, always, that it may occur sooner than my commonsense says it will be.

All my love, my dear one. Your own Phyllis

Between this letter and her next one to Barry, Phyllis receives a letter from Queenie Garrod. This leads to a meeting, described by Phyllis at the end of her next letter.

18 January 1943, from Queenie Garrod (London), wife of Lieutenant Bob Garrod to Phyllis
Dear Mrs Baker, Thank you very much for your letter. I quite appreciate how you felt with regards to letting me know your good news. Thank you also for making enquiries at the Royal Signals Association.

The War Office sent me another notice extending my allowance to July. I would be very grateful if you could give me some idea to the procedure when once you have been notified that your husband is a prisoner ...

I sincerely hope that it will not be very much longer before I shall have some news of Bob + the other men in the Unit.

Yours Sincerely, Queenie Garrod

22 January 1943, from Phyllis to Barry (received, no date). Letter 9
My Darling, It is now ten days since I sent your last letter. The delay is due to an abortive attack of 'flu ... I still feel a bit queer and heady, but I think that is due to suppressed excitement ...

Recent events have settled the question for us of whether we went to stay with your people or not. It is definitely not worth it, after staying here [in safety] so long for Robin's sake ...

Phyllis's reference to 'recent events' is one of the rare allusions in her letters to the war itself. Barbara and Alan's house was in Wye, Kent, under the flight path of incoming German planes, and there had been at least one random attack on villages in that county already that year. It was therefore thought unwise to take Robin there for a prolonged stay. While in some ways this was a relief, Phyllis looked forward to Barbara's company and was finding life at the White House very restrictive and her mother's health very unpredictable.

Sunday, 24 January (same letter)
Yesterday was a very full day. Busy all morning in the kitchen, making pastry etc. and in the afternoon I did my usual Saturday afternoon trip to Amersham, to see the play. This week it was 'No Time for Comedy'. Do you remember it? It was the play we saw in town on the last day of your embarkation leave. I enjoyed it far more this time – no doubt because I hadn't got that awful sick feeling in my tummy, 'only 4 more hours, only 3 etc'. Oh darling, I get periodical waves of longing for you that almost drive me silly. This last week I've felt all in a whirl – partly 'flu, but mostly just wanting you so much that I couldn't sleep or eat properly. I've got myself in hand now, I think. Which is as well, as Mother is very queer today. I think it's as well we're not going away just now. I don't feel a bit my own mistress living here, but the restraints are not merely those of living in a house not ours. Every time I want to do something, which I would do without thinking if it were my house, I realise that it would be too much for Mother. What I most miss and long for, is to be where I could invite my friends to visit me. If it is fixed a month or so ahead, I can occasionally arrange to have people here, but there is always so much formality about it, that I don't often ask …

On Friday evening I was looking at a postcard sized enlargement of one of the snaps you took just before you went abroad. A group containing your parents, Mother, Phil, Enid, Robin and me. There is not one of us that does not look much more than eighteen months older. Mother and Barbara in particular, I think. Your mother is working much too hard, and her eyes look so tired. But she will not admit it, and keeps up not only her own heart, but that of anyone who has anything to do with her, Joycie's death must have been a bitter blow to her.

I've a nasty feeling that this letter is not being full of cheer, as it should be. But I know you know that we are not always on top of the world, but neither are we in the dumps for long. While you were just 'missing', I made the most wonderful plans for us and our family, for after the war. Now I know for certain you are alive, I feel the smallest cottage … would content me, once you were home. I now live for the day when I shall get a message from you. To know that you are well, that the accident of last January [see Barry's letter of 21 Jan 1942, p. 44] has not had any permanent effects … Do you still want to stay in the army?

From these letters and from family stories we know that the army was not a favoured choice of career for Barry. Phyllis dreaded the idea of serving abroad and of having to send young children back to Britain, not seeing them for months or years.

(Same letter)
If only I could send you books! I know that is what you will want more than anything ...

Darling one, I'm telling you all the odd things that have or are happening, because it is difficult to touch on really important things without risking on running against the censor ... Did I ever tell you that I met Bob's wife (Queenie Garrod) in town one day? It was a rather unfortunate meeting, in some ways. She is working in the Ministry of Supply in the Holborn district. And I asked Daddy if he could tell me of a good place to get a decent meal there at a reasonable price. He said 'Yes, the Old Bell Inn, in the middle of Gamages'. It was not until we were in there that I discovered that it is one of those solid eating houses for hungry business men. Eight to a table, and don't waste time talking. Have your meal then make way for the next man. I felt all the time that Mrs G. was trying to be a little more 'refeened' than she normally was ... it was difficult to get more than monosyllables out of her. Very heavy going. She is very pretty indeed, and I felt an awful snob for my feelings about her, but how I hated to hear her refer to 'Barry' as if she was an old intimate friend of yours. I was probably pretty insufferable too!

Dear One, here is the end of my allowance of paper.

All my love, dearheart. Your own wife, Phyllis

Phyllis, an ardent liberal, thought of herself as a modern, open-minded woman, but the class divisions that were part of any English upbringing of that period had been drilled into her. She found herself unable to ignore the fact that Queenie said and did things she, Phyllis, had been taught to avoid.

Because of the delays involved in censorship at both the British and the Japanese end, people were encouraged to limit correspondence to immediate family. This partly explained why Phyllis, Barbara and Alan took turns to write. However, one or two others also felt impelled to write.

One such letter was from Kurt Abrahamsohn/Kenneth Ambrose. In 1935, when Barry was an undergraduate, he needed to improve his German in a hurry. With the help of friends he set up an exchange visit with the Abrahamsohn family in Stettin, who were Jewish. First Kurt (aged 15) came to stay with Barry's family in Kent, then Barry lived for a month with his family in Stettin. In 1936, with the growing restrictions for Jews in Germany, the Abrahamsohns sent Kurt to boarding school in Britain. In 1938, as the situation in Stettin and Berlin deteriorated further, Kurt undertook the increasingly desperate task of getting work, permissions and permits to allow his family into Britain. Both Barry's and Phyllis's parents, Alan, Barbara, James and Lilian, agreed to sponsor Kurt's parents, and they and his sister duly escaped. Many other members of his family were, even as Kurt wrote this letter to Barry, perishing in the Holocaust.

Barry and Kurt Abrahamsohn
at Stettin [Szczecin] in 1935.

30 January 1943, from Kurt Abrahamsohn to Barry (received after liberation)
Dear Barton, You can perhaps imagine how glad we all were when at long
last the news came a little while ago that you were alive and well. Of course,
just how well you are we still don't know, but we very much hope that you
are bearing up and managing somehow.

Well, Barton, there are lots and lots of things I should like to tell you, but
I don't know what the Censor would pass, and I had rather this letter got to
you with little news than that it was full of them, but was held back. The
main thing I want you to know is that we haven't forgotten you, and that we
are looking forward to the day when you will be back here again.

My parents and Ilse (and myself of course) are very well. As far as our daily
life is concerned, you would hardly notice there was a war on. A month or
two ago, Phyllis brought Robin up to London, and we all went to see them at
Francis Bacon's place. It was really nice. You have got a lot to look forward
to when you come back, Barton.

Well, all the best to you, and we haven't forgotten you, so don't forget us. With kind regards from us all, Yours Kurt.

Six months after writing this Kurt was accepted into the RAF.

9 February 1943, from Phyllis to Barry (received after liberation). Letter 10
Well, darling, it's at least another fortnight since I last wrote. This business of having to type the letters is a nuisance in some ways ... I wish you could see him [Robin] when he is dressed up in an old coat of Paul's for the garden, with Wellington boots. He looks so grown up, and is so thrilled with the two pockets in the coat. He struts round with his hands in his pockets. The other day he wanted to go down the garden, and as it was lovely out I let him, though with some misgivings, because we have had so much rain that the mud was very deep and slushy. He was returned a little later by his Grandad, who said he found him lying yelling in the mud by the rabbitry, with his hands in his pockets. He refused to remove them, and was therefore unable to get up! He was in a filthy state, and had to be half undressed, but his hands were spotless! ...

I expect you would like to know a bit about me, darling. But it's not easy to write about myself. I've got out of the habit – the delightful habit – of feeling that there is someone to whom one can say exactly what one is thinking, and who is interested in the smallest details of one's concerns. Yet I know that if when I do receive a letter from you, it does not tell me all about yourself, rather than the events going on around you, I shall be very disappointed.

Sunday, 14 Feb (same letter)
No, darling, I hadn't completely forgotten you. But the last few days have been difficult, and I feel it's rather my fault, and I must do something about it. I have had nightmares for the last four nights, and it's all because you aren't here ... It is because the general outlook is so much brighter, and 'after the war' doesn't seem so far off, that I've taken to dreaming instead of doing, I fear. It is impossible to tell you what I really want to in these sort of letters, but I am keeping a diary letter for you to read when you come back, so that you can get some idea of what is happening now – so far as your family is concerned.

The brighter outlook Phyllis refers to may be the progress America is at last making in the Pacific war and perhaps Rommel's retreat in the Middle East. Sadly, Phyllis's diary has never come to light; she or Barry may well have destroyed it on the grounds that it was too intimate for anyone except Barry to read.

On Friday I took Robin to Watford ... Owing to the times of buses and trains, he had had no tea but some biscuits I carried, by the time we got home, he was very thrilled to sit in Grandad's chair, eat a piece of toast and cake, while Mummy had her supper. I'm afraid the reaction came next day, when he came in from a rest during which he had not slept, and started to cry

– sort of screaming crying, and wouldn't make any effort to stop, or allow me to do anything for him. He got himself so worked up in the end that I was desperate, and Daddy said would I leave him to him. I did, and they retired together …

Dear darling one – you are never out of my thoughts – and have all my love. Phyllis

10 February 1943, from Barbara to Barry, typed (received after liberation)
My dearest Barton, I wonder if you write to us and the letters just don't arrive? Or if you are not yet allowed to write. Knowing officially that you are a prisoner was very wonderful but of course we long for more, to know whether you are well, just something from yourself. So far no news of Roger has come through at all; poor Roger, I wonder if he knows of Joy's death.

We have just had John home for four weeks after his long course of training as a Navigator. He is now Sergeant Navigator (Bombing and Wireless) which is wonderful work considering his great handicap.

John, Barry's youngest brother, suffered from severe asthma. He had struggled to lead a normal life at school and had to sleep with oxygen cylinders under his bed.

Barbara's letter goes on to talk about Alan's health and repeats information about Robin and other family members, then continues:

John spent a day or two at our little farm whilst he was at home hoping to do some ditching: he did too much the first day and was smitten with a baddish attack of asthma which a local doctor dealt with very effectively. Here, he did a lot of excellent work in the garden … he looked very fit indeed when he left.

[She writes of her publishing hopes and of Aunt Ada]. This letter tells you nothing of our love and longing for you; it is there all the time even when we are very busy as people must be in these days. God be with you darling and help you and all prisoners.

Dad and I join in sending you our very very best love, Ever your loving mother Barbara

P.S. I find I haven't mentioned Phyllis! If you get letters you will get hers so will know that she is well but she will not tell you how bravely she is dealing with life, we love her very much. B.

A month later, Barbara writes again. Hearing nothing back, those who write send the same news over and over again in the faint hope that at least one letter will get through.

13 March 1943, from Barbara to Barry (received after liberation)
My darling Barton, I do so wonder whether you have had any news from home yet … We haven't heard of Roger either, some names seem to have been broadcasted to Australia so some people are happier …

(Young) Alan's Christmas present arrived this week. He sent us tea, cigarettes, Turkish delight, and crystallized dates, a wonderful present. I wish I could have sent it to you.

Phyllis rang us up from Birmingham; she was staying with Lionel and looking after him and the baby whilst Joyce is in hospital for a few days, there was I think nothing serious the matter. Phyllis sounded as if the change was doing her good, she is so brave and patient. We have not seen them since Christmas as it would be silly to bring them here just now, but some day darling, we must all pack into Wilks farm and be altogether anyhow for a little time. You will love it there dearest.

Apart from their house at Wye, Kent, Barbara and Alan owned a small farm nearby. The Wilks farmhouse appears to have been rented to tenants, who also ran the farm. Members of the family went there regularly to help, to holiday or to gather the produce – mainly cherries.

My page is finished dearest. You know how greatly we love you and continually think of you and pray for you,
Ever your loving, Mother.

Phyllis must have spent a lot of the war travelling to look after friends and relatives (and taking a break from restrictions at the White House). She stayed with her brother in Birmingham in mid-March, but by 24 March she is staying with her dear friend Helen Smijth-Windham again.

24 March 1943, from Phyllis to Barry (received 4 August 1944). Letter 12
Dear Darling, First of all I want to tell you that the experiment of bringing Robin here has been an unqualified success. He has got rosy cheeks, a good appetite, and is so full of cheek that it is impossible to help laughing at him sometimes, when one should not. It delights my heart to see the way he plays with the others, so happy and contented. You should see this household. So very feminine, but with photographs of handsome men all over the house. I've put your photograph up on the mantelpiece in the nursery beside the others, and now Robin informs all and sundry that that is his Daddy, next to Simon and Joanna's, and Rosemarie and Peter's. These last two belong to Helen's housemate, Marie Adams. Do you remember her? She was so very ill when Rosemarie was born, and you had lots, and lots of roses sent to her from the YO's [Young Officers]. Her husband (Ian Adams) is a full Colonel now. It looks as though Smidge may be at any minute (though this unfortunately means a decrease in pay). Smidge has also got a D.S.O. I feel very army minded here.

I hadn't a hope of writing to you in the few days I was at home, before coming here, and found when I got here that Helen has no typewriter here, and have only just managed to borrow one. While I was at home, I had to spring clean all our things, so that the room could be done while we are away. I've had out all your things, aired them, and found no moth. Robin was very thrilled by all your things, but insisted that your thick dressing gown was Daddy's rug.

26 March (same letter)

I had to stop at that point, as the children woke up from their afternoon rest. In the evening we had a visitor. Yesterday I left early, and went down to Farnborough. I've seen the remains of our car, dear, and it's a depressing sight.

Early in the war a farmer had allowed them to park their car, a Wolseley Hornet, in a corner of one of his rough pasture fields. She was jacked up with her axles supported on four piles of bricks.

It's not even worth taking away as scrap. It has been completely stripped, and then used by the children in the neighbourhood as a handy target for stones. We shall have to put that down as a dead loss, and I'll cancel the registration number ...

I am in a state of great indecision at the moment. Robin has got on so well here that I am not looking forward to taking him back home. In this village there are a number of young mothers with husbands away, or only here for weekends. If I could get a cottage, I feel very tempted to set up on my own, taking other children, on a Paying Guest basis, for short periods. Many of my friends have young children ... I want a proper nursery for Robin. That I can see no way of achieving at The White House, nor of having other children to be with him. If only it were not in a danger area, Wilk's Farm would be a fairly obvious place to go ...

Wilks farm was simply too close to the coast and on the incoming/outgoing route for German bombers.

The White House has so many advantages, particularly financial, but it is no good saving money at the expense of Robin's well being. There is no doubt about it, the atmosphere at the White House is not very good for Robin, for Mother is even more of an invalid than when you went away, and I have not been as well as I might be. I think I miss being with young people rather. It's such fun here, where one can say what one likes almost, without fear of upsetting some one's feelings. Also I can talk about you to my heart's content, and the others of their husbands ...

Helen says I am to give you her best love. I'm not so sure about it, but I suppose I'd better pass on the message as she gave it [Helen was 'quite extraordinarily pretty'] ... Helen and I are sitting by the nursery fire, waiting for the midnight news to come on ... It's over now, and I nearly fell asleep, thinking of you. My darling, I find it more and more difficult to put into words in each letter just what I am thinking and feeling. Yet that is just what I am hoping you will have done for me. How I long for some words from you, dearheart. I long and ache for you all the time, and when I am in bed at night, I let my mind wander back over some of our many many happy memories, till sometimes I can almost feel your presence, or the feel of your lips on mine. Then I feel warmed and comforted and can relax, still pinning my faith on the future, in the sure conviction that as far as our relationship is concerned, it will all be as wonderful as it was, and as I dream it will be. It is so lovely to feel as certain as I do of your love, and the assurance that you place an equal faith on me. Where I am afraid of failing you is over Robin. He is so lovely, and so close to me, that it is not easy to see him in proper focus all the time. We seem to have a much closer relationship to each other than most of the mothers and young sons that I know. It is rather a terrifying thing, the smiling blind confidence he has in 'Mummy'. One thing I can say now, and that is, that if you could see him now, you would find him all that you could desire, I do believe. This visit here seems to have removed all his little troubles. My problem is, how to keep him in this state, so that he may continue to grow in the way you would wish him to do.

Now, my darling, it is 2.15am, and more than time I was in bed. I go to try to dream of you as you were in the past, and will be in the future, and to worry as little as possible, for all our sakes, about what is happening to you at present. I really do trust, my darling, that the knowledge that whatever may happen, I'll be waiting for you, with a baby who is learning about Daddy as fast as I can teach him, is of use to you at the present moment.

All my love, my own darling. Your wife, Phyllis.

Chapter 16

Thailand: April 1943

Wampo [Wang Pho] Viaduct

On 29 March, when the job at Tha Kilen was finished and after, as Milner noted in his diary, 'receiving many orders and counter-orders from the Japs about our move up-river', they marched on to Wampo South. On 11 April Baker [Barry] is listed as Quartermaster, and 27 Line Section now numbered about 45 men. One of those lost was Signalman J. Grierson, who had at some stage been sent back down the line to Nong Pladuk camp, where on 9 February he died of beriberi.

> Most of our jobs so far had been quite straightforward – clear the track of undergrowth, bamboos and trees and then dig enough earth to build up the embankment to the pre-planned level surface. At the end of each day's work we marched up and down on the newly placed earth stamping it down firmly. I remember the Japanese engineers shouting 'Orr men stepping very hardly'.
>
> Our next task was to be quite a different 'one off' job, unlike the usual jungle clearance and embankment. Wampo is at the 114km mark, and when we reached it in early 1943, was quite a new camp, the rains had not started and the camp was quite dry and fairly clean. We were by now dying off quite frequently but not more than one or two each day and we were still on two bowls of rice per day, not one.

The railway from Tamarkan [Tha Makham] onwards to the Three Pagodas Pass was built along the eastern side of the River Kwai Noi. Most of the camps were also situated on the eastern bank and as close to the river as possible, as this was the only source of water. However, rivers meander so the railway, taking the straightest possible line, could be anything from half a kilometre to many kilometres from the camp. This resulted in daily marches to and from the worksite, sometimes a grim slog especially in the wet season, over rough terrain and frequently in the dark.

> Near the village of Wampo the river makes a sudden eastward loop into a rocky gorge and almost cuts into the line of the railway and here it was necessary to build a viaduct about half a mile long to carry the rails over the gorge beside the river.
>
> Our camp was set up on the west bank, opposite the working site as the gorge made it impossible to build a camp on the east bank. We had to cross the river from the camp to the site, morning and evening, but as it was in the

dry season the water was quite shallow and you could walk on the bottom most of the way and only had to swim in the middle.

The camp was located on the edge of a forest of teak trees, which were to be the source of timber for the construction. We were a big group, a thousand or more I think, still commanded by Milner. One half of the group worked on the trees preparing the beams, the rest, of which I was one, worked in the gorge. No. 27, much reduced in numbers but still a coherent body, were there too.

Our first job was to clear rocks and boulders from the planned route of the viaduct, which we did by drilling and blasting. The holes were made with a rock drill. One brave man holds the drill while two others smite the head of it with sledgehammers. We Linemen were used to sledgehammer work and did not often damage the hands of the drill holder but some of the other parties suffered several damaged or broken wrists. There was no power machinery of any sort in the whole construction, just hand tools.

Barry and 27 Line Section had another advantage over so many of their fellow prisoners – they had been 'hardened up'. That is, they had lived and worked in Malaya for several months, had travelled in the jungle and encountered heat, monsoon rain, tropical insects and disease, had negotiated with locals in a mixture of languages and had slept in tents. The vast majority of men on the railroad

Remains of the Wampo [Wang Pho] viaduct from a postcard in the 1990s.

had either lived in a barracks with bed, board and medical attention for years, or had arrived in the tropics only days before capture.

By the time of the midday tea break our holes had generally gone in deep enough, and while we rested and drank our tea (no midday rice now), the Japanese engineers packed the holes with plastic gelignite and set detonators and lengths of safety fuse in them. There might have been as many as fifty blasts set off at once and it was important, both for us and for the Japs, to make sure they all went off. In the afternoon we shifted all the broken rocks and carried them down towards the riverbank.

When all the boulders had been cleared we set about making the concrete foundation piers, all built by hand with hand mixed concrete. We worked in small groups of eight or ten men, collecting sand from the riverbank, chips of rock for ballast and cement. Once the concrete was made, it had to be carried to the site on the usual rice sack stretchers. Wet concrete makes a very heavy load. The Japanese engineers had already set up wooden shuttering for the piers about five or six metres long, two wide, and deep enough to bring the top surfaces all up to the same level.

While we were clearing the rocks and building the piers, the other half of the group were felling teak trees. Very tiring work, as fresh teak is extremely hard. The trunks when felled were cut to length and then squared up by Japanese engineers using an adze. I have seen one of their engineers square up a log fifteen foot long and around two foot thick in one morning's work.

When the concrete piers were nearly finished, 27 Line Section and others rejoined the timber party and started the very heavy task of carrying the squared timbers down to the riverbank. The intention had been to float them across the river but some of the PoWs who had worked in the Burma teak forests insisted that green teak is so dense it will not float. The Japanese were unconvinced but the first trial proved the point. From then on we swam the beams across the river fastened to bundles of bamboo to keep them afloat.

A few elephants with their Burmese mahouts helped in this work of shifting the beams down to the river but they were the only 'powered machinery' on the job. They seemed extraordinarily precise, even fussy, in their handling of these heavy loads seemingly without any orders from the mahouts. There were not enough of them, of course, and we had to do much of the carrying ourselves. I reckon these beams must have weighed around ¾ of a ton (or tonne) each, more or less, depending on their length. At first we tried to get them up on to our shoulders like undertaker's men with a coffin. But the edges were too rough and sharp, so instead we used the ever-present bamboo poles. Eight or ten stout poles pushed under the beam and then lifted with one or two men at each end and the beam could then be carried down to the river looking like a giant caterpillar.

There were no cranes, simply intricate bamboo scaffolding fastened onto the rocky cliffs above the site and multi sheave pulley blocks fastened to it.

Sketch of the building of the Wampo viaduct by PoW Will Wilder, 1943.

A long rope over the pulleys with 50 PoWs tailing on to it served to raise each of these beams into its proper position, where they were then all fastened together with dog spikes.

When the trestles were in place, held up by more bamboo props, then the even heavier horizontal beams which connected them together all had to be heaved up into place by the same method and then spiked together. With the crudest estimate there must be between 500 and 1,000 beams in the viaduct. While we were doing this other groups of PoWs had laid sleepers and rails on the prepared embankment and were ready to go on over our viaduct as soon as each section was completed. Part of the railway had already been built from the far, northern end of the Wampo gorge, so that within a day or two of our group's completion of the viaduct, sleepers and steel were in place and wagons were passing over our work.

We PoWs who had built it were actually carried forward for a short section of our next march in railway trucks over the viaduct. I remember it as a very scary proceeding. The train went at a walking pace and at each rail joint, with its sudden change of direction, we felt that the wheels might easily jump the track and tumble us all down into the River. We got over without

Wampo [Wang Pho] viaduct 1943, photograph by Renichi Sagano (courtesy of the Thailand–Burma Railway Centre).

incident but I heard that the engineers kept a working party permanently on the viaduct with crowbars to lever bogey wheels back on to the rails if they came off.

I have to admit that when this job at Wampo was finished we PoWs felt a certain mixed-up pride in the work. We could see the completed viaduct and it worked and we had built it ourselves without mechanical aids of any sort beyond hand tools and a few elephants. I was left with a great admiration for the skill and planning ability of the Japanese engineers and an ever-growing bitter hatred for our guards.

It may have been at the completion of the viaduct or simply on an ordinary evening, but on 20 April Milner noted, 'Baker [Barry] has made a mandolin out of half a biscuit tin, some wood, and strands of steel telephone cable. We have one or two men who play it very well and they had quite a concert here last night.'

Chapter 17

Britain: Spring 1943

The missing story

In letters over this same period from Phyllis to Barry we hear only about the joys and trials of her day-to-day domestic and family life. Using this account of the war years leaves, of course, a vast untold story. Phyllis does not, *cannot*, talk about the continuing major event in her life – the war. She was living within thirty-five miles of central London and her father went to his London office every day. Bomb damage; noise of overhead planes; fear of invasion; rationing of food, petrol and clothes; bad news of friends and relatives; newspaper reports of success and failure on various fronts; these were all part of daily life, on top of her enduring anxiety over Barry. We hear not a word of any of this. Robin, while in later life remembering the rabbits and dogs and even a large container of pigswill in the backyard of the house, as well as dramas such as getting locked in the bathroom, remained unaware of the war.

From a practical point of view, Phyllis was living in relative luxury. James and Lilian Bacon had started the war in comfortable circumstances. As it progressed, they, like others, had to learn to live on less, with less help and to find ingenious ways – such as the rabbit breeding – to make up the shortfall. At the same time, many in Britain, including the families of Barry's men, as is clear from letters to Phyllis later in the war (see below), suffered much greater deprivation and difficulty. We can only imagine all these circumstances in the background of the mainly cheerful letters that Phyllis and Barbara write. Phyllis does, however, allow herself the comfort of telling Barry about her concerns for the future.

In April she started a letter that took nearly a month to write. She was trying – as in earlier letters – to plan for the present and the future without any clue about the length of time Barry would be away, but assuming that he was alive and would one day return. Phyllis was clearly chafing at the restrictions of living with her parents but unable to settle in her mind what would be the best solution, given that Robin was her main concern.

23 April 1943, from Phyllis to Barry (received after liberation). Letter 13
Dear darling, if I didn't have to type this, which makes one stop to think what one is saying, and was not therefore very conscious of the censor, I could write you a real letter tonight. It is 11pm and I have been re-reading all the letters you have sent me since you left Britain. It has somehow brought you much nearer to me for a while. Sometimes you seem so far away, that I have to make myself sit down to write a letter to you. Do you

remember the days when we each wrote to each other every day? How we resented being as far apart as we were then, and how inadequate we thought a weekend a month, and all holidays, were, to be together. And now we have been married 3½ years, and Robin is the cheekiest imp of a son that ever a father who hasn't seen him for 2¾ years can imagine. He is very conscious of your existence now, and recognises any photograph of you at once. He talks of when Daddy comes home, and asked me (only it was really a statement) if Daddy will play with Robin when he comes home …

Just at present I want you more than ever, because I want you as I always do, and I also want you to tell me what I ought to do. In my last letter I told you that I did not know what to do for the best about Robin. He does so love other children, and is so much easier to manage when he is with them, that I feel I must make a change and get with other children. Either by setting up house on my own (too expensive) or sharing with someone else (who?), or by taking a job with/where other children are.

At this point, as had happened before, Phyllis set the letter aside and did not take it up again for another fortnight. The reasons for these long gaps within Phyllis's letters can only be guessed at. Apart from the restricted times at which she can use a typewriter, her mother's health and the demands of a toddler, there was also the correspondence from 27 Line Section wives and mothers to deal with. These things might explain why she struggled to sit down to write, but not why, having started them, the letters 'just won't go'.

Two factors that must have inhibited her writing come to mind. One is the lack of permissible subject matter – no war, or bad family news, for instance. There is also a limit to the amount of hopeful chat about their future that she can bear to write. So she returns time and again to the only safe subject – Robin. However, it was probably a second, more subconscious factor that so often froze her hands on the keys. She was a problem solver by nature, but to make any plans to solve her current dilemmas she needed to know if Barry was alive or dead. Each time she tried to communicate with him she had to face her fear of the answer to this question. By now there were probably rumours of the treatment of Far Eastern prisoners; these too preyed on her imagination.

11 May (same letter)
Do you remember the big red brick house at the bottom of the fields on the way to the village? I heard confidentially from the agent that it had been taken, and a nursery school run on the Montessori system was to be installed there. I was thrilled, rang up at once, and arranged an interview with the new tenant for as soon as she arrived. I had great hopes that by getting in before the news became public I might be able to get a residential staff or secretarial job, with Robin as a boarder. But alas! it turned out that the school was not just starting, but moving up from another part of the country, and already had a full staff. They are quite prepared to take Robin (they have three other boarders of his age), but I am not prepared to part with him.

Once again the letter stalled as she hit another impasse in her need to plan the future. It was nearly a week before she returned to it.

16 May (same letter)

Darling, I'm probably going to get a wigging from Mother, but I just must sit down and finish this letter to you. I have had letters from four more next-of-kin of the men in your section to say their men are PoWs …

Dear darling, we really have been hectic here for about a fortnight. Spring cleaning, and the men in to repaint the kitchen. Also, your mother has been very ill, and though she is now recovered (there is nothing for you to worry about) she must go quietly for a bit, and is coming here to stay for a bit, so Mother is busy organising the house (and me) in preparation. I can't type up in my room, as they can hear me, and it's not worth having a row with Mother as I'm going away soon anyway. (They get so worried at the time I get into bed as it is. With lots of sympathy for me, they can't fully appreciate how much I dislike going to bed). But all day and every day I am thinking of you … very much encouraged by the course of events at the present moment …

At this date North Africa is once more in Allied hands and the Americans are pushing hard in the Pacific theatre.

Robin wears a Jimmy [Royal Signals] badge 'like the one on Daddy's coat in the picture'. He took a long time to get hold of the idea that I was Mother's girl as well as his Mummy. One night I said to him 'If I am Nanny's girl, and Robin's Mummy, I am Daddy's what?' He thought hard for a minute, and then triumphantly proclaimed 'Dear' …

Every day now I watch eagerly for the post – one wonderful day, a letter from you will come, perhaps. And then perhaps I shall be able to realise that you really are there, alive and waiting for our reunion. Always now I think of the past, and only realise with my mind, not with my emotions, that you must inevitably have changed a lot. Only my darling please don't let anything you have or are suffering take away that light touch that was so essentially part of you. It was that which comes back to me almost more than anything else when thinking of that mad summer, and our two years engagement.

This letter is going all wrong. Partly I know that Mother and Daddy are waiting for me to come upstairs, and though my heart and mind are just full of you, there is so much I want to say, that I ought to dally and pick my words. But I must send this off in the morning – you will have such a big gap without a letter. I really will try to be better about writing. Since I definitely decided to try for a job, two days ago, I have felt much more at peace in my own mind, and better able to concentrate on things. But I shall have to give up dreaming so much if I am going to make a success of it, I fear. Though of course you know it already, I'll just repeat – I love you completely, with every little bit of me. Please never, for one moment, doubt or forget that.

Your loving wife Phyllis. ROBIN SAYS HE SENDS HIS LOVE TO DADDY.

During May 1943 there is a trickle of letters from 27 Line Section. These are nearly all from families who have finally heard from the Signals Record Office, more than a year after the fall of Singapore, that their men are prisoners.

8 May 1943, from Marjorie Parker (Glossop), wife of Driver Ernest Parker, to Phyllis
Dear Mrs Baker, I am now able to tell you that my husband Dvr. E. Parker 2587178 has been reported a Prisoner of War in 'Tai Camps'. I received notification of this from Army Records Office on 6.5.43.

I am very thrilled, but sorry to say that none of the other Glossop Girls have heard any news as yet, but there are great hopes.

I will take this opportunity of thanking you with all my heart Mrs Baker for your unceasing comfort through those long weary hours of suspense.

My very kindest regards & wishes for your husband's speedy return.

Yours Sincerely. Marjorie Parker.

These tiny bits of news must have cheered everyone up as they suggested that the men had all been taken prisoner and might even be 'safely' together still.

Barbara, who has been seriously ill, is staying with Phyllis and her parents. She writes cheerfully to Barry.

28 May 1943, from Barbara, The White House, (received 2 Aug 1944). Letter 42, seventh on parents' string. Hand printed in ink which has transferred when folded.
MY DEAREST BARTON, I AM SITTING IN THE ANNEXE. THE ROOM YOU AND PHYLLIS USED TO HAVE. DAD, JOHN AND I ARRIVED A WEEK AGO + JOHN + I ARE STILL HERE. NOW FOR THE NEWS YOU MUST MOST LONG FOR. PHYLLIS

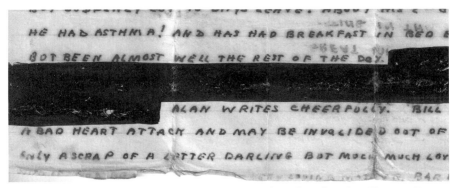

Part of the original censored letter dated 28 May 1943, Barbara (from the White House) to Barry, (received 2 August 1944).

IS WELL + LOOKING AS PRETTY AS I HAVE EVER SEEN HER; PARTLY I THINK BECAUSE PALE SUMMERY COLOURS SUIT HER FAIRNESS SO WELL + PARTLY I EXPECT BECAUSE THERE IS A HOPE OF A LETTER FROM YOU IN JULY OR THEREABOUTS. WE HAVE JUST HEARD THAT ROGER IS A PRISONER, RICHARD [his son and Barry's cousin] MUST FEEL VERY VERY HAPPY. ROBIN IS TRULY THE GRANDPARENTS DREAM COME TRUE. HE IS FRIENDLY +, DARLING, SO EXACTLY LIKE YOU WERE AT TWO. HE CALLS ME NANNIE BARBARA BUT ALAN IS ONLY ALAN WHICH PLEASES DAD VERY MUCH BUT WILL SHOCK ADA I FEAR! LILIAN AND JAMES ARE PRETTY WELL AND AS SWEET AS ALWAYS. JOHN WAS NOT EXPECTED AT ALL BUT SUDDENLY GOT 10 DAYS LEAVE. ABOUT HIS 2ND DAY HERE HE HAD ASTHMA! AND HAS HAD BREAKFAST IN BED EVER SINCE BUT BEEN ALMOST WELL THE REST OF THE DAY. [two lines blanked out by censor] ALAN WRITES CHEERFULLY. BILL HAS HAD A BAD HEART ATTACK AND MAY BE INVALIDED OUT OF THE ARMY. ONLY A SCRAP OF A LETTER DARLING BUT MUCH LOVE COMES. BARBARA

Chapter 18

Thailand: Spring 1943

Walking, walking, long time walking

Difficult as this period was for relatives in Britain, for many of the men of 27 Line Section 1943 was the nadir of their lives as prisoners. Between 26 April and 8 May Milner's group were dispersed. Most went on a long 120km march upriver. But as Barry notes:

> At one stage of the march we were ordered to detail a party for special duty elsewhere. Colonel Milner had no choice but to select the required number of men from the group and this included eight men from my dwindling numbers in 27 Line Section.

These men are among those unfortunates who were later placed on the infamous transport ships to work on the docks in other parts of the annexed countries or in Japanese ports or mines. These ships were unmarked and several of them were torpedoed or bombed by the Allies. (It should be noted that Britain did not mark all PoW or internee ships either.) From Barry's post-war records and correspondence we can name most of the men who either then or at a later stage were transported to Japan: Earnshaw, Signalman Henry Farrell, Harrison, Driver Leonard Holmes, Driver 'Big Jock' Jardine, Murrell, Parker, Signalman Thomas

Henry Farrell in about 1940.

'Big Jock' Jardine and Isla in
about 1940.

Potter, Signalman Leonard Russell, Signalman A. E. Walstow, Driver Lawrence
Whitton, and Driver Alf 'Dabber' Woodend. It is clear from post-war letters that
friends chose to stay together. Only half of these men would survive.

By this stage of the war not only had 27 Line Section been dispersed (Barry
probably had no more than thirty-five of his original sixty-eight men still with
him), but Army units had been overridden by the Japanese allocation of men to
one group or another, especially as the sick were left behind and then, if they
recovered, attached to another group passing through. Many men from Malaya
Command Signals, including Barry, remained in No. 2 Group Thailand, but
others from 27 Line Section were in No. 4 Group. The structural hierarchy of the
Army remained in place and the soldiers' training meant that these PoWs, unlike
the conscripted Tamil, Malay and Thai men (and women and children) in railway
work camps, could organize and look after themselves. However, they had little
control over where they were sent or with whom.

North from Wampo

We packed up and marched on northwards from Wampo [Wang Pho]. For
the next hundred kilometres we passed through the camps shown on the map
[p. 80]. Some I remember because we must have stopped our march

overnight, others because we stayed there, camped and built some more of the embankment, but I cannot remember which was which.

On this march I still carried my rolled up valise with the remains of my kit in it, including my paper-backed Racine and the portrait of Phyllis. The ornamental cardboard frame of this picture, supplied by the studio had begun to disintegrate in the hot wet weather and I feared that the photo might also be spoiled. I cut a suitable length from a piece of thick bamboo leaving a knot at one end, then rolled up the photo and pushed it into the open ended tube. The end was then closed up with a bunch of rags.

I had a strange encounter on one of these long marches, which took me back to the happy days at Kota Tinggi, before the Japanese invasion. I think I mentioned that I studied Malay language under an elderly munshi who taught me, among other things, the art of Malay poetry, the Pantun.

During the march after Wampo, on the way up river towards 211 kilo Camp [Nam Chon Yai], the weather became gradually worse and we were slogging through rain and mud with no comfort at the end of the day's journey. I often passed the time by talking to myself in Malay and repeating some of the pantuns that I could remember. On this particular occasion I was marching beside a stranger whom I recognised as probably a Dutchman as his dress was different from ours, but he had no rank badges or any other recognition signs. I started to say aloud a particularly apposite pantun, which goes:

Jalan-jalan, sa-panjang jalan,
Singa-měnyinga di-pagar orang,
(Walking, walking, long time walking
Looking over neighbours' fences,)

At this moment, half way through the pantun, the man beside me joined in and recited the last two lines,

Pura-pura měnchari ayam,
Ekor mata di-anak orang.
(Is he perhaps searching for a lost chicken?
But the corner of his eye is looking at his neighbour's daughters.)

At the same time he put a finger to the outer corner of his eye, which was exactly what my munshi had told me that a Malay would do.

This episode cheered me up very much during a wet and miserable period of our long march northwards, and we spent the rest of the day talking Malay to one another; mine very stumbling and uncertain, his accurate and fluent. I lost touch with him and found no other Malay speakers in our group.

This was early May 1943 and still raining most of the time. Our march up from Wampo had been increasingly disagreeable as the route alongside the river became more and more muddy and the dry creeks and river beds draining into the Kwai from the east all began to fill up, so that we were repeatedly forced to wade or paddle through the muddy water. You can easily imagine how we looked forward to a warm and dry welcome at the camp where we would pass the night.

Each of the camps we passed through was under the general control of a British CO, a Lieutenant Colonel. The quality of each of these COs showed up very clearly in the general state and appearance of the camps and even more clearly in the welcome we received. We were by now no more than 400 or so, but the sudden arrival of so many wet and hungry men so late in the evening would strain the hospitality of any Regiment. It was raining most of the time so space had to be found for us overnight in the huts that were already often overcrowded. At some camps this was done willingly and cheerfully, at some very reluctantly.

The Japs did provide a few extra bags of rice and in some camps this was added to the general stock and we were invited to feed with the regular occupiers on whatever their caterer had provided. In other camps we were merely allowed to use the cookhouse after the regular users had finished with it.

One particular Camp stands out in my memory. I cannot even remember the name of the place, it may have been Kinsaiyok at 172km or Kanyu at 152, but what I can remember is the unusual name of the CO, Lieutenant Colonel McOstrich. This was a semi-permanent staging camp and we stayed two nights there. The location was fortunate as there was a spring or stream above the camp. The CO had arranged a series of troughs made from split bamboo which carried running water to many sites in the Camp, especially to the cookhouses so that the weary task of carrying buckets of water up from the river was no longer required. We were offered clean dry accommodation in well-maintained huts and two good meals a day. I think there must have been a village nearby as I remember setting off the next day with my little bag full of hard-boiled duck eggs and a few peanuts.

We left McOstrich's camp much more cheerful but still very hungry, thin and generally suffering from dysentery and/or malaria, and arrived at the large semi-permanent camp of Tha Khanun.

Milner's diaries show that the march North from Wampo took them through Tarsao, Kanyu, Kanyu 5, Kinsaiyok, Rintin, Hindato, Prencali [Prang Kasi?] and Takanoon [Tha Khanun].

The end of the road, 211k Camp
Tha Khanun (also called Takanoon or Tarkanun) was a large, well-organized camp with several doctors, proper arrangements of huts for the sick and some drugs and equipment for treatment. The river was still just large enough for barge traffic, accounting for the almost adequate rice ration, the good organization of this camp, and why it had become a medical centre and holding area.

We hoped that we were to stay there and build a section of embankment, but our group still under Colonel Selby Milner, and gradually getting smaller, was ordered to move on further North.

We were to form a new working camp about 7km upriver; that is to say at about the 221km mark. From some variation in the starting point of these distances the new camp had the name of '211 kilo Camp' [Nam Chon Yai camp] and was the furthest point I reached up the river. It also included the most miserable period of my whole life.

When we reached the site of 211 it was, as usual, raining and there were no preparations at all, in particular there were no huts or latrines or cookhouses. Our Jap OC, it may have been Captain Noguchi, pointed out a heap of green tents which were to be our homes for the next few weeks. Our first task was to clear a space in the undergrowth and bamboo clumps to make our camp; we then set about pitching the tents. There were not nearly enough to accommodate the whole group but fortunately these tents were supplied with separate fly sheets, and these extra sheets could be pitched on improvised bamboo poles to provide extra cover although without ends. One of these fly-sheets made our cook house but there was none spare for the latrines which had to be dug in the open. We crammed into these tents for the night and within a few days managed to construct a few double bunk type sleeping platforms which gave everyone at least two foot of bedspace.

There was no barge traffic up to 211 camp and our rice ration came up through the jungle paths on a hand cart or carried on our backs by ourselves. A 50kg bag (1 hundredweight) is not an impossible burden for a fit man, but by now most of us were far from fit and were anyhow already fully occupied building the new section of railway, so that the rice ration was small and became steadily smaller.

On our first morning at 211 we were roused out very early, in the rain and in darkness for a full scale tenko. Through the medium of a Japanese interpreter who spoke very little English, Noguchi told us that the progress of the railway building had fallen far behind schedule and that this was caused by the idleness and incompetence of the British workers and their officers. This was an attempt to thwart the Emperor's plans, an act of treason, for which the only punishment was beheading. These stern measures would, however, be relaxed if from now on we all worked twice as hard as before and built our allotted stretch of embankment in record time. This speech in fact, amounted to what had become recognized as a 'speedo', which meant longer working hours and more harrying, shouting and beating by the guards.

Noguchi then announced the number required for the working party which was virtually the whole nominal strength of the group less a very few men detailed for camp construction and the tea men. Colonel Selby Milner then took it on himself to explain to Noguchi that about a quarter of the men were so weak from dysentery and undernourishment that it would be impossible to produce a party of that strength. Milner was immediately slapped and beaten as he had expected to be. He repeated the protest almost daily.

Noguchi then pointed out that the rice ration, now down to a very few ounces, would be calculated strictly according to the number of men who went out to work. This put Milner and his officers (me included) in the unhappy position of being forced to detail for work men who were too weak to stand, simply in order to swell the numbers who would be counted for rations. It was quite usual to see a man actually suffering from a malaria rigor being supported between two others on the march out to the railway site. Such men were, of course, no use for actual work and a few of the guards accepted this and did not look too closely if a man spent his working day lying on the ground.

We still had a doctor, Oliver Braham of the Royal Army Medical Corps (RAMC), who had plenty of knowledge and skill but no drugs and no equipment except what he happened to be carrying with him. He saved me a great deal of misery on one occasion, when I had accidentally touched some kind of jungle nettle which produced a viciously itching rash on both arms right up to my shoulders. I asked Olly if there was anything he could do for me and quite unexpectedly he produced a leather wallet packed with loaded hypodermic syringes. Most of them were morphine or other painkillers, but he also had a few of adrenaline which he told me was just what I needed. He gave me the shot and the rash disappeared in a very short time: wonderful and unexpected relief. Olly died soon after that and we were left without any medical personnel.

Barry has here confused two men – Dr Mark Gordon Braham, whom he knew well and who died in late 1944, and an untraced 'Oliver'.

During a 'speedo' PoWs would get up in the dark and return in the dark. Sometimes the only meal of the day would be late at night, queuing on muddy paths in continuous rain. Maintaining hygiene in these conditions was almost impossible. Then, on 26 May 1943, an entry in Milner's diary reads: 'Cholera has broken out at Takanoon'. During June Signalman Jim Bridge, one of the four Glossop boys, died at Tha Khanun of either cholera or amoebic dysentery. Barry remembers:

One day a few dysentery cases started violent vomiting as well as producing sudden dehydration and death within a day or two. Men who had served in India recognised the symptoms of cholera and our CO immediately informed Capt Noguchi who insisted that all possible or probable cholera sufferers should be moved out of the main camping area. We arranged some kind of shelter for them but could not provide any treatment, as none was available. The only useful treatment for cholera other than a previous immunisation injection, which we had not received, is a continuous drip of normal saline to counteract the dehydration, considered to be the immediate cause of death. This treatment was used later on at Chungkai but was quite impossible in our primitive conditions. The infection came, of course, from the river, our only source of water.

The onset of this cholera epidemic came as no real surprise. We had heard rumours of it at a camp further up stream from us and we heard reports of

Jim Bridge in 1941.

corpses seen floating down the river and lying along the sides of the jungle paths.

The cholera spread rapidly and it soon became impossible to bury the dead so, on the advice of those who had experience of such epidemics in India, we started to burn the bodies. We used a pit with alternating layers of bamboos and bodies, and it was one of our tasks when we marched back from the railway work to collect the bodies and put them into the burning pit. The fire was kept burning continuously by a small duty party. We never ran short of fuel.

Noguchi continued to demand impossible numbers for the working party and Colonel Milner continued to register his daily protest, and to earn his daily slapping or beating. Towards the end of June 1943 I found it increasingly difficult to swallow and digest even the small ration of watery rice porridge that was our daily portion. Several others in the camp had the same experience and we rapidly became so thin and weak that we were no longer able to get out to the working site. We had heard of some PoWs judged as useless mouths having been sent in barges down river to one of the base camps, but we had also heard stories that most of these sick men were dead on arrival. I carried on for a few days trying to do something useful in the camp or cookhouse, but eventually gave up and with no appetite almost stopped eating too.

At this point Selby Milner told him that if he could do nothing else he might as well make the crosses for the PoW graves. Looking back, he felt that this apparently heartless instruction stopped him, just in time, from lying down and dying.

Noguchi decided to make up a party of useless thin men and send them down to Tha Khanun. We were a group of about twenty, I believe, unable to walk and barely able to stand, it was assumed that we would soon die, which most of us eventually did.

Milner's diary notes: '23 June 43 Capt. Baker evacuated to Takanoon seriously ill ...'

Beyond the call of duty
Barry recalls:

> The day chosen for the evacuation was a Sunday, one of our rare 'yasme' days, so other fitter men were free to accompany us on our trip through the jungle. We had about 7km to walk to reach the barges going to Tha Khanun. Two of my men helped me, one carried my pack and I was supported between the two of them. After a short distance we found that we were making poor progress and one of them took me on his back and carried me the rest of the way. The two names of Douglas and Corporal McWhirter are in my mind but I cannot be at all sure that this is a true recollection.

Gibby Douglas is surely correct, but the last time Barry saw McWhirter, according to his notes at the time, was in Ban Pong in November 1942. (Other possible names are McCarthy or Wilson, or perhaps his batman Reg Hedges.)

> We were welcomed at Tha Khanun by a proper reception committee of doctors and orderlies who first examined us very thoroughly to make sure that none of us was carrying a cholera infection and then did whatever they could to restore our strength.

Dr Robert Hardie of the RAMC kept a diary of the whole period of 1942–1945. In 1943 he was working in Tha Khanun. Hardie has an entry for 2 July 1943:

Charlie Wilson in 1940.

'Parties of sick men, in an appalling condition, keep arriving here by barge from further up river, where conditions are evidently much worse than here.' Another entry records: 'A lot of very sick men are coming down from 211 camp in a shocking condition – gaunt spectres of men, riddled with malaria and food deficiencies. One can do very little for these people. They can't assimilate the sort of food we have except eggs, of which we have very few.'

> Dr Hardie may well have been one of the MOs who cared for me at Tha Khanun and saved my life.
>
> After we had been thoroughly tested we were all weighed on a beam balance, built in the camp and calibrated against a 50kg rice sack. My weight, about average for the group, was noted as 5 stone 13lbs, or 37.5kg.
>
> I found that I could eat the well-cooked rice we were offered with the addition of a meaty soup and the occasional egg and in a few days made quite astonishing gains in weight and strength ...

By 16 July 1943 Milner records: 'Had a note from Beaver at Takanoon, cholera is apparently stamped out there. Baker is better.' Barry recalls:

> When the barges arrived to take us down river I was able to carry my bedroll on board myself, and even to help other sicker men with their kit. Some of the group which came down from 211 with me were already dead but some survived and I believe we were by now probably fitter than some parties from other up-river camps who were waiting with us for the barge trip.
>
> I really cannot remember much of that trip down the river. It was a motor-ized barge with a crew of two Siamese boatmen and one or two Japanese guards. We stopped at various camps on the way and we may have spent the nights ashore but most of the time we lay in a heap in the bottom of the barge. A few of us died and were unloaded at the next camp and eventually we arrived at Chungkai.
>
> Once again we were received by a team of PoWs, who seemed quite used to the arrival of parties like ours. We were washed down with buckets of river water, the two or three dead removed, and disposed of, the rest of us helped up from the river to the camp and installed in one of the many huts waiting for us.

Chungkai, a large base camp, had become a receiving station for the sick men sent down from the upriver working camps and grew into a well run hospital camp over the next year. Towards the end of July 1943, when Barry arrived, the camp was struggling to accommodate, never mind treat, the incoming sick.

Although Barry survived, Driver Jimmy Grant, who reached Chungkai Camp ahead of him, died of dysentery and cardiac beriberi on 2 July. Signalman Reginald Jennings died in Tamarkan [Tha Makham] Camp on 18 July of beriberi/malaria and Murrell attended his funeral. Signalman George Hobson, the second of the Glossop boys, died at Kanyu or Tarsao [Tha Sao] 2 on 8 August.

Jimmy Grant in about 1940.   Reg Jennings in about 1940.

Chapter 19

Britain: Summer 1943

Silent summer

By June 1943, while Barry and his surviving men battled to keep their diseased and skeletal bodies alive, Phyllis was still living at home with her parents and finding this increasingly tricky.

9 June 1943, from Phyllis to Barry (received after liberation). Letter 14
At last they have gone to bed and left me in peace to write to you. I find it almost impossible to write to you with other people round me, and very difficult to write during the day time at all. Just lately, for some unknown reason, Mother and Daddy have been going to bed so late that I could not possibly start typing to you without a long disagreement with Mother. We have been rather busy lately – your parents and John came here on May 21st. John was ill, and your mother supposed to be convalescing after her recent illness. Alan went after a week, John after ten days, and Barbara after a fortnight. Two days before she went, young Jeremy Charles came. I am looking after him while Joyce and Lionel have a holiday. He really is a very good baby, so happy and contented, when food is not in question – then he is very impatient if it is not forthcoming in speed and quantity to suit him! His one drawback is his terrific weight. By the end of the day, I really feel quite exhausted. He is only a few pounds lighter than Robin, though a year and a half younger! However, it is good solid bone and muscle largely. He can only intimate his views by sounds. When annoyed, he swears so hard that, as Enid says, you can almost hear what he is saying! But enough of young Jeremy. Robin loves him, but all the same has suddenly developed an 'I want Mummy' complex ...

   I am very worried that I cannot find my copy of my last letter, and apart from not wanting anyone else to see it, I can't remember what I told you in it. However, you must have gathered that I am looking for a job ...

Phyllis writes at length about the pros and cons of working at a school in Somerset in which Robin would be a boarder. The salary would be low, the possible snags with regard to Robin unknown, and the distance from her invalid mother a big concern.

   I'm rather hoping that you will come back with some definite ideas on what you want to do. If I can help it, you are not going to be debarred from doing anything you want because you have a wife and son for whom to provide. It is far far more important that you should be working at something you really want to, than being in a safe job, where you will have no outlet for your (not inconsiderable) capabilities. Poor Alan is so afraid I am going to urge you to chuck the army, without regard to other possibilities. But I'm not going to … all I can feel at present, is that once I have you back, nothing else will matter a twopenny damn … Now, goodnight, dear darling one. I hope I dream of you.

Your own Phyllis

Another person who felt a need to write to Barry was his old schoolmaster, Maurice Kirkman. It is difficult to comprehend the roll-call of death of the young men such teachers had sent hopefully out into the world.

25 June 1943, from Mr Maurice Kirkman (Tunbridge Wells) to Barry (received after liberation)
Dear 'Old Boy', Having heard of your whereabouts from your father, I send this word of greeting. I sit on the Common, as I write, under a couple of lime trees, with a background of waving grass and a distance of green English June, with a band of blue against the sky: such a view as you can imagine – and recollect …

Do you know those quaint lines by an old 17th century poet? –

My soul, sit thou a patient looker-on:
Judge not the play before the play is done.
Her plot has many changes: every day
Speaks a new scene: the last act crowns the play.

Yours, as <u>always</u>, M.C.K.

In early July Barbara writes a very ordinary letter, but it turns out to be her last wartime one to Barry. Perhaps uncertain of the latest regulations, this is typed *and* in capitals.

12 July 1943, Barbara to Barry (received after liberation)
MY DEAREST BARTON, I FEEL THAT PERHAPS IT IS MY TURN TO WRITE TO YOU AGAIN … YOU ARE NEVER OUT OF OUR THOUGHTS FOR VERY LONG. HE [young Alan] IS STILL WHERE HE WAS BUT JOHN HAS MOVED TO DAD'S BIRTH COUNTY [Norfolk] BUT I DOUBT HE WILL BE THERE LONG …

I HAVE BEEN VERY BAD ABOUT WRITING LETTERS SINCE WE CAME BACK FROM OUR HOLIDAY, IT IS THE VERY BUSY GARDEN AND KITCHEN TIME OF THE YEAR SO I HAVEN'T HAD MUCH TIME OR ENERGY FOR A LETTER. JOHN HAD 48 HOURS LEAVE EIGHT DAYS AGO WHICH SIMPLY FLEW … OUR TENANT [at Wilks Farm] HAS HAD TO GIVE UP … AND WE ARE LEFT WITH A HOUSE THAT WE CANNOT LEAVE EMPTY OR GOVERNMENT WILL TAKE IT OVER, CANNOT LET WITH ANY CERTAINTY OF BEING ABLE TO GET INTO IT ONCE THE WAR IS OVER … IT IS JUST SOMETHING TO THINK ABOUT BUT COMPARED TO OUR REAL SORROWS AND WORRIES IT IS JUST NOTHING AT ALL. DO YOU REMEMBER THOSE PEOPLE YOU ONCE STAYED WITH

WHI[L]ST YOU WERE UP AT CAMBRIDGE, THE ABRAHAMS? THEY LIVE IN TOOTING AND THEIR SON [Kurt Abrahamsohn, see p. 99 above] HAS BEEN ACCEPTED FOR THE R.A.F. IN THE PILOT/NAVIGATOR/BOMB AIMER CATEGORY …

DARLING I WRITE TO YOU OF ALL THESE LITTLE THINGS SO THAT YOU WILL BE IN TOUCH WITH US BUT I AM SURE YOU KNOW THAT THEY DO NOT SEEM VERY IMPORTANT ONLY THE THINGS THAT ARE AND THE THOUGHTS THAT ARE MUST JUST REMAIN IN OUR HEARTS. GOD BE WITH YOU DARLING ALWAYS AS OUR THOUGHTS ARE WITH YOU. WITH DEAR LOVE FROM US BOTH, EVER YOUR LOVING MOTHER, BARBARA

During July yet more letters from relatives of the men in 27 Line Section arrived for Phyllis. Some of them have actually received PoW cards from their sons/ husbands; writers also mention their friends receiving cards. The following letter is typical:

13 July 1943, from Mary Grierson (Lockerbie), wife of Signalman J. Grierson, to Phyllis
Dear Mrs Baker, Just a few lines to let you know I have at last been fortunate in receiving a postcard yesterday morning from my husband saying he is a PoW in Japanese hands and is safe and well. The postcard is dated 'July 1942' – there was no name of camp but perhaps that will come later.

I suppose it is not possible to send parcels or anything out there but if you have any details as to what I can do, perhaps you would let me know and I shall be very Grateful for same.

Yours Sincerely, Mary Grierson.

It is difficult to convey the extent to which all these relatives were living from day to day, hoping for a card or information from the War Office. They could not help dreaming that at any moment order would be restored, that at the very least they would, like relatives of German-held PoWs, be able to send comforts out to their men or know that their letters are arriving. Those such as Phyllis, who have had notification from the Records Office of their relative's PoW status, but no direct communications, became increasingly anxious. Those who had heard nothing at all from any source must have felt very lonely and despairing by this stage. On the other hand, those, like Mary Grierson, who receive direct but out of date news entertain what is often false hope (see above p. 106).

On 17 July the British Postmaster General issued a revised leaflet detailing all the restrictions to be applied to mails: they were to be short; in typed or blocked letters; in one of four approved languages; only from close relatives/friends; no more than one a fortnight, and NO enclosures, handmade envelopes or labels. Subject matter was to be purely personal and to exclude mention of anything to do with the armed forces, economics or politics. For many relatives, writing while bearing all this in mind, and with never any reply, must have been a complex, soulless chore.

Chapter 20

Thailand: Summer 1943

Chungkai, storyteller & lady almoner
Meanwhile, Barry was recovering at Chungkai. In this camp the number of inmates varied, but it housed very approximately 12,000 to 15,000 men of many different nationalities. All through spring and summer of 1943 starving and diseased PoWs from the upper reaches of the railway trickled downriver to the bigger camps such as Chungkai. In October the two sections of the railway, in Thailand and Burma, joined up at Konkuita, 260km from the start point at Nong Pladuk. Completion was two months ahead of schedule. From then on, sick and dying men poured into Chungkai transported by barges or on the railway itself. Six men of 27 Line Section had already died on the railway and five more were never to return, but the remnants of 27 joined Barry at intervals over the next year.

The now generally accepted number of Allied prisoners who died on the Thailand–Burma railway, according to the late Roderick Suddaby of the Imperial War Museum, is between 12,000 and 13,000, approximately a fifth of the 61,000 who were sent to work on it. However, this number is dwarfed by the deaths, between 80,000 and 120,000, among the vast, uncounted gangs of Chinese and Indian coolies and some Malays, used over the latter stages.

From the summer of 1943 until February 1945 Chungkai became Barry's home, though of course he never had the security of knowing that he would be there for so many months. He described aspects of his life there in precise detail, though occasionally his memory for the sequence of events has been garbled by the passage of time, so dating has been corrected.

Chungkai was a big camp. It was dotted with clumps of bamboo and banana trees and rows and rows of huts. The Camp was roughly divided into two sections, the fit and the sick, each half with about ten huts, around 100m long. There were of course, cookhouses, Jap huts for the guards and great ranges of latrines all with roofs to keep the rain out but no walls, to ensure a good draught.

I was soon among the fit, and joined in with parties who went down to the river or the railway to meet the parties of sick men as they arrived.

Our Medical Officers – MOs – (there were several of them) examined each newcomer and marked him sick or fit, and the British camp commander and Chief MO decided where the new arrivals were to be accommodated. We lined up with rice-sack stretchers and carried the worst cases up to the

Drawing by Jack Chalker of a river barge unloading sick and dead POWs at Chungkai in 1943.

sick huts, which were each reserved for some particular illness. Most of them were dysentery and beriberi or general malnutrition. Benign tertian malaria (with paroxysms every 48 hours) hardly counted but other varieties were more serious.

A pattern of conduct for the rest of our times as PoW was already beginning to form. The Jap engineers endlessly called for more working parties of fit men to go up the line to carry out repairs and maintenance work. The line was already being bombed by the Allies. Our OC had to choose and detail suitable men to fill these demands, and the choice naturally fell on those men who were not actively engaged in camp duties. So everyone sought for a useful employment, and from taking the sick up from the river or the railways into their huts, I graduated into looking after them in various other fashions.

My first and simplest job was basically as a storyteller or rather reader. I would take a likely book from the camp library and sit down on the end of a bed space in one of the sick huts, and read a chapter or two. Then I would move down the hut, twenty or thirty yards, and read the same piece to another lot of sick men. This was judged to be a useful employment, so I was not called on to join a maintenance party.

These camp libraries were very simply set up. To join you had to contribute a book. Most people managed to keep at least one book with them in the camps, and once you had contributed your one book you were free to borrow another one from the shelves. In a camp of this size, where no services of any sort were provided by the Japs, there were endless opportunities for finding useful work: building huts or mending the roof; carrying water; digging latrines; making paths through the mud; collecting fire wood and, of course, cooking. Yet there were still many quite fit PoWs who seemed content to lie in their huts and eat their three bowls of rice without contributing anything. These men seemed surprised when they were detailed for an up river working party, and pretty soon everyone in the camp was busily employed or at least looked as if he was.

Under the guidance of our friendly Siamese we learnt to turn bamboo into bed slats. The original split bamboo slats had all been lashed in place but the lashings all had to be cut so that the slats would be removed when they became infested with bed bugs as they soon did. We had a weekly ceremony of 'slat bashing' when all the bed slats were taken outside, passed quickly over a bright fire and then vigorously slapped together. This seemed to destroy the bugs – but they came back.

Several PoWs had brought up musical instruments on their original trip from Singapore, and then been forced to dump them at Ban Pong. To our surprise much of their kit, carefully labelled, was later transported up to the appropriate camp and reunited with its owner. Chungkai soon developed a handsome orchestra based on a couple of piano accordions, and a few violins.

We enjoyed the performances but these jolly functions contrasted harshly with our work in the sick huts, which got steadily worse as more parties of sick and dying arrived from up river. We were burying ten, fifteen, or even twenty every day, and it was disconcerting during my readings to become aware that one or two of my audience were never going to hear the next chapter. The funerals were carried out by the Unit or Regiment to which the man had belonged, with the appropriate prayers and Last Post on the bugle. The Scotsmen of course had a piper instead, who played 'The flowers of the forest are all taken and gone'.

After a few weeks of this the Jap commander complained of this continuous mournful music, and ordained that there would be only one funeral daily when all the dead were to be buried at the same time. A very neat graveyard was set up with wooden crosses to mark each name.

There were, of course, many bodies buried hastily on marches or burnt during the cholera epidemic in the upriver camps, with no marked graves at the time.

The graveyard at Chungkai was embellished with rows of red cannas, which grow particularly well in Siam. During the rainy season when the river rose up to its flood level, the ground water level must have risen above the level of the bodies in the graves. The cannas must have profited by the extra fertilization and grew to astonishing heights, well over head level.

One of the most difficult jobs for senior officers and doctors was management of the minimal pay. Small sums had been allocated to officers, and even smaller amounts to Other Ranks, from early in their captivity. Barry misremembers this as a novelty in Chungkai. By the time he reached Chungkai he had long run out of his lucky windfall savings, and these small sums mattered. The PoW military commander of each camp had to decide, with the consent of his colleagues, whether the money should be distributed to each individual or taxed for the benefit of the sick.

How much the Japs decided to pay us I do not know, but it was to be subject to deductions for the rations and accommodation that they were providing for us (!). This money in Japanese printed wartime paper notes was handed over to the British CO for distribution, who immediately impounded half of it for Camp welfare. This meant in fact, buying extras for the men in the sick huts.

After my reading aloud sessions in the sick huts I was given a very different and uncomfortable job, that of Almoner for some of the huts. The job of Almoner, or 'Lady Almoner' as it was called, involved the actual distribution of goodies bought from the welfare fund, to the sick men in the huts. The most useful purchases were eggs, honey, palm syrup, and occasional pots of vegemite, the Australian marmite. There was, of course, not nearly enough for everyone, the MO in charge of a particular hut would give me a list of the men due to receive these extras and the quantities for each one.

I did not at first realize the difficulty of the job but it became clear soon enough. Most of the very sick men got nothing at all because, as the MO told me, they would die anyway. The extras, very carefully husbanded, would go to those men who were able to profit from them and might just recover with their help but who would die without. At least I was spared the agony of deciding who got what, but every day I was faced with the need to find answers. 'I am much sicker than Joe, Sir, why does he get two eggs this week and I get none?' An unanswerable question to which I had to find some reasonable answer day after day. I talked to the other Almoners and had no comfort from them, all in the same position as I was. 'Tell them Orders is Orders, and you are just doing what you are told to do.'

Chapter 21

Britain: November 1943 to February 1944

Down to twenty-five words

In the second half of 1943 there was a major event for the family: Barbara and Alan moved to San Francisco to help with propaganda broadcasts on the World Service to Malaya. Fearing that Barry might suffer if their work ever came to his captors' notice, they stop writing altogether. So Barbara's letter of 12 July 1943 is the last she or Alan wrote to Barry during the war.

Less easy to understand is that between 9 June and 2 November 1943 Phyllis wrote just one letter, number 15 (now missing). Then, some time in September, Phyllis and Robin moved in with an army wife near Warwick, to live on the *au pair* system. There are no letters explaining why, but it may simply have been the culmination of various plans suggested in earlier letters. Phyllis continued to keep in touch with the relatives of 27 Line Section.

On 11 September 1943 Post Office staff were told that Far Eastern PoW mail, already restricted to typed capitals, was now to be limited to twenty-five-word messages. Staff members were asked to tell relatives themselves until the printed handout with this information became available. There were notices in the press and on the radio, but Phyllis failed to pick them up.

On 2 November she borrowed a typewriter for a morning and typed a long letter about her doubts over whether Barry received mail, Robin's desire for a little sister and her efforts to save for the future. She finished:

> *2 November 1943, from Phyllis (at Hill Wootton, near Warwick) to Barry. Letter 16*
> ... TO ONE IDEA I HANG ON FIRMLY, NAMELY, THAT YOU WILL NOT BE WASTING YOUR TIME MORE THAN CAN BE HELPED, AND WILL BE LEARNING ALL THAT YOU CAN FIND ANYBODY TO TEACH YOU. ALSO, IF I KNOW ANYTHING OF YOU YOU WILL BE DOING A LOT OF HELPING OF OTHER PEOPLE, TOO. SO MANY PEOPLE HAVE SAID TO ME THAT IF ANYBODY COULD 'TAKE IT', YOU CERTAINLY COULD. AND THANK GOD I KNOW THEY ARE RIGHT, MY DARLING. NEVER FORGET THAT I LOVE YOU, WILL YOU? EVER YOUR OWN PHYLLIS

This letter was returned by the censor; an enclosure from the GPO reads: 'The Japanese Authorities require that letters and postcards ... shall be limited to 25 words and shall be either typewritten or written clearly in block-lettering ...'

Below is Phyllis's next surviving communication. She cannot say much in twenty-five words. Her sister Enid's marriage to Eric Furness a week before is not mentioned in this one, for example. This slip has the number three on it but other slips are unnumbered.

17 December 1943, from Phyllis to Barry (received January 1945)

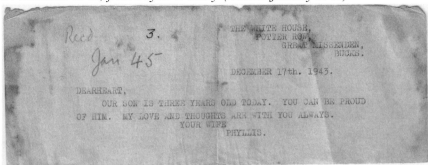

Around Christmas Phyllis received more letters from relatives of 27 Line Section men to say they have had PoW postcards from their men. She has still had nothing from Barry. She wrote another circular letter from Warwick asking them to note the new address.

31 December 1943, from Phyllis (in Warwick) to relatives of 27 Line Section
Dear _____, There is some mail from Far East prisoners being distributed now – I do hope you will be among those who get news. If not, remember that the Japs say there are still over 30,000 names to come.

May the New Year bring you early and good news; perhaps by this time next year we may be in full correspondence with our men (<u>not</u> as PoW's), if nothing more.

Did you hear the wireless programme after the news to-night? In greetings from the Allies, Britain was represented by the march of the Royal Corps of Signals.

I have heard nothing since I wrote last year, but am full of hope for the new year – a real hope, not just the vague optimism of 1943; I trust that if you do not feel the same now, you will soon have reason to.

This letter took her some time to copy, and we have a second version dated 2 January 1944. In the latter it becomes clear that apart from the circular letters she also wrote to many relatives individually.

2 January 1944, from Phyllis (in Warwick) to relatives of 27 Line Section
Dear _____, When the last list of names came through, I heard from quite a number of people within 2 or three days. At that time one of my family was taken dangerously ill. I fear that I did not reply to a few people, though I tried to do so. If you were one of those to whom I did not write, I hope you will understand that it was not because I was not rejoiced to hear the good news.

If you get any news direct from the Far East, or hear anything from a reliable source that you think may interest others, or cheer those who have had no word, I'll be very pleased indeed to pass it on.

I have heard nothing since I wrote a year ago, but am full of hope for the new year – a real hope, not just the vague optimism of 1943.

There were many replies over the next two months; some wrote to say they had had cards last July or over Christmas. One of these was Tina Douglas, whose husband, Gilbert 'Gibby', probably helped to carry Barry when he was too weak to walk, on the journey to Tha Khanun (see above p. 124). She wrote:

4 January 1944, from Tina Douglas (Glasgow), wife of Driver Gilbert Douglas, to Phyllis
Dear Mrs Baker, Many thanks for your kind letter which I appreciate very much.

I had intended to write to you this week, so this is the reason I was doubly glad to hear from you.

I wanted to tell you that I received a postcard from my husband on Hogmanay and even now, I am still excited. He says he is in excellent health, is working for pay, and is interned in No. 2 PoW Camp Thailand. Not much, is it Mrs Baker? Yet those few words mean such a lot to me after these long weary months. I had been feeling very despondent as only recently I lost my only brother on the Burma front, so with this blow and the absence of news from my husband, I was really depressed. Now however I feel that this card is a good omen for the new year, and already I feel a lot better.

I am really sorry that you are still without news from your husband Mrs Baker as I can understand your feelings, but as long as you keep that courage which you so often imparted to me – well something must turn up soon for you.

Here's wishing you the best of luck in the New Year and may you hear from Cpt. Baker very soon.

Yours Very Sincerely, Tina Douglas

Other relatives wrote to say that, like Phyllis, they have still heard nothing from their men. Some have still not even been notified that their men are prisoners.

12 January 1944, from Mr A. D. George (Birmingham), brother of Lance Sergeant Cyril George, to Phyllis
Dear Mrs Baker, I am writing to thank you for your letter addressed to my late mother, Mrs George, who passed away in February of last year.

I am the elder brother of L/Serg. C. George, who was I believe attached to your husband's unit, and I should be extremely grateful of any news you may be able to obtain in the future as to the safety of our relatives.

Unfortunately we have not so far been amongst the lucky ones to hear from the Far East but feel quite confident about the safety of (in my case) my brother. Many people in this district have had news during the last few weeks and I should like to reciprocate your hopes, that you also will receive more news of your husband.

I believe you are attached to the Red Cross and was wondering if when you have the time, whether you could give me an idea of the number of men who have not been reported prisoner or otherwise since the 'missing' notices were sent through.

Thanking you again for your letter. Yours faithfully A. D. George

Cyril George had died of dysentery two months after capture.

In spite of this silence, there were some lines of communication to the Japanese prison camp authorities – perhaps via the Red Cross. Mrs Grierson wrote to Phyllis.

17 January 1944, from Mary Grierson (Lockerbie), wife of Signalman J. Grierson, to Phyllis

Dear Mrs Baker, I thank you for the nice letter received a few days ago. I wrote you during the month of September last and often I wondered why I had not heard from you but I understand how fully your time would be occupied and I do hope that you and all your family are now enjoying the best of health.

You see, Mrs Baker, I received a postcard from my Husband in August but it had taken just over a year to come from the time it was written, and he was fit and well then, next came the War Office communication confirming that he was a PoW.

Just a few weeks later the War office notified me that my husband had died from malaria in Thai Camp and that the date of his death unknown. I wrote the Regt. Paymaster last week to ask if any further word had come through but have had no reply yet.

I do hope you receive more word soon of your Husband.

Wishing you all the best and may 1944 bring you more good news.

Yours Sincerely, Mary Grierson.

While devastating for Mary Grierson, this letter may have given false hope to others that if they had heard nothing their men were still alive and well. Phyllis keeps sending the brief permitted typed slips.

January 1944, from Phyllis to Barry (received October 1944)

ROBIN A GREAT COMPANION NOW. 'DADDY' ALWAYS IN OUR THOUGHTS. YOU ARE A VERY REAL PERSON TO HIM. I ALWAYS HOPE. ALL MY LOVE, PHYLLIS

February 1944, from Phyllis to Barry (received October 1944)

SMIDGE HOME AFTER NEARLY FOUR YEARS. ROBIN AND I ARE GOING TO SHARE HOUSE WITH HELEN. BOTH WELL, AND SEND ALL OUR LOVE, DEARHEART. PHYLLIS

Chapter 22

Thailand: Late 1943 to Early 1944

Hospital orderly

During this period, as the silence in Britain lengthened and communication was reduced to a few words, Barry, now fit, became more actively involved in the attempt to save lives. What his account fails to mention, but others do, is that apart from the sight and sound of men in extreme pain, with wounds open to the bone, there was an unbearable stench and fly infestation in the sick wards. The uncontrolled bowels of the sufferers in the dysentery huts and the stink of gangrene in the ulcer wards required heroic self-control of their helpers. He writes:

> For some months more and more men with large infected ulcers had been arriving at Chungkai from up-river camps. These ulcers were nearly all in the legs and were caused by scratches from the thorny bamboo, which like most wounds in the jungle soon became infected and ulcerated. If the sufferer were fit and strong the ulcer would sometimes heal. My own small ulcer in my left hand did just that and no scar is now visible. Many did not heal but instead steadily increased in size.
>
> There were whole huts full of them in late 1943 and early 1944 and acting as a dresser in these wards became one of my hospital duties. There was a large group of volunteers, 300 or more, officers and ORs who did odd jobs all around the sick huts to help the small group of RAMC doctors and orderlies. We had no previous training and we just did what the doctors told us to do.
>
> For now I simply had to clean out the raw ulcer and remove the rotten necrosed flesh from the edges. We used a homemade antiseptic dressing. After cleaning and dressing, the ulcer was covered with a piece of rag or banana leaf. These rags, mainly torn up sheets, were carefully preserved, boiled daily after use and hung up in the sun to dry. They may have been sterile, or nearly so, but they were the best we had.

Apart from his hospital work, Barry's main role in camp was as an inventive maker and mender ('Makeshift Baker') at which he excelled. In late 1943 he had become involved with creating props for the theatre but had more time on his hands after the Japanese closed the theatre for some infringement of the rules.

> With the closure of the theatre, I re-joined the group of volunteer orderlies in the ulcer ward and here met Dr Jacob Markowitz for the first time. Some

Cleaning out tropical ulcers with an old spoon and no anaesthetic at Chungkai (drawing by Jack Chalker).

months back there had been a conference of the doctors in Chungkai to consider how to treat the increasing number of these ulcers, the patients often dying of septicaemia or simply general weakness and debility. There were, of course, no antibiotics regularly available though small quantities of one of the sulpha drugs did appear occasionally. The doctors decided that when an ulcer patient had a life expectation of not more than a fortnight then the limb, almost always a leg, would be amputated. Markowitz got to work immediately to sort out the backlog. It is recorded that he took off over a hundred legs in his first month.

The doctors had a supply of Dental Cocaine and this was used as a spinal anaesthetic, very suitable for leg amputations. As I worked up and down the ward with the other volunteers, cleaning and dressing the ulcers we would regularly be asked 'Will it be my turn soon?' Most of the men were anxious to be freed from the misery and pain of an ever growing ulcer, and were prepared, even anxious, to undergo the risk and pain of an operation. I worked for a short time as a member of Dr Markowitz's team. The operating theatre, during my brief job, was in the open, without a roof as it was the dry season.

The area was surrounded by screens of rice sacks on bamboo frames. The patient was brought from the ward on a bamboo stretcher whose arms were then fitted into notched bamboo uprights. My job was to tend a small fire under a cut-down paraffin can in which the instruments were boiled.

I had to fish out the instruments with homemade bamboo tongs and to lay them on a piece of sterile cloth on a small bamboo side table. We had, as I recall, two scalpels, a bone saw, and several retractors made from table forks. What kind of stitching thread and ligatures he used I cannot remember.

There were no comforting pre-med drugs, so the patient was immediately rolled onto one side and one of Markowitz's assistants inserted the needle into his spine and injected a suitable dose of cocaine. Marco usually had one or two doctors assisting him. When tests showed that the anaesthesia was satisfactory a very tight tourniquet was placed around the patients upper thigh or groin and the operation proceeded.

Marco said that he expected to do a femur amputation in twelve minutes. The amputation of the lower leg took longer, about fifteen minutes, as two bones are involved, and the artery also divides into two. I believe about 80% of patients survived these operations, a great advance on certain death in a fortnight. Many of the ulcer patients would have preferred death to a continued endurance of their miserable condition.

There were no painkillers and the next few days must have been agonising after the anaesthetic had worn off. These patients, referred to as the 'Amputs', lived all together in a separate hut and no doubt comforted one another. By the end of the War most of the survivors were getting about on some sort of bamboo prosthesis.

War is full of anomalies:

We had one birth in Chungkai, one of the Japanese guards brought in a Siamese woman who had been in labour for two days with a cross presentation. Markowitz, or one of the other doctors, got her up into the knee and elbow position and somehow managed to turn the foetus, possibly by pulling down an arm, so that the proper presentation was achieved and the baby was born naturally.

Goods for these and other operations were supplied very secretly by Mr. Phi Boon Pong, a Siamese merchant and barge trader. He and his family also, at great risk to themselves, supplied batteries (referred to as 'canary seed') for the secret wireless sets. One might ask if the canary had been singing and this meant, 'Is there any news'. Boon Pong was publicly honoured after the War.

There were several other brave underground suppliers, but without Boon Pong the death-toll would have been many times higher. He, with his courageous family providing cover, continued to trade with the Japanese while supplying the PoWs secretly with money and exceedingly dangerous and banned items until the end of the war.

One sad irony of the PoWs' shortages, especially in the medical department, is that Red Cross parcels had been sent and, at least later in the war, did arrive.

Phi Boon Pong Sirivejjabhandu and his 13-year-old daughter with a Japanese soldier in about 1943 (courtesy of the Thailand–Burma Railway Centre).

A few were distributed, but many were pilfered by their captors or simply left in warehouses undistributed. According to Barry, this was:

> [For] an extraordinary but perfectly logical Japanese reason: to distribute food and comfort parcels from abroad would mean that the PoWs were deprived of these things, a reflection on the policies of the Japanese High Command and hence of the Emperor himself. Since the Son of Heaven was a God and could do no wrong, these parcels were not needed and would not be distributed.

One medical necessity, blood, unlike most of the drugs they so badly needed was, of course, always available. The difficulty was how to transfuse it safely given the problem of incompatible blood types; yet the surgeons knew that it could be a crucial life-saver when operating and in cases of extreme debility, of which there were all too many.

> In early 1943 Markowitz and the other Medics in Chungkai started a bold treatment for men who were simply very weak from continuous dysentery and avitaminosis (vitamin deficiency). They set up a blood transfusion clinic. I knew my blood group and I believe most of the soldiers did too. The

transfusions were not quite direct donor to patient but as the blood could not be stored both men concerned were together and met one another.

About one pint of blood was drawn off from the vein in the donor's elbow, and the donor was then invited to sit up. He was given the large pot containing his own blood and was then instructed to stir it and whip it with a pair of bamboo chopsticks. This produced a degree of coagulation and the solid matter, the fibrin, could be withdrawn with the chop sticks. When the MO decided that the blood had been successfully defibrinated it was transferred directly into the sick man's arm. This process was used, I suppose, to reduce the danger of clotting where there might have been some uncertainty about the blood groups. The bribe or payment for each donor was a cup of tea with sugar and condensed milk, a rare treat.

After one transfusion I had a very happy encounter. While walking through one of the sick huts a man of my own section, No. 27, stopped me and said, 'Sir, yesterday I had some of your blood, and last night I dreamed about a woman for the first time since capitulation!'

In Chungkai a fit man could give blood once a fortnight. Barry recalls giving at least a dozen transfusions, as did most of the other hospital workers. The Australian doctor, Colonel 'Weary' Dunlop, who took over from Markowitz in early 1944, records in his diary a figure of 300 successful transfusions at Chungkai.

Chapter 23

Britain: Spring to Summer 1944

Barry is alive

By a roundabout route, Phyllis's dreams finally came true. A card intended for her, but addressed to Barbara and Alan's home in Kent, was forwarded by the zealous Post Office to San Francisco, arriving on 27 January 1944. They cabled Phyllis immediately.

Undated, from Barry to Phyllis, a pre-printed Imperial Japanese Army card (post-marked Kent, January 1944)

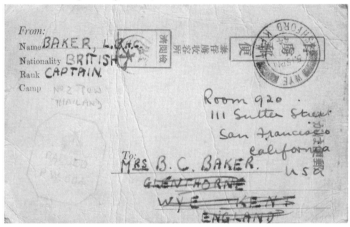

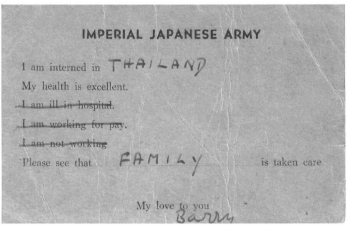

It is something of a miracle that this 3 ½in × 5 ¼in piece of card travelled successfully from the Thai jungles to Britain and from there to San Francisco (and back to Britain again, and is still here today).

However, only one day later, on 28 January 1944, Sir Anthony Eden gave a speech in Parliament. His opening words were, 'I fear I have grave news to give to the House … it becomes my painful duty …' and he went on to describe in appallingly blunt terms the conditions prevailing in the railway camps. He talked both of general conditions – disease, starvation and thousands of deaths – and of individual and barbaric atrocities.

> *2 February 1944, from Mrs Tina Douglas (Glasgow), wife of Driver Gibby Douglas, to Phyllis*
> Dear Mrs Baker, I expect you will be feeling just as I feel – not very far from being heartbroken, after the revelations of the Jap outrages.
> It is only we who have dear ones out there, who can fully understand it, and this statement given in parliament, has given us more anxiety.
> I suppose Mr Eden was forced to give it, yet how much better we would have been living in a fool's paradise.
> We knew of course that things were very bad, but this is more than we bargained for.
> Most maddening thing of all is that nothing can be done about it.
> To us it seems incredible that in this age of civilisation men can treat fellow beings in this atrocious manner.
> All we can do is to wait, hope, and pray to God that our dear men can suffer this torture, until something can be done for them …
> Yours sincerely, Mrs G. B. Douglas

Barbara, writing a long letter to son John, is also torn by the mixture of good and bad news:

> *5 February 1944, from Barbara (San Francisco) to John*
> Darling, have I told you that we've had our first post card from Barton? … We sent (young) Alan a cable as well as Phyllis because the first news of the atrocities was published the day after the card arrived & we thought it might help him a bit to know that we'd had a card. Of course Anthony Eden's statement took a bit of the comfort away, still the signature and the words (Thailand & Family) that Barton had added were written quite firmly & well so we hope very very much that what the card says is true. He must be terribly hungry I'm afraid & here we are in America with food abounding …

With the arrival of the card, Phyllis had at least the relief of having evidence, for the first time since February 1942, over two years previously, that Barry was probably still alive. She refers to the card in her next extant typed slip:

March 1944, from Phyllis to Barry (received, no date)
POSTCARD RECEIVED WITH GREAT JOY. FAMILY ALL WELL AND SEND LOVE.
KEEPING FILM RECORD OF ROBIN FOR YOU. LOVING AND HOPING ALWAYS.
YOUR WIFE PHYLLIS

She must have written immediately to some of the 27 Line Section relatives
because Tina Douglas replied:

9 March 1944, Tina Douglas (Glasgow), wife of Driver Gibby Douglas, to Phyllis
Dear Mrs Baker, Many thanks for your nice letter, and let me say how glad
I am to know that your husband is safe and in the same camp as my own
husband. [Relatives naturally assumed that 'Camp or Group 2' referred to a
fixed prison camp.]

Things seem to be moving a bit now, with the Japs getting a foretaste of
what's to come, so maybe a few more blows will make them decide that
better treatment of their prisoners would be beneficial.

Also that twenty five words included the date, which I had not known, so
I'm hoping, that my previous notes, have got through.

I was most interested to hear that you have a small son Mrs Baker, as I am
very fond of children, and having one of my own, I know what a comfort he
must be to you. My little boy is nearly seven, and it's due to him that I kept
going during the long period which his daddy was posted as missing.

It will be a wrench parting from him to take a job, but in the circumstances
I think it would be best for you and will help to keep you from worrying.
Often I have wished I could take a job myself, but having my father and sister
to look after, (they are doing important work) along with my son, I seem
always to have plenty to do ...

Badly off as we think we are, it's so much worse for them, not knowing
how things are at home or how their dear ones are faring ... so it's up to us to
be as brave and patient as our men, and who knows, it might not be too long
before they return, when we will be able to make up to them a little for what
they have gone through.

Hoping this finds you and your little son well and happy.

Yours very sincerely Mrs G. B. Douglas

On 22 March there was another instruction from the War Office about post.
From now on, pre-stamped airmail postcards are to be used for Far East PoW
mail. These small official cards permitted typing or block capitals and twenty-five
words only.

*9 May 1944, from Phyllis to Barry, official PoW card, hand printed (received
October 1944)*
POSTCARD RECEIVED FROM YOU. ALL WELL HERE. ROBIN GROWING FAST.
ALWAYS TALKING OF WHEN DADDY COMES HOME. WE KEEP HAPPY FOR
YOU. ALL OUR LOVE, PHYLLIS

9 May 1944, from Phyllis to Barry, official PoW card, hand printed (received October 1944)
DEAR ONE, HANNAH AND [young] ALAN ARE NOW OFFICIALLY ENGAGED. ALL YOUR FAMILY AND MINE ARE SAFE AND WELL. YOU ARE ALWAYS IN MY THOUGHTS. YOUR PHYLLIS

June 1944, from Phyllis to Barry, official PoW card, hand printed (received October 1944)
SORRY THERE HAS BEEN A GAP. ROBIN HAS HAD WHOOPING COUGH. QUITE BETTER NOW, FULL OF BEANS – JUST STARTED DANCING CLASS. ALL MY LOVE PHYLLIS

In July, to her joy, Phyllis has further evidence that Barry is still alive.

Undated, from Barry to Phyllis, a pre-printed Japanese Imperial Army card (post-mark Kent, July 1944)
I am interned in [then in hand-written capitals] *No2 PoW CAMP, THAILAND*
My health is excellent
~~I am ill in hospital~~
~~I am working for pay~~
~~I am not working~~
Please see that *WHOLE FAMILY* [in hand-written capitals] is taken care
My love to you *Barry Custance Baker* [in hand-written lower case]

This card, like the first, was forwarded in error to his parents in San Francisco. The tiny variations in this second communication (e.g. his distinctive family name) show that Barry is thinking about ways to confirm that he is the true author of these cards. Phyllis continued to send the limited official PoW cards:

July 1944, from Phyllis to Barry, official PoW card, hand printed (received, no date)

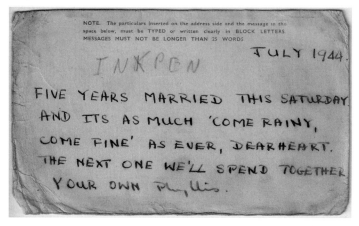

Chapter 24

Thailand: 1944

Clinging to hope in Chungkai

By early 1944 the demands of the railway were reduced to having groups of
PoWs sent up to maintain and repair its fragile structures. By keeping busy in
Chungkai Camp Barry began to hope that he and the remnants of 27 Line
Section might possibly survive. Apart from his hospital work and his role as
'Makeshift Baker', he continued to fill his days preserving the remnants of his old
life. He writes:

> Sometime at Chungkai I acquired the materials to preserve the two, the only
> two, objects from my PoW days that I still have with me now: my re-bound
> Racine and the framed photo of Phyllis.
>
> The Japanese had given an order that all books must be censored for fear
> that they might contain something critical of the Japanese High Command
> or of the Emperor. There was only one censor in the camp and he had
> some difficulty in reading English, but luckily the stamp he used was a very
> simple character, which our camp expert forgers had no difficulty in copying.
> The official censor was quite satisfied with the explanation that these books
> had already been passed by a censor in another camp.
>
> The Racine, from my Cambridge days, was a typical French paperback of
> the 1930s with a stitched binding. The 650 pages were suffering from its
> rough jungle journeys and barge trips and it was very frail though still com-
> plete. I found a bookbinder in the Camp who agreed to repair it. I had done
> some small job for him and this was by way of repayment. The paper covers
> were completely tattered and he replaced them with sheets of cardboard and
> covered the whole job with a piece of gas cape (military mackintosh). The
> book survives today.
>
> Phyllis's photo frame was quite different as I did that myself. I preserved
> the picture in a bamboo tube during my up-river journeys, but I now wanted
> to display it over my bed space and needed a proper frame. From a pair of
> black leather leggings I cut four strips about 18mm wide and stitched them
> onto a piece of cardboard to make the frame. It was strengthened with neat
> corner pieces, the thread used was pulled off a piece of khaki webbing strip
> and the holes made with a sharpened piece of a bicycle wheel spoke. Another
> piece of cardboard made a separate back cover, which was hinged onto the
> front with a strip of gas cape and the framed picture now hangs over my desk
> almost as good as new.

Fayer portrait of Phyllis (1939) in frame made by Barry in Chungkai in 1944.

Survival was still a very precarious business. In early 1944, with the railway base camps overflowing with sick, semi-fit and even some fit men, the Japanese now had a large labour force available in Thailand. They began sending more prisoners down to Singapore to be shipped to Japan or other parts of their territory. A group of about nine men of 27 Line Section were in the 'Japan party' heading for Manila aboard the *Osaka Maru* in March. Another handful of men from the section followed in the *Hofuku Maru* in July. These, and many similar vessels, became known collectively as 'hellships' because of the appalling conditions on board.

Kongsi
Survival in the worst conditions upriver often depended on having one or two very close mates. Later, in big camps such as Chungkai, friendship groups of a different sort enabled men to cope with the strange conditions of living at close

quarters with thousands of other men. Barry, like many others, sought to cement these friendships.

During our fairly stable period at Chungkai in 1944, many of us found that we had drawn together into small self-protective groups of friends generally with some common interest. These small groups acquired the title of Kongsi, a Chinese word meaning a business group or merchant company. My group, formed quite unconsciously, included Joe Hepworth, John Perret and my particular friend Patrick H. Stephenson. I don't know why these kongsis began to form but they did and were recognised. We did not feel antagonistic to others but simply ready to support or help one another. Nothing was said, simply an understanding among a small group of people with some sort of common interest. This kind of grouping did not happen much in the up-river camps while we were still building the railway, probably because we all had the same interest in common, that of staying alive somehow. At Chungkai and later at Kanchanaburi we all felt fairly sure that we were going to live through it all and we began to develop our own personal interests and to take an interest in other people's lives.

Joe's father was the owner of a Shoddy Mill in Ossett, Yorkshire, the biggest in the town, which as everyone must know is the world centre of the trade in Shoddy. We did not know this and in fact did not know just what shoddy was (old woollen cloth goes to the mill where it is shredded by violent machines and turned back into a mass of very short staple fibres, which are called shoddy). Joe was only too willing to tell us all about it and all about ''epworth's' as he always called the mill.

John Perret was an industrial chemist researching for the Dunlop Rubber Company in Liverpool. Most of his work was in the new science of plastics. He and others were trying to develop a butyl polymer, which would replace natural rubber for motorcar tyres.

Perret had an ambition to carry out a series of experiments to test his pet theory. He was convinced that the very simplest of micro-organisms, not even yet discovered, would have the same characteristics as very large pure chemical molecules. None of the very complex molecules like DNA, had yet been discovered and although some of the internal structure of the atom was already known, the vast array of sub-atomic particles had not yet been even imagined. His thesis would be that the most complex molecules gradually shaded into the simplest of living organisms without any clear dividing line.

He would spend hours explaining to Stephenson and to me just how this theory would work out. We, with only a basic understanding of chemistry, would only listen and wonder.

Pat Stephenson was an engineer of the most traditional type, apprentice, craftsman, master. He had worked for the British United Shoe Machinery Company, in Nottingham, and was able to give me useful hints on how best to mend our boots or make our sandals. He later specialised in motorcars

Pat Stephenson, self portrait photographed in a mirror, probably in 1941.

and was a test driver for the ERA (English Racing Automobiles) racing team, though never a race driver. He was called up in Wartime into the Ordnance Corps and was rapidly commissioned and promoted to the rank of captain.

On the railway Pat was remembered for one particularly outstanding feat. In one of the up-river camps, the lorry that brought up the rice rations broke down completely and it was found that the big-end bearings in the con-rods had melted. To repair such damage would normally call for the use of a fully equipped engineering workshop with specialized tools and supplies. The rice supply for the camp depended on this one lorry so Stephenson stripped the engine down in the jungle, using only those tools available in the vehicle's own tool kit. The con-rods were separated from the pistons, the damaged bearing metal removed and new bearings cast with solder supplied by the Japs. Solder is not the same as bearing metal, but is a fair substitute. The newly cast bearings then had to be scraped by hand to make an exact fit on the bearing surfaces of the crankshaft and the whole engine then re-assembled. I believe the molten metal for the casting was prepared in a ladle over a wood fire. When the job was completed the motor started up again and ran well.

With this group of a businessman, a chemist, and an engineer, I was treated as a mathematician and theoretical physicist, though most of my useful work in the camps was simple making and mending with improvised gear. I gained the proud nickname of 'Custance Makeshift Baker'.

I did, however, make one truly scientific and useful contribution to camp life.

In Chungkai several musicians had tried to build fretted instruments but ran into difficulties. During his first year at Cambridge Barry had studied musical theory and knew the 'magic numbers' for major chord frequencies. To get from these numbers to a working set for an instrument required seven-figure logarithm tables – not available in Chungkai – but Barry did a set of complex calculations.

I gave the table of values thus calculated to a number of ambitious instrument makers. There were a number of instruments in Chungkai, built on this principle, including a mandolin and a giant fretted double bass plucked not bowed and all of them worked adequately. I believe that my figures were passed to other camps up and down the river.

Chapter 25

Britain: Autumn 1944

News of the 'hellships'

Although the war would run for nearly another year, and Phyllis must have gone on sending cards, this is the last dated communication from Phyllis to Barry as a PoW that has survived:

> *September 1944, from Phyllis to Barry, official PoW card, hand printed (received, no date)*
> THE PLAYSHED AND POTTING SHED ARE BEING CONVERTED INTO A BUNGALOW FOR US AS LONG AS WE WANT IT. SEE YOU SOON NOW. LOVE PHYLLIS.

By late September 1944 Phyllis had moved back to live in her parents' newly converted sheds. Her mother's continued ill health was almost certainly one of the concerns that brought her back.

During the summer and autumn of 1944 many of the infamous Japanese transport ships were torpedoed or suffered aerial bombardment by the Allies. Rescue from the water by either side was limited, but in early September some 150 prisoners were picked up by the Allies after the sinking of the *Hofuku Maru*, about 60 of whom were British PoWs from Thailand. They included men from the Royal Corps of Signals. Interest in their accounts of imprisonment was intense, and on repatriation months later the War Office debriefed each survivor to try and ascertain the fate of the 40,000 British troops missing in the Far East.

Phyllis, thinking about Barry's men, started sending out letters some time in October to relatives to collect information; the first replies started coming in at the beginning of November.

> *4 November 1944, from Vera Randle (Preston), wife of Signalman Horace Randle, to Phyllis*
> Dear Mrs Custance-Baker, Thank you very much indeed for your very interesting and most helpful letter. It is most encouraging for all of us to hear any news at all of our men in the Far East and to know that there are people working to glean any kind of news possible. The last time I heard from my husband was December 23rd 1943 and the card had been written in the February of the same year. I am not sure if you have my husband's rank and number so to make sure here it is, Signalman Horace Randle 2346001, no nickname that I know of, in civil life he was a timber selector. My name is Vera and we have no family, my address when he left Britain was 9, Somerset

Rd, Deepdale, Preston, Lancs. I will always be most grateful for any thing at all that you can let me know concerning our men so let me thank you once more for your personal interest and let us hope and pray that before very long we get some satisfactory news.

Yours very sincerely Vera Randle.

Phyllis, contacting the War Office, realized the immensity of their task in finding out about the thousands of missing men from these few rescued individuals. She was determined to help. She did not have names and addresses for all the men in the section, but she did have some names (and addresses) of people connected with the men – possibly fiancées, or simply friends. She sent them the following letter:

24 November 1944, from Phyllis to any people for whom she had addresses who might have access to any members of 27 Line Section
Dear _____, In the winter of 1941–2, I forwarded to you a letter from Malaya, from a man in my husband's unit. I don't know from whom the letter came, and it may be someone with whose next of kin I am already in touch. But in case not, could you send me, if possible, the name and address of his wife or parents, or if not, just his own name and number?

Yours Sincerely

With the help of Queenie, the wife of Lieutenant Robert Garrod, who had also run the Clipper Mail service, she decided to compile a dossier of information, including photographs, about the men in 27 Line Section. She wrote to Queenie and enclosed a copy of the letter (see below, 29 November) that she had written to the relatives to bring them up to date with her efforts so far.

24 November 1944, from Phyllis to Queenie Garrod (London), wife of Lieutenant Bob Garrod
Dear Mrs. Garrod, The enclosed letter is a copy of one that I have sent to all the next of kin on my list, and on the one you gave me. I don't think there is anything more I can tell you, except perhaps that the Government are going to give us a chance to send a ten word cable to our men, just as soon as the clerical staff can make the arrangements. But that is not for publication at the moment. Also, if they can raise enough paper and staff, there will be a special number of the 'Far East' journal, dealing solely with the news the survivors have brought. But that is not yet quite certain. I gather that there were very few officers on the Transport ship that was sunk – and none among those rescued by the Americans.

One of the greatest troubles of the interviewers is that of accurate identi-fication – so I thought that a small dossier of 27 Line section might help them, and speed up news for us – if there is any. As the deaths were at the rate of one in five, we cannot possibly hope that all the men in that section have come through all right; but only one wife has written to say she has been notified by the War Office of her husband's death in camp. As Mrs. Grierson is also on your list, you probably know that already.

The following people on your list are either friends or their relationship to their correspondents was unknown to you when you gave it to me. Could you tell me if you are still in touch with any of them, and if you know who their correspondent was? They are:- Miss McElduff. Mrs. G. Gould. Miss Kenny. Miss Robinson. Miss Austwich. Miss Roberts. Miss O'Dea. Miss Irvine. Mrs. Phipps. R. G. Perry. Miss Moffatt.

I suppose you don't by any chance know how many men there were in the section? The Signals Association said they would give me a list, but were blasted out of their offices almost immediately, and are only just getting back to normal again. I don't know how you feel about it, but the news these boys have brought back got me down for the moment worse than anything else we have heard so far – which doesn't help anybody at all! [End of letter missing]

Phyllis struggled to find out the exact number of men in the Unit as this had varied somewhat. When first formed it comprised seventy-two men of all ranks. However, all Barry's post-war notes and nominal rolls list sixty-nine, including the two men lost before the fall of Singapore. A letter after the war from one of the men refers to 'L. Kennedy, one of the original members of 27' (see p. 229). He is not among the sixty-nine, so we must assume that three men either missed the original boat, stopped off en route to the Far East or were re-assigned after their arrival in Singapore.

29 November 1944, from Phyllis to all the relatives of men in 27 Line Section for whom she has addresses
Dear _____, You must, I know, be anxiously awaiting for news that the men rescued from the Transport ship may have to give.

I had a long interview on Nov. 21st. at Curzon Street House with one of the men who interviewed the survivors, and this is all I could learn.

No news of any individual can be sent to the next of kin till all the interrogations are complete, so as to avoid any mistakes of identification, and this will take many weeks. To begin with, there are over forty thousand men to enquire about. As the men could not be kept at the War Office without leave for this time, they have been sent home, and all are returning for duty to the War Office in six weeks time, where they will stay till they have given every scrap of information they can. In the meantime, it is useless to write to any whose addresses you may learn, as they cannot possibly cope with the floods of letters, which they are sending on to the War Office. Can you imagine how you would feel, if you got your man back on leave, and found 500 letters in the first post for him to answer? Besides, each one has news of different men to give.

Ivy Graham, mother of Driver George Albert Graham, writing to Phyllis on the same day from Barrow-in-Furness says, 'One of our local boys has got home. He was one that was picked up. But I have not seen him. His father ... said he had to go away because people were stopping him and asking so many questions and his nerves would not stand it.' Phyllis continues:

> While there can be no denying the fact that thousands of men have died in Siam, there are two points to help us. After the railway on which they were working was completed, conditions became very much better, and any man who pulled through to October 1943 should be alright now.
>
> The men who were being taken to Japan were all picked for their physique, and that is how those that were picked up survived the five days in the water. But when the Japs reported the sinking, they referred to 'the survivors', not knowing we had rescued any. So they must have picked some up, and have of course been asked for a list by our Government. So even when the men give us a list of their fellow-passengers it cannot be certain that they died at sea. They have asked the Government to make another statement soon about the present improved conditions so as to reassure relatives.

Sadly, this reassurance did not take into account the great numbers of men who, as a consequence of working on the railway, died later in the base camps. As Barry mentions in his memoirs, they died every day, from ulcers, dysentery, malaria and vitamin deficiencies. Many also died in the holds of transport ships or drowned after they were sunk. Others had fetched up in labour camps in different parts of the Japanese 'empire' such as Sumatra, where they were building another railway, in the unspeakable copper mines in Taiwan, or in Borneo, where they died in conditions as bad as, or possibly worse than, in Thailand. Phyllis did not know any of this; besides her aim is to uphold spirits. She continues:

> These [rescued] survivors are men from all camps and regiments, and quite a number are regular army men. There are several Royal Signals men among them. One thing I can most earnestly assure you of, is that the War Office will get all the information they possibly can for us, and the men, of course, are just bursting to tell all they can. During the two days they were in camp, after arrival, being medically examined and re-equipped etc. they gave up every minute they could to answering questions. But to give you some idea of the difficulties, several men might say 'Oh yes, we know Harry Jones, of — regiment, he was in Camp—'. But they can't be certain which of 4 Harry Joneses in that Regiment this one might be, and it would be a dreadful mistake to give news to the wrong family.
>
> About the cables we have been promised – the Japanese Government proposed it, asking the British Government if they were prepared to foot the bill (30 shillings per man). They were at once told to get on with it, and so far as can be known, are doing so. But it will take weeks, probably months, before all the thousands of men can get, fill in and return the forms, and then the cables be sent.

Meanwhile the various possibilities of broadcasting are being explored, but unfortunately that is very open to abuse, and on security grounds can't be widely used yet. There are staffs of qualified people in Britain, India and Australia picking up and recording all messages purporting to be from prisoners and they are sent on at once, if they can be identified as genuine.

While we are waiting for these men to return to the War Office, I suggest you send me any questions you want to, and I'll take them up all together. If I haven't got the number, name and rank of your_____, let me have them at once, and also please tell me if he was not called by his first Christian name, or had a nickname in common use – so many men were only known to their comrades by nicknames. Also, please give his civilian employment; if married, the names of his wife and children; if engaged, the name of his fiancée; and also the address you were at when he left Britain, if you have moved since then. If there was anything outstanding in his appearance, such as height or colouring, a squint or a broken nose – anything which might serve to help the memory of someone who has only seen him once, or met him without learning his name, please mention it. If you have a good snap-shot, that might help, but please don't send me any big photographs.

The most maddening part of our lives, at present, is our complete inability to do anything, and I hope it may be a little help to you to feel someone is trying personally to get news for you, though of course we can't hope that even the united efforts of 57 willing men [the British PoWs picked up by the Allies after the sinking of the *Hofuku Maru*] will produce information, good or bad, of over 40,000 men.

One thing stands out clearly from all accounts – our men are showing a magnificent spirit. It is very hard for us to be courageous at the moment, but it is the only tribute we can make if we are to be worthy of them. May we all be given the strength for it.

Chapter 26

Thailand: Chungkai 1944

Chorus girl

One way in which the men were showing spirit, not only in Chungkai but in all the other camps when they were able to, was in providing entertainment for each other. Erratically during 1943 and more consistently thereafter in Chungkai, enterprising individuals and groups put on concerts, shows and straight plays. Barry's Lieutenant, Bob Garrod, was involved, and for Barry the theatre provided not only his best distraction but some lifelong happy memories:

> I was co-opted into the early productions as a stage carpenter and odd job man for the Dutch director Joop Postma. Later on a fine new theatre for plays was built and used by several different groups of producers. As a small, slim, handsome young man and a good dancer, my true potential as a chorus girl and romantic actress was eventually recognised. Most of the shows were mixed variety concerts with a line of chorus girls.

Leo Britt, a Corporal in the RASC, had worked in the theatre and became the mainstay of this activity. There is a rare photograph of his most successful show, 'Wonder Bar'.

> Leo put on a number of straight plays in which I had minor parts. Leo was very strict with us 'girls'. Report to the theatre after first rice and from then on wear skirts and high heels to become used to moving like a woman. Some of us became anxious that we might possibly be becoming 'too too' girlish, and to prevent this we kept a stock of barbells and weight bars (bamboo and logs) behind the stage, which we could lift from time to time as an assurance that our manly muscles were still there.
>
> The autumn and winter of 1944 was the period of Leo Britt's main activity and his troupe considered themselves as the Chungkai Repertory Company. We often had two or three shows in preparation at once. Word rehearsals in the morning, stage in the afternoon and show in the evening. We had no electric light of course, but the stage was quite well lit by two or three petrol lamps that were operated by my particular friend Pat Stephenson.
>
> The parts for the plays were either copied out from books, which we happened to have in the camp, or more often written down by someone who knew the play well from having acted in it or produced it before the war. In Hay Fever I had a longer part of an older woman, one of a group of friends who meet at a country house weekend party, at the home of a very famous

'Lichten Op' revue poster, 1944. The cast included Bob Garrod and (Barry) Custance Baker (Collection Museon, The Hague, Netherlands).

A scene from 'Wonder Bar' at the Chungkai Theatre, May 1944.

actress. Mostly mixed up couples having violent kiss and cuddle scenes and dashing outdoors to avoid each other; 'Anyone for tennis?' I actually wore a pretty white tennis frock with a pleated skirt and white shoes, which I made myself.

In my best scene (in Hay Fever) twisting around on a very hard bamboo sofa with the host I was often worried that our kisses might cause giggles or rude comment from our brutal and licentious audience, but we got away with it and the host, Leo himself, once whispered to me, 'They're taking it OK, do it just once more'. So we did, and the Japs, who came every night and sat in the front row, just loved it.

A small part with Dickie Lucas, the main leading lady at the time, in a Café Colette show, has given me my best-loved anecdote. We did a dance routine to the tune of 'Yam', a popular song of the thirties. We danced separately and then as a pair, finally in the chorus line. When walking back to my hut after the show I overheard two soldiers, one of whom I knew, discussing the show. 'Those two fucking tarts, they were more like real fucking tarts than any fucking tarts I've ever met'. My best theatre crit.

Other members of Barry's original unit, 27 Line Section, who fetched up in Chungkai, were also stars of the stage. Bob Garrod acted in a very successful production of 'Night Must Fall' in June 1944.

Chungkai Theatre poster by Geoffrey Gee, June 1944 (de Wardener papers, Imperial War Museum).

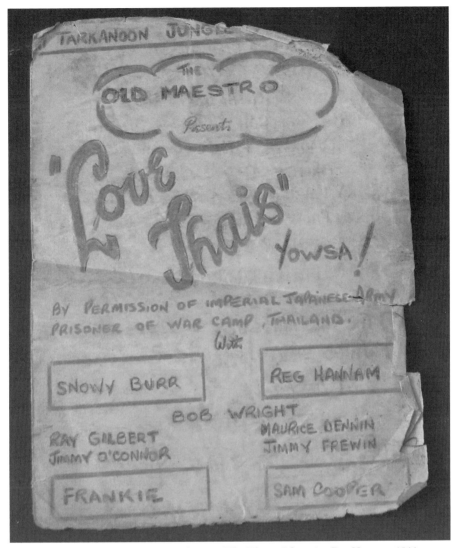

'Love Thais' concert programme in Tarkanoon [Tha Khanun] featuring Reg Hannam, 1944.

In the same month, another member of the unit, Hannam, was still on the railway doing maintenance work but in spite of this also performing regularly. There was clearly a flourishing cabaret act in Brankassi [Prang Kasi] Camp which Hannam and his friends performed to entertain their mates.

Hannam appears to have worked continuously driving lorries along the path of the railway for much of his time as a prisoner. On 13 November 1943, when a friend gave him a birthday card, he was upriver at Tarkanoon [Tha Khanum], where another concert programme shows him starring in an extravaganza compèred by Leo Britt. It is difficult to overestimate the morale-boosting effects of these theatrical performances. The enthusiasm and dedication of those who performed were crucial to the survival of many of their fellow PoWs.

The theatre was fun, but it was fun against a grim background:

> Between theatrical engagements in the latter part of 1944, I went back to the sick huts to help the band of volunteers who were permanently working there. This time I was put into the dysentery ward where our main duty was to help the patients to walk to the latrines or carry those who could not walk. The amoeba attacks the lining of the bowel, causes bleeding ulcers and the patient may die from loss of blood through continuous bloody stools or more often from ulcers, which perforate the wall of the colon and allow infected matter to leak out into the intestinal cavity. This causes peritonitis and a fairly quick death. This was going on all the time alongside our gaiety in the theatre and provided a gloomy background to our jolly stage shows.
>
> Towards Christmas 1944 I was back in the theatre with Leo Britt's company where we put on two shows. Another event was staged at Christmas itself with the help of Gibby Inglefield who had been a choral scholar at St John's Cambridge. The stage carpenters built a set of choir stalls, which were set diagonally on the stage and lit from the front so that they seemed to disappear into the darkness of a chapel. On the night, one night only, the choir was placed in these stalls hidden behind a mosquito netting gauze curtain. A radio announcer with a microphone in his hand stood alone in front of the curtain and told the audience that a radio broadcast of carols from King's College would now be presented. The gauze curtain was raised just like a pantomime transformation scene and disclosed a group of choristers in white surplices lit up by our two Tilly lamps and little oil lamps disguised as candles, in a row of stalls which really did appear to stretch away into a dark interior. Members of the audience told me that the illusion of the interior of a College chapel had been very convincing and nostalgic.

By late 1944 the prisoners were aware that the war was at last going the Allies' way. The Americans were recapturing island after island in the South Pacific; the Chindits, Allied Special Forces working behind the lines, were making steady progress in the violent jungle war in Burma, not far from the PoWs; and the Allies were advancing steadily in Italy, Russia, France and Holland.

The PoWs who were in camps where rare secret radios survived began, at last, to believe that they might survive and one day be free.

> This news raised the spirits of all the PoWs, even the thousand or more in the Sick Huts. So our next performance, Cinderella, in which I had a small part as the Fairy Godmother, was presented in an atmosphere of hope and confidence, and it was the happiest show that Britt put on, the last one in fact.

Basil Peacock, a veteran of the First World War and a major in the Royal Artillery, was in Chungkai that Christmas of 1944. In his book, *Prisoner on the Kwai* (1966), he mentioned this performance:

> In the evening we all went to the pantomime and laughed uproariously. I cannot now remember a single joke, but I shall never forget the sight of Cinderella (one of our younger and prettier subalterns) going to the ball in a golden coach and waving to us like royalty. The scenic effect was so good and ingenious that no one laughed, all applauded such stage-craft.

After Cinderella closed, Barry remembered:

> Leo Britt chose one more play to put on the Chungkai stage. It went into full rehearsal but was never actually shown. This was a stage play called 'Outward Bound' and included a young couple in love. Leo Britt decided to give these two parts to Dickie and me, boy or girl, and after a few dull rehearsals we decided to learn both parts and to play boy and girl on alternating nights.

However, something in another production angered the Japanese – a regular occurrence – but this time with severe consequences.

> The affair ended with several actors or producers being severely beaten or put into one of the punishment cages and the theatre being completely closed down. No more plays or concerts, so I went back to work in the sick huts, before anyone could detail me for an up-river working party.

Barry's reminiscences about the theatre in Chungkai in 1944 are somewhat sketchy. For an accurate, full and entertaining history of the theatre in the lives of the PoWs see Professor Sears Eldredge's online book, *Captive Audiences/Captive Performers: Music and Theatre as Strategies for Survival on the Thailand/Burma Railway 1942–1945*.

Chapter 27

Britain: December 1944 to May 1945

Phyllis and the War Office

From November 1944 onwards Phyllis received a flood of correspondence full of intimate details about the missing men. Some correspondents she knew already, but many others now send details. The mother of James (Jimmy) Grant describes him as, 'Medium build & fresh complexion just an ordinary healthy young man' (Jimmy had already died of dysentery and beriberi, in July 1943). For her dossier, Phyllis created a simple page of information for each man in the Section (p. 165).

Several relatives of Far Eastern PoWs from other parts of the Royal Signals or even from other regiments also got in touch. Phyllis created abbreviated pages for these men too. One of them, Lance Corporal James Stewart (known as Albert), had a friend in 27 Line Section. His father wrote to Phyllis.

1 December 1944, from James Stewart (Glasgow), father of Lance Corporal James Albert Stewart, to Phyllis

Dear Mrs Baker, I have had the privilege of reading the contents of your letter of 23rd November, which you sent to Mrs Farrell [mother of Henry Farrell], Glasgow. Here I want to thank you for your very earnest endeavours regarding the whereabouts and Welfare of our Relatives who are unfortunately Prisoners with the Japanese. My Dear Wife has been confined to bed due to Mental strain for the last 4 Months caused through the uncertainty of the whole rotten business. I would be very gratefull to you if you would include my Sons name in your list of inquiries. I understand that Mr Baker was a Captain in the RCOS. My Son was also in Signals & knows Mrs Farrell's Son. & I hope that they are together My Son is known as Albert & went to Malaya about the end of 1941. He is single and lived with us at Bearsden. We have had 3 Field Cards from him in 1943 the last one on 23rd December 1943 with little news to Console anyone I have indeavoured to contact the relatives of his Captain Reckie of Edinburgh without success. Perhaps the following address will assist you in your inquiries.

L/Cpl 2336746 James Albert
Royal Corps of Signals
PoW Camp No2 Thailand

He was employed in the engineering dept. of the Post office before enlistment.

I regret the scrappy nature of this letter but I am sure you will understand just what my feelings are at the moment & how gratefull we will be to you

Dossier page for John 'Scotty' Walls.

for any information that will help us to carry on & still have faith. On behalf of Mrs Stewart & myself I wish you to accept our sincere thanks for the splendid work that you are doing and I pray God that your efforts will be successfull & that we will be priviledged to hear from you in the near future

Yours Very Sincerely, James Stewart

PS enclosed please find a small snap of my son. [see overleaf]

Phyllis added Lance Corporal James Albert Stewart to her dossier.

J. Albert Stewart and his father
in about 1941.

Two days later Phyllis received a letter about another Signals boy, Corporal James Stewart. This letter was from a Mr William Stewart of Stranraer, whose son, like his namesake above, was an engineer in the PO in civilian life; but this James Stewart *was* a member of 27 Line Section. These letters illustrate the difficulties of identification experienced by the War Office and the complexity of the task Phyllis had set herself.

A few days after this, Mrs Farrell wrote to give Phyllis some helpful information about her son for the dossier.

7 December 1944, from Mrs Farrell (Glasgow), mother of Signalman Farrell, to Phyllis
... Although there was nothing outstanding in his appearance, the following might be of help. Before he went overseas he had a tattoo done on his right forearm, it began at the wrist, and went almost to the elbow. It was the figure of a highlander in full national costume, it was coloured and very unusual and would be the first thing to catch the eye. On his left forearm he had a scroll with the words; 'DEATH BEFORE DISHONOUR' and underneath a bird in flight with a letter bearing the word; 'MOTHER'.

Ruth Hobson, wife of one of the four Glossop boys, wrote her third letter to Phyllis.

3 December 1944, from Ruth Hobson (Glossop), wife of Signalman George Hobson, to Phyllis

Dear Mrs Baker, Many thanks for your most interesting and helpful letter, it is very kind of you to go to all this trouble for us, and it does certainly help to know that someone is personally doing their best for us. Especially when they are, as you can say, at the very centre of things. Your heart must ache many a time like mine and we can only pray for strength to bear it.

I am enclosing a snap of my husband taken in Malaya soon after they arrived there, I have marked my man with a cross. He is of average height about 5′ 5″ and of a slim build. His hair is medium brown and blue eyes. The only prominent feature is his nose, which is rather big.

His name is George, and he has no nick-name that I know of. My name is Ruth, we have no children and were married Dec. 23rd 1939. Our home address is as it was when George left Britain.

In civilian life my husband was employed at John Walton's Bleach-works, a firm which belongs to Tootal, Broadhurst, Lee, Co. Ltd., but which always goes under that name. His dept at that time was Anti-Crease, you will remember Tootals Products are famed for their crease resisting properties, that was a part of his job, treating the material to be crease resisting.

My husband was very fond of sports, football, cricket, table-tennis, and in football usually played left outside or inside.

I can't think of anything else which might help, but if anyone got to know him very well he would probably mention Dinting, a part of Glossop where he lived before we were married ...

Once more thanking you for your help. I trust we may soon have news and I hope all the members of your section have received news by now, I refer to those men who were still reported missing when you last wrote.

We shall have to possess our souls in patience a little while longer now, may God Bless you.

Yours Sincerely, Ruth Hobson.

George Hobson, so vivid a character in his wife's letter, had been dead for fourteen months when she wrote it.

Letters from the relatives of the men in 27 Line Section now flooded in. These families, as mentioned above, came from every part of society. A long letter relating to Signalman William Bamford began:

Undated, from Mrs Hanlon (Manchester), aunt of Signalman William Bamford, to Phyllis

Dear Madam I am writing on behalf of my sister Mrs Bamford as her and her husband is no scolar and I have to do all the writing for them, now in regards to her son William Bamford which is a prisoner his Mother had a card from him last July 1944 to say he was alright working with pay ... as far as we know he had no nick name just Willie he did not speak very clear the last time we seen him but he had false teeth before he went oversea but we did

not have the pleasure of seeing him with them in before he went away ...
now I do hope and trust you may be able to send his mother some good news
concerning her son as he is their only child and they are just living for their
boy ...

Willie had already died of septicaemia from a tropical ulcer in Tha Khanun on
30 September 1943. He was, according to another PoW, a 'good kid, 100% well
liked by everybody. Died quickly'. Out of kindness, fellow soldiers usually told
relatives that their son or husband had died quickly. Given the diseases from
which they died this can rarely have been true.

*Undated, from Mrs F. Tomkinson (Manchester), mother of Signalman David
Tomkinson, to Phyllis*
Dear Mrs Baker, We Thank you so much for your Letter it is so Kind of you
to Let us have some news and I am sure you Like ourselves are always Glad
to receive What ever news we can of our Loved one. And it is so nice to
Know that so many are doing their uttermost to get news of the Boys that
will Bring a Little Comfort to us who are Watching and waiting so Patiently
for News of those Poor Soul's who appear to us to be Forgotten Men Cast
into Horrible Prison Camps With the Worst of Brutes that one could
Imagine It is Really getting us down and Nothing seems to be getting done
about it. We hear Nothing from our Boy and We dont Know if he is getting
our Letters he is sure to be as upset as we are and all we can do is hope and
Prey that God will give him strength to Carry through to the End. And this
has upset us more now these Boys that have landed in Britain We read that
the War office has Forbidden them to say anything about Conditions of the
Prison Camps so our Loved ones must be suffering agonies Were it not so
the War Office Would not have Worried what they told the Public.

   Well dear I hope and trust that you will be instrumental in getting news of
our Loved ones from these Boys We feel and know you will do all you can to
Ease this terrible strain that is almost to Breaking Point. This is the Third
Xmas and still we know nothing it is High Time Something Was done for
these Poor Souls who are Perishing out There Well Dear you ask me to send
you our Dear Sons Name and No [number] it is David Lloyd Tomkinson
and no 2346404 Rank Signalman his hair is Fair and of a Very Pleasant But
quiet Disposition We call him David at Home he had no nickname and in
civil Life was an electrician no he is not Married and his Fiancée is called
Joyce Pallard and We are still at the same address that he went away from
Thanking you once again and we hope and Prey you will soon hear from
your Dear Husband and that he is quite safe and well.

   In closing I Remain yours Faithfully, F Tomkinson

David Tomkinson was one of eight lads who got separated from the rest in
Changi in 1942 and sent to Java. At this stage no one knows where they are.

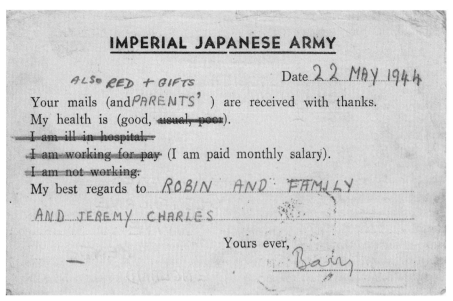

Dated 22 May 1944, pre-printed Imperial Japanese Army card (received 2 January 1945.
'Red + gifts' means Red Cross gifts).

Over Christmas two more postcards from Barry arrived, dated 15 January 1944 and 22 May 1944. They have taken 11 months and 7 months respectively to reach Britain. Unlike the first two, forwarded to his parents in San Francisco, these are delivered directly to Phyllis, and the second contains a hidden message. Jeremy Charles Bacon, a nephew, was born in May 1942. Barry can only have known of his birth through receiving letters, so including this name was his way of telling

Jeremy Charles and Robin in 1944.

the family that he had heard from them and was truly alive. This must have given Phyllis an enormous lift.

On 5 January 1945 Phyllis sent out a last request for information for her dossier. She also posted her November letter to further relatives from a list of 27 Line Section personnel that she had been sent by the Royal Signals Association. She received many replies.

Arnott's wife, Margaret, wrote, 'This letter is going to be rather difficult for me to put together, as I went almost completely blind over a year ago.' However, she manages to type a letter describing her husband: 'He is 6′ tall, slim build, fair hair, going slightly bald at temples, blue eyes and rather uneven teeth but very nice. He was a very keen footballer having played for a short time professionally with Larne F.C.' Mrs Russell wrote to say her husband could be recognised by the tattoos of Indian girls on his upper arms and one below the elbow saying 'Man's ruin'.

Some letters, like the one below from Olive Whitton, are written in beautiful copperplate. This is in a different hand to the first letter Olive sent and had probably been dictated, as there is a marked absence of punctuation.

7 January 1945, from Olive Whitton (near Manchester), wife of Driver Lawrence Whitton, to Phyllis
Dear Mrs Baker, In reply to your card just received re not answering your previous letter I am very sorry that I overlooked it and as I am now working I haven't much time for anything these days so I am away from home from

Lawrence Whitton in about 1940.

6am until 7pm so you see I am well occupied and I am glad to say I have just received another postcard from my husband from a PoW Camp in OSAKA and he still says he is in excellent health & working for pay so I think he may be alright now from the bad news of the ship that was sunk and I thank you from the bottom of my heart for all you are doing on my behalf my husbands address was Driver L. Whitton 11416, Royal Corps of Signals and the address at the time he went away is the same as this letter. and he was commonly called Lol. And Baby's name is Joan, he work in the brickmaking trade before he joined up, so thanking you again for all you are doing to get news for us I remain

Yours Sincerely Mrs Olive Whitton.

Another, rather ordinary, response to Phyllis's request for information is worth recording, because of what came later.

9 January 1945, from Mrs G. M. Potter (Hounslow), wife of Signalman Thomas Potter, to Phyllis

Dear Madam, Thank you for your letter of the 5th of January.

I should be glad of any news of my husband. Sig. T. Potter Thai Camp. He is tall, broad, dark hair and brown eyes. (3523809)

Thanking you for your trouble and kindness.

Yours truely [*sic*] G. M. Potter

Sometimes the information Phyllis was seeking for her dossier for the War Office was embedded in an outpouring of the kind of worries besetting all the relatives.

Undated, from Mrs Alice Lane (Portsmouth), Signalman Arthur Newton's grandmother, to Phyllis

Dear Madam, In the first place I am not very good at letter writing, so I must ask you to excuse me if this is badly written.

First of all I must thank you for your letter to me concerning my grandson.

But as far as I know, and I also hope he was not in that Ship that was torpedoed. For the last two cards that I have had from him was from Borneo. the first one was addressed from Borneo alone, but the second one I had on Christmas morning, and this is what he says

I am interned in Sandarkan.
My health is excellent, I am working for Pay.
My love to you and all at Home.
    Arthur Newton.

And I can tell you that it was a Godsend to me. He is my Grandson and I brought him up from a Baby having lost his mother and father. and unfortunately I lost my Husband so I was forced to put him and his brother into the National Childrens Home and he had just finished serving his time at the printing Trade, when he was called up. so I don't think I have seen him for about 3½ years. In the first place he was sent to Malaya, and no doubt you know what happened their, when the Japanese got their. So having received that card at Exmas it is a little bit assuring don't you think so, although they are such a long time before they reach you, one never knows as they are not dated, as their is a person who lives close by me, and I believe her Husband is in Siam well he wrote her a card in May and she has only just received it. But I must tell you that I send him a Japanese P.C. one a fortnight and I address it as this. A. H. Newton 2361041. Signalman, British. P.OW. Sandaka. Borneo, and I also have to put my address, but of course whether he receives them or not that is another matter, but it is not for want of trying for I do my best. and occasionally I write to the Red Cross in fact I sent to them at Christmas asking them to put a message of 10 words through for me so you see I am not backward in doing all I possibly can to try and let him hear from me.

I am every so sorry for the Relatives and friends of all those poor fellows that were on that Ship In fact for all those who are going through such a terrible time in this bitter cold weather, it is Heartacheing when you think of it all. not only our poor fellows but all of them, that has been done to Death, I sometimes wonder why God lets such things happen, although we have been bombed out of our home, that is nothing compared to what they are going through. I am sorry to say that I only have one Photo of my Grandson and that I cannot spare, but I have one that was taken at the Home if you would care to see that. Well I think I have told you all I know, and I wish I knew more, but I do hope what I have said is correct so I will just go on living in hopes and trust in God and pray that we may come together in not so long a time so wishing you all success in your most trying work

I remain yours very Sincerely, Mrs Alice Lane

Arthur Newton is another of the boys who disappeared to Java in 1942.

Finally, on 12 January 1945, Phyllis went to the War Office and handed in her dossier to a Mr Rogers. (A note attached to the dossier reads: 'This relates to RC of Sigs personnel F[ar] E[ast]. Please examine in detail & let me know what I am to tell Mrs Custance Baker.') Mr Rogers did not know this at the time, but he was going to hear a lot more from Phyllis between now and late 1945.

Not everyone replied in time for their relative's details to be entered into the dossier. Mrs Agnes Graham, wife of Driver George Albert Graham, wrote apologetically, '… when I received your letter I could not write to you as I had burnt my arms rather badly at work. I hope you will excuse the bad writing.' As she lived in Barrow-in-Furness, her work is likely to have been in munitions or ship-building, with explosive materials and molten metal a continual hazard. Agnes then went on to describe her husband: 'Rather tall with blue eyes and light brown hair inclined to wave which gives it a frizzy appearance. Rather short sighted and wears glasses when on duty.' Luckily, George Albert's mother, Ivy Graham, had already sent Phyllis the vital information, so he had a page in the dossier.

Signalman Potter & Signalman Riley

The winter of 1944 and the spring of 1945 were the best and the worst of times for the relatives waiting at home. Many of the men rescued from bombed or torpedoed Japanese transport ships were PoWs who had worked on the railway; they brought direct news of their treatment. Both the scale of losses and the suffering of prisoners in the Far East camps were extremely distressing; yet the

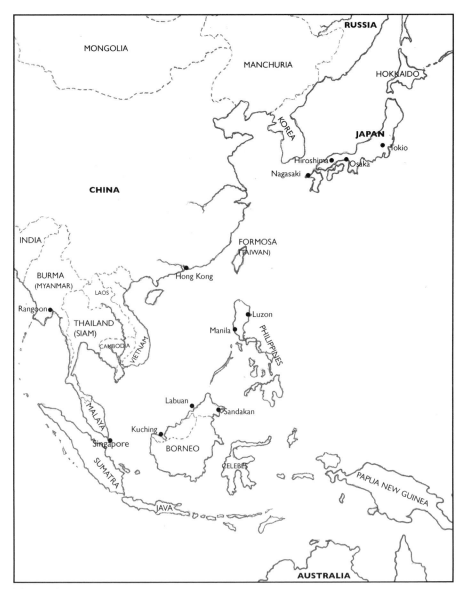

The Pacific Region in 1942.

possibility of any news of the missing men after the years of silence was tantalizing. In January 1945 there was a high-profile rescue by American troops of
mainly American PoWs from Cabanatuan, on Luzon in the Philippines. Among
these men were another twenty-three British survivors of the *Hofuku Maru*.
Unlike those rescued by the Allies days after the original sinking, they had been
recaptured by the Japanese and imprisoned again on Luzon. They included
Thomas Potter of 27 Line Section and Walter Geoffrey 'Geoff' Riley of the
5th A/A Group (M) Signal Unit, Royal Signals.

The story of their life on the 'hellship', their recapture by the Japanese after
reaching the island of Luzon and their dramatic rescue by the Americans was
recorded by Geoff in a book, *Dishonourable Guest*, privately printed by his son
Stephen J. Riley. When the names were published Phyllis, still in touch with
Mr Rogers, sent out another circular letter.

*1 March 1945, from Phyllis to all the relatives of men in 27 Line Section (another
copy of this is dated 28 February 1945)*
Dear _____, This is just a note to tell you that the interrogation of the
survivors [from the earlier rescue] is still in progress. The men had such a
bad time from the general public that they were granted an extension of
leave, before this work was started.

Meanwhile, I learn that so far news has been learnt of only one man from
our section. But among those rescued in the gallant dash raid on Luzon was a
Signalman Thomas Potter, who was in 27 Line Section. It will probably be
at least two months before he gets back here, but when he does, we may hope
for more news. It is 18 months since he left Siam, but even news that old will
be welcome, and he will at least know all the men we are enquiring about. So
the War Office would like to keep your photographs till then. I will write
again immediately there is news.

There is a misunderstanding about dates in Phyllis's letter. It is eighteen months
since Potter left the railway, but actually only nine months since he left Thailand/
Siam. She also wrote personally to Thomas Potter's wife, and received this disconcerting reply:

*14 March 1945, from Mrs G. M. Potter (Hounslow), wife of Signalman Thomas
Potter, to Phyllis*
Dear Mrs Custance Baker, Thanks for your letter. I do hope you and your
mother are quite better now, I was so sorry to hear of your illness.

My husband and myself go our own way and do not see each other, so I am
not likely to see him on his leave. The war office will, I suppose, inform me
of his arrival – so immidiately [*sic*] I know anything I will let you know. I am
sorry that I will not be able to help you more. And I do hope my husband will
be able to give you some good news.

Please will you keep the above to yourself, and not mention it to my
husband.

Thanking you for your trouble, you must be a very nice person.
Sorry for my poor English, but I think you will understand it.
Wishing you good luck and good news.
Sincerely yours, G. M. Potter

On 27 March Phyllis wrote to Thomas Potter but sent it via Mr Rogers at the War Office. There is no further clue to what was happening here. Several relatives wrote to Potter and he clearly replied to as many as he could, but we hear nothing more from Mrs Potter.

Everything moved so slowly. The War Office, hampered by war damage, natural caution and the logistics of obtaining and relaying correct information to desperate relatives, was unwilling to commit itself or even hand out such information as it obtained.

Meanwhile, correspondence from relatives (even relatives of men not under Barry's command) continued to arrive for Phyllis. There were over eighty letters in 1944, the bulk of these in November and December, and about a hundred in 1945. Among these, on 1 April 1945, is a second letter from Mr James Stewart of Bearsden, Glasgow, father of one of the men in Phyllis's dossier but not in 27 Line Section (see above p. 164). He had been lucky; his son James Albert (known as Albert) Stewart was among those now free in American hands. He promised to send Phyllis information as soon as possible.

Some time at the end of April, Phyllis, with the dossier (or her carbon copy) at this time in her hands, interviewed a Sergeant Smith from the Royal Signals and his wife. Smith had been rescued after the sinking of the *Hofuku Maru* and knew Barry and other men from 27 Line Section. Phyllis had a notebook and scribbled entries (hence the inconsistent punctuation) for each man that Smith remembered. For example:

Appleton. Saw him in June '44. Excellent condition. Down ? Tech. Party due for Japan but hadn't left. Worked with Smith as Cook after completion of railway in Tamarkan [Tha Makham] hospital camp. One/or 2 attacks/malaria but survived them well, often spoke of his children and wife.
Bridge. Died 1943??
Canning. Tropical ulcers on leg in Thailand sanatorium. April 1944. Ulcers healed unable to straighten his leg. Very clean. Mentioned wife & mother. Health otherwise O.K.
Dawson. Seen end Jan 44. Condition pretty fair. No party for Japan then. ['Japan party' are the groups of men selected to be shipped to Japan.]
Douglas. June 44. Sick in 1943 but recovered. Worked in Japan cookhouses as servant which gave him extra. Mentioned both wife and son. Kept out of trouble.
Earnshaw. 1944 June. Health quite good. Mentioned fiancée [Mary Chitham] a lot. (sister?) Packed up on railway in 1943 August. No party for Japan.

Billy Dawson in 1941.

<u>Farrell</u> Plumber? Friend of Walls? Last seen June 44. Health fair. Trouble with asthma. Kept bright & cheery. In hospital October 43. Down for new San. (?) Looked after by Thai Red X.

<u>Garrod</u> 43. Last August 1943 Condition quite good – bright & cheery. Not due for Japan. Mentioned wife.

<u>Gimson</u> has been seen.

<u>Graham</u> [Driver George] June 44. Quite good health. Pelagera [pellagra = lack of vitamin B3] – but recovered by June 44. No party for Japan.

<u>Harrison.</u> Early 44. Quite well.

<u>Jennings</u> June 44. Quite well. (Didn't take [??] on railway) Not on railway.

Jennings is one of the identity hazards the War Office feared. He *did* work on the railway and in September 1943 the War Office had written (correctly) to Mrs Jennings to say that her son, Reginald, had died of beriberi malaria on 18 July

1943. But scepticism had long since set in among the relatives, and Mrs Jennings had still sent a photo and information about her son to Phyllis for the dossier. She will have been given false hope by this incorrect sighting in 1944.

Johnston. June 44. Might be sent on draft to Japan. Always speaking of his wife and children. Well & cheerful. Knew Barry. Kept going very well.

Jones. June 44. Working in hospital dispensary. 2 camp. Not changed – keeps well.

Kittwood Last seen early 44. Very seriously ill – malaria.

McDonald June 44. Good health. Worked on railway 10 months – Then hospital orderly in Tamarkan [Tha Makham] camp. In original 27 Line in France.

Parker. Same cargo boat for Japan. Probably killed.

Plane [no note]

Russell June 44. In quite good health – quite cheery. Always speaking of wife & 2 boys.

Walls. Speaks of wife and son. June 44. Well and cheerful. Pretty good health.

Woodend. On draft. Possibly drowned. Potter will know.

Whitton Last seen June 44. O.K. Sent Japan. Excellent health. Speaks of wife and child.

William Kittwood reported as a PoW.

Jack Plane in 1941.

In early May we have one letter from Phyllis, to an unknown recipient, describing her interview with Smith. She has, in the understandable confusion of that period, some of her details incorrect. Smith was not rescued at Luzon but was one of those rescued soon after the sinking. This letter is definitely written to a close friend or relative of Barry's family; she refers to Barry as Barton, which is what his family always called him.

> *3 May 1945, from Phyllis (at the White House) to a relative or friend of Barry's parents, carbon copy of a typed letter*
> Dear _____, Last week I met one of the men rescued on Luzon, who gave me good news of Barton. I saw Sig. Smith's wife first, who said she heard her husband speaking of Capt. Baker: 'He's the man the Japs can't do anything about – he laughs in their faces.'

This description of Barry's behaviour is somewhat at odds with his policy of keeping a low profile. However, it may, for obscure reasons, have been a successful and disarming ploy. In *The Prisoner List* Richard Kandler quotes his PoW father, Reuben, on a Captain MacDonald, who 'had an extraordinary knack of managing the Japanese: if he didn't like what they said, he'd just laugh at them. Not with them, but at them. Just laugh in their faces. Don't ask me why, but somehow this clicked – they didn't mind it.' Perhaps it came across as flattery.

The letter continues:

> Sig. Smith was in one of the working parties on the Siam railway which Barton supervised. He says his (Barton's) health is 'excellent' as health goes there. He had only two light bouts of fever: his chief trouble was small tropical ulcers, but even when they were worst, he had refused to stay in camp, but gone out with the men. I asked if he had been forced to work on the railway, but was told no – though as often as not he got down to it alongside the men. Smith knows he had had at least three letters from me – and still had a large photograph last June! He also still had a much beloved knife, and 'was always making things'. A guitar and some wooden soled sandals, with tops made from old ties were among these things.
>
> Smith told me 'the men out there just reckon he's "tops"', that he never hesitated to do anything he could to help the men or ameliorate their conditions, and that he was held in great respect by them.
>
> Next week another of the survivors who was in Barton's unit [Potter] is coming to London, and has written to say he would like to meet me, and give me news. 'Capt. Baker was fine' was his description of him; both these men last saw him at the end of June, 1944, so this is the most recent news I could hope for.
>
> I know you will be pleased to hear this cheering report, and rejoice with me. Do you know that John has acquired a bar to his DFC? One day we may learn what for – but not from him, I imagine!

Jack Earnshaw in 1941.

Phyllis then wrote to all the relatives of men about whom she had received good news from Sergeant Smith. These relatives had, of course, no conception of the way Far Eastern PoWs had been moved around from camp to camp. Thus Corporal Jack Earnshaw's father replied to Phyllis:

Undated [1945], Verdi Lindley Earnshaw (Twickenham), father of Corporal Jack Kenneth Sunderland Earnshaw, to Phyllis

Dear Madam, Your letter regarding my son received with great appreciation regarding your untiring effort to collect news for the relations of our men of the Signals Corp in the Far East, and also congratulate you on the good news of your husband. I hope the day is not far distant when our loved ones will be returned to us, it will be a real blessing to forget this horrible nightmare, and enter our normal life once again.

I have forwarded your letter to my Son's Fiancée, whom I have always kept in touch, I feel for them so much, their young lives being wasted under such trying conditions, you see my boy lost his mother over 7 years ago, he has always been a good boy, we were great pals, and that is why I miss him, the fears of his present ordeal and his unknown future are always with me.

I am sorry to have to say that the two men who were interviewed have been mistaken in his identity, he was in No. 2 camp Thailand in Jan 1944, and we also had a postcard just after Christmas dated May 1944 from Thailand, hard luck but don't think I am disappointed, I thank you for your kindness and your splendid help.

Yours Sincerely, V. L. Earnshaw.

Chapter 28

Britain: May to August 1945

Delivering bad news

On 1 April 1945 Barry's middle brother, Alan ('the Bimbashi'), docked in Britain and on 12 April he got married. Little brother John flew back from Canada to be best man and Robin was a page. John returned to Canada and on 10 May he and his pilot, Maurice Briggs DSO DFC, performed some brilliant aerobatic displays in Calgary. They were fêted and later set off from Calgary airport for the next leg of their tour. On their final turn over the control tower, they made contact and crashed. Both were killed.

Alan's wedding in April 1945
with John (left).

Alan and Barbara received the devastating news in San Francisco. John had written a letter for his parents in 1943 when he started flying on sorties.

30 August 1943, John Baker to Barbara and Alan. The envelope reads: 'IF I AM MISSING please open and send this to A. C. Baker' (he had updated the address to San Francisco)
Dear Mum & Dad, You will only get this letter in the event of my being reported missing or killed; which though not exactly probable is quite a possibility in this very violent life.

Please do not worry more than you can possibly help; there is a considerable chance of my returning in a few days or weeks, and a very good one of being a PoW. And if by chance I am killed, then you must just take a little more concern in your own lives and those of Barton & Alan & their off-springs. Mourning is of no use & there could be no better thing to die for ...

Among the many letters to Barbara and Alan received after John's death, is the only communication we have from Lilian, Phyllis's mother.

13 May 1945, from Lilian (the White House) to Barbara and Alan
My very dear Barbara and Alan, What can I say to express my very deep sympathy with you – if only you were here that one could do something to help you.

You know how we all loved John – he was one of the dearest lads I have ever met – modest, brave, loving & true ...

Everyone loved John – family, friends and colleagues – and for Phyllis, through much of the war, he was her closest link to Barry. But like everyone around her she had to keep going. She interviewed Thomas Potter and made notes on her dossier. One of the men he remembered was Sergeant Hunt, who died early on in Changi in 1942. Potter remembered him as the 'finest fellow I ever met. Coolest man in action I ever saw'. In late May or early June, Phyllis, who assumed the War Office had informed next-of-kin of known deaths, wrote to Sergeant Hunt's mother, only to discover that she was first with the news. In response to her apologetic letter, Mrs Hunt replied:

12 June 1945, from Mrs Bertha Hunt (London), mother of Sergeant G. L. Hunt, to Phyllis
Dear Mrs Baker. Thank you so much for your kind and sympathetic letter. Please do not feel sorry you were responsible for me hearing the sad news about Gordon before hearing it from the War Office. I would far rather have heard it from Potter than by a cold printed form, which I shall no doubt receive in due time.

I certainly do feel proud to hear Gordon spoken of so highly, he was a lovely lad.

I am very sorry to hear of the death of your brother-in-law, what a lot of sadness this war has caused.

I would rather you kept the snap until all enquiries have been made. I really don't think there is anything more you can do for me and thank you very much for all you have done.

I hope it will not be long before you have more news of your husband.

Yours very sincerely

B. E. Hunt.

In June Phyllis sent her dossier back to Mr Rogers and asked about whether the War Office had informed other relatives of men known to have died. He replied.

20 June 1945, from Mr Rogers at The War Office to Phyllis

Dear Mrs Custance Baker, I have received that fearsome dossier from you safely. As a matter of fact I am just back from a fortnight's interrogation of men from Luzon and of course as a matter of routine put every Signalman's name before the Royal Corps of Signals survivors. At the moment I cannot say whether or not we managed to get any information about the Section in which you are interested as the 'processing' takes a little time. But all the next-of-kin will be informed should we have any news good or otherwise.

As you had also been in touch with Signalman Potter I really think we have between us covered the ground! I still have about five Signalmen to see so perhaps I had better hold onto your records for the time being.

Did you manage to get any news yourself? Presumably not otherwise you would have been sure to have told me!

Yours Sincerely G. T. H. Rogers

Relatives who had not heard from Phyllis since she interviewed the survivors were beginning to wonder why she had not been in touch.

22 June 1945, from Mrs T. Carr (Harrow), mother of Signalman Stephen R. Carr, to Phyllis

Dear Mrs Custance Baker, I forget whether I answered your last letter. I've been wondering if you have had any news of my son Stephen R Carr who was in the same unit as your Husband, I've been making various enquiries, one way or another, but no one seems to know anything about these unfortunate men in Malaya Camps. I'm beginning to feel extremely anxious even if they are safe would they survive the climate after all this time.

I've only had two cards from him since he was taken prisoner, that was in 1943. Anything could happen in the meantime, perhaps he has been moved from Malaya. It's all very exasperating, but the [sic] is one consolation, our forces are getting on, & in time they will hop into Malaya. What a lesson we have learned? The Japs are no longer the simple people of bygone days but a cunning, crafty, & I will say a clever race, anyway we were hoodwinked, as far as the war is concerned, let's hope it will soon come to an end.

Yours Sincerely, Mrs T. Carr

Stephen Carr in about 1940.

She was right to feel concerned; Steve Carr had died of dysentery on 3 November 1943 after the end of the speedo period on the railway. Phyllis knew that he was dead but had to wait for the War Office to inform his relatives. She wrote again to Mr Rogers from a different address.

19 July 1945, from Phyllis (Sherburn Cottage, The Nookery, Angmering on Sea) to Mr Rogers
Dear Mr Rogers, Thank you for your letter of June 20th. I should have answered it before, but I have been moving around the country rather a lot this month.

I am very anxious to know if all the next-of-kin who have to be told bad news have yet had it. Naturally, I don't want to 'put my foot in it', but those people whose next of kin are on my list, and who still haven't heard from me, are wondering why. [She lists thirteen men.] I did not tell you of the news I learnt of my husband for two reasons – I knew you would know I'd heard from Potter at least; and as several of the survivors knew him, you would get the 'official' news, & I wanted to have a War Office letter to send out to his parents in America. Needless to say, it has been an immense comfort to me to get such relatively recent (& good) reports.

Your sincerely P. Custance Baker

The men Phyllis was asking about were those reported by Potter and/or Smith as dead or assumed to be drowned; some in Malaya, others in Thailand on the railway, yet others on troopships, in particular the *Hofuku Maru*. Phyllis felt bad about withholding such information, but was unable to distribute it until it had become official. Letters like the one above from the mother of Stephen Carr were difficult to deal with, and the War Office were cautiously slow.

Although the thirteen men listed by Potter do not include Jennings, whom Smith thought he had seen in 1944 and the War Office thought was dead, Potter must have confirmed his death as Mrs Jennings wrote to Phyllis on 29 June to thank her, '& especially for the message about my son. That is indeed a comfort to know that much about him.'

The news from the end of July into early August 1945 must have been tormenting to Phyllis and all those waiting. The end of war in the Far East appeared imminent, but not totally certain. By 11 August she would have heard about both the atomic bombs on Hiroshima and Nagasaki and the Soviet invasion of Manchukuo. It was with muted relief that Phyllis wrote once more to Mr Rogers.

11 August 1945, from Phyllis (at the White House) to Mr Rogers
Dear Mr Rogers, May I trouble you for the return of 'that fearsome dossier'? The news is such that I don't think it is of any further value, and I would like to return the photographs to their owners.

Can you please tell me if the next of kin of the men mentioned in my last letter have been notified that they are dead or missing?

You will no doubt be exceedingly busy now for some time – it seems too good to be true that the war in the Far East is really over!

Yours Sincerely, P. Custance Baker

The War Office must finally have sent the dreaded letters out to the widows and parents of the men known to have died, and Phyllis could at last send her condolences. The letters she wrote were individual, personal letters, and are not therefore in the preserved collection. However, in 2011, Michael Taylor, great-nephew of Ruth Hobson, widow of George Hobson, got in touch with me; she had kept her letter from Phyllis and the family kindly supplied a copy.

17 August 1945, from Phyllis to Ruth Hobson (Glossop), wife of Signalman George Hobson
Dear Mrs Hobson, Before this I have tried to write to you – but it is difficult to find words that are not trite. That you have my very deepest sympathy you will know. But the mere fact that the same news may come to me at any day makes any facile attempts at consolation impossible. I can only hope that apart from any spiritual comfort of your own beliefs, you may be blessed as I am with loving parents, parents-in-law, brothers and sisters. I am thankful

too, for you, that the news reached you before our hearts were so lifted with hope by the news of Japan's offer of surrender.

If there is any practical way in which I can be of service to you, I trust you will tell me at once.

From the greatness of your own grief, you will I know be glad for me, that I had a good report from the men rescued on Luzon. It is now nearly 15 months since I last heard of my husband.

Yours very sincerely, Phyllis Custance Baker

George and Ruth Hobson on their wedding day, 23 December 1939.

Chapter 29

Thailand: Early 1945

Bridge over the River Kwai

By early 1945 Allied bombing raids on the railway line were becoming increasingly frequent. While these gave the prisoners hope, sadly they also killed numbers of PoWs housed close to the line. The Japanese continued to send men up or down river to repair the damage. In early 1945 Barry was still in Chungkai. He remembers:

> Around about February 1945 a large working party was suddenly called for and it was formed of almost the whole of our old 2 Group many of whom had found their way to Chungkai. We were to march a short way down stream to Tamarkan [Tha Makham] to repair the big bamboo bridge built by Lieutenant Colonel Toosey's group. It had been damaged by bombers – Canadian Flying Fortresses, I believe. There was a raid in progress when we arrived, so we spent several hours in the slit trenches. The bridge was repaired quite soon and the railway was running again in a few days.

As a prisoner, Barry kept nominal rolls of his 27 Line Section men with notes of deaths or the last time and place he saw any man of his unit alive. At Tamarkan he met Hannam, also repairing the bridge. Reg Hannam had been working continuously, driving lorries up and down the railway. He later told his family about a bombing raid as he was repairing the Tamarkan bridge. In one of the coincidences of life, fifty years later, Barry's and Reg's grandchildren were unknowingly together in the same class at school.

Barbed wire at Kanchanaburi (Kanburi) camp

Barry remembers:

> Soon after working on the bridge PoW Officers were separated from Other Ranks and concentrated at a big camp at Kanchanaburi or Kanburi. It was now a real enclosed prison camp with a bamboo fence and an outer barbed wire fence with sentries patrolling between them. Our work now simply consisted of raising the level of the camp above flood plain by digging and carrying endless quantities of earth from outside the area and spreading and firming it. Very dull heavy labour.
>
> The huts, when we arrived in March, were almost derelict and as soon as the ground was levelled we rebuilt huts of much better quality than the old ones. The Japs must have realised by now that the War would be over soon

and, possibly fearing war crimes trials, now became even more energetic in seeking out any diaries or other written materials.

There were now frequent searches by the very intimidating Kempi Tai, aimed at discovering hidden wireless sets or any written records. The Kempi gave the impression of being bigger and taller than the average Jap soldier. They wore very clean well fitting, uniforms, high boots, and a holstered pistol on their leather belts. They also each had a leather whip hanging by a loop from the wrist, which they were ready to use in case of any lack of respect from a PoW. Each Kempi was accompanied by two ordinary Jap soldiers armed with rifles and fixed bayonets.

Our guards seemed almost as anxious as we were that these inspections should not discover any infringements for which they might themselves be held to blame, and would often drop a hint that an inspection was due. We suffered more and more regular tenkos and were often kept on parade for extra hours if some possible discrepancy had appeared or if someone was noticed as being late with his ceremonial bow.

From earlier less enclosed camps most COs had learned the trick of always achieving an exactly correct number on parade. This was done by carrying out a few fake burials, so that there were always a few extra men in the camps. The Japs were only interested in numbers.

The fake burials of a rice sack or two full of earth would be marked with some invented name, Corporal A. N. Other, or more often, Private Parts. When a tenko was called for the CO would, if necessary, tell one or two men to hide, or parade everyone to cover anyone who might be astray. At Kanchanaburi, it would have been harder to hide any extras as the camp was too open.

At Kanchanaburi, with its surrounding barbed wire, open layout and intense level of supervision, the prisoners had to abandon this particular subterfuge.

Barry was not involved in theatre here (in fact he remembers none occurring), and activity was generally very restricted. Camp life became very dull and filled with anxiety. Around this time he received some of the twenty-five-word PoW cards that Phyllis had sent, so at least he knew that she and Robin were well and prospering. Physically he was doing well too.

Kanchanaburi was a large town and of course, in the very populated rice belt area of Siam so rations were fairly adequate. I had by now run out of money except for my Japanese pay, which I still spent on eggs and peanuts. Our three bowls of rice were often flavoured with fish or meat stew and sometimes fresh vegetables which were grown by ourselves in the camp, and I settled to my best weight of 8 stone 7 lbs, 54kg, and was in quite good general health by now. Most of the men in the camp were healthy by now as all the serious dysentery cases or other sick men had died. We had very few deaths at Kanchanaburi.

This was, of course, an officers' camp, and they had generally better resources – higher pay, more assets left to sell. Yet all accounts suggest that this was an uncomfortable and unpleasant period, including the particularly inhumane treatment of an interpreter, Captain Bill Drower, by Colonel Noguchi. On 28 May 1945, Noguchi and other guards beat up Bill on the flimsiest of pretexts and then confined him to a tiny cell 'forever' on one small ball of rice a day. He soon had beriberi, malaria and eventually blackwater fever. He remained there for eighty days. On 16 August 1945 the war ended and he was pulled, unconscious, from his cell. Everyone worked to keep him alive until he could be transported to a hospital. Noguchi was hanged for this and other war crimes in 1946.

Barry continued to keep himself going:

> There were rumours of an impending move to a distant area, which would entail a long march so most of us tried to get as fit and strong as we could. I took up skipping and found I could do a thousand skips without much difficulty.
>
> To prepare for the probably long march I built myself a proper Bergen rucksack using bamboo poles for the frame and pieces of my old valise, bedroll, for the sack itself. Since the bad days of 1943 I seemed to have acquired quite a lot of kit. Everyone hid all their loose papers and diaries as I did.

The anxiety induced by the Kempeitai was clearly greater than at any time previously and Barry buried his diary 3 feet deep in an old latrine in Kanchanaburi Officers PoW Camp. He drew the sketch map below, but was never able to retrieve the diary.

In September 2012 the family got in touch with the Thailand–Burma Railway Centre (TBRC) at Kanchanaburi and sent them a copy of these maps. The General Manager, Terry Manttan, went to some trouble to locate the spot where the diary was buried. Sadly, it has now been thoroughly built over.

The last 200km, Nakhon Nayok

In the early summer of 1945 the order finally came to move. The only information given as they marched in an east-north-easterly direction was that it was a very long way away – approximately 120 miles. Part of this journey was by train and barge, but there was plenty of marching too.

> We did it in three days and nights of marching, with brief over night stops in Buddhist monasteries. I have a clear picture of a very large hall with a smooth stone floor on which we all fell sound asleep with no difficulty at all. We, still under Selby Milner, were not the first to arrive as various smaller advance parties were already there.
>
> Nakhon Nayok, I remember as a well-built and well-run camp. There must have been a town of that name not far away as the rations were fairly adequate, though no one grew fat. Many Siamese hung around the camp trying to buy or barter any valuables, which we might still have and I decided

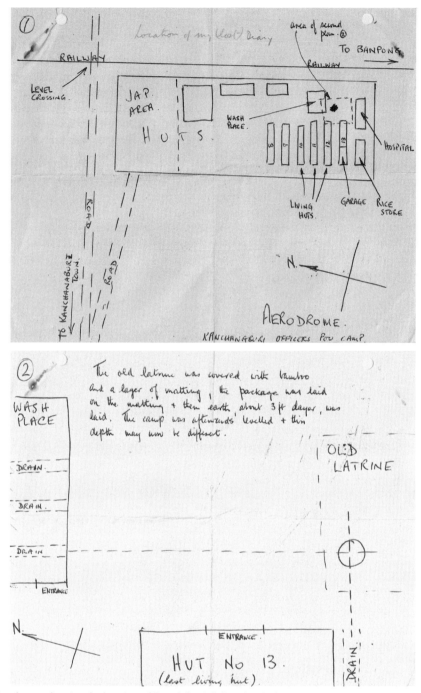

Sketch map showing the location of Barry's buried diary in 1945.

that the time had come to part with my gold signet ring that Phyllis had given me. The crest itself was on an engraved stone, which I cut out and stitched into the back of a cloth belt which I then owned. The gold brought me a modest sum of Japanese printed paper money with which I was able to buy my usual duck eggs and peanuts and, as a special treat, a pot of honey.

The news, which we now heard quite frequently (on wireless sets hidden by brave men), told us that the end of the war was in sight. The War in Europe had finished a month or two ago, Russia had belatedly declared war on Japan, all the islands held by the Japanese had been recaptured, most of their navy had been sunk and the USAF (United States Air Force) was continually bombing the Japanese mainland.

The Japanese, now facing defeat, and possibly anxious about future investigations into their policy on the railway and elsewhere, carried out more and more searches for written paper of any kind. Amazingly, the radio, transported from Kanchanaburi, re-assembled in Nakhon Nayok and working again, was never discovered.

Part Four

Picking up the Pieces

Letter from Reg Hedges (Barry's batman) to Phyllis in October 1945.

Chapter 30

Britain: August 1945

Peace at a cost

On 6 August 1945 an atomic bomb was dropped on Hiroshima, on 8 August Russia declared war on Japan, on 9 August another atomic bomb was dropped on Nagasaki and on 15 August Japan surrendered to the Allies. On that day, with Emperor Hirohito's address to the nation, the Pacific war was officially over. Barbara and Alan in San Francisco were near a source of the latest news and sounded more certain and joyful than Phyllis had in her letter of 11 August to Mr Rogers at the War Office.

15 August 1945, from Barbara (San Francisco) to Phyllis
My darling Phyllis. It has come at last. Peace. But your hearts and our hearts are still full of anxiety until we know that our Barton is free. Will the Japanese army everywhere obey the Emperor? We must wait a little while. God be with you darling in these still anxious days. Yesterday, when I heard all the sirens & the bells & the hooters & the shouts I wept again for John & for all Barton has suffered but now I must be full of hope as I am sure you are: you are both young & food & happiness & long hours of sleep will restore nearly all that these years have taken from you.

Barbara writes of the possibility of Barry returning via San Francisco. She gives her contact details to pass on to Barry and her brother-in-law Roger, interned in Changi, in case this should happen.
Barbara continues:

This is not a news letter darling. We have been very busy for several days not leaving the office until 11pm. & getting back there at 5 or 6am with a bit of sleep in the day time. Yesterday I only went in the morning but Alan did a very long day & we both came down at 5.45 this morning. It has been very tiring for everyone but the result at this end at any rate was well worth any amount of weariness.

Alan doesn't think we'll be here very long. Once Singapore is handed back there would seem to be nothing useful to be done from here. We must just wait & see.

No more dear Phyllis, I'm going home for a rest & then back for my evening's work, Alan, strong man! is staying on in the office.

xoxox Robin. xoxox Phyllis. From Barbara.

We can only imagine the excitement and trepidation over the following weeks and the long, long hours of waiting for news. Phyllis wrote to Barry on 22 August but this letter disappeared into the chaos on the other side of the world and never reached him.

Chapter 31

Thailand – India: Freedom

An American paratrooper

The end came to us quite dramatically. Our wireless told us of 'Atomic Bombs' on Nagasaki and Hiroshima and unconditional surrender by the I.J.A (on 15 August 1945). Our Commander informed Noguchi and asked what news he had from his headquarters. His reported answer was that he had no outside communication for some days except pigeons, which were all dead. He was then introduced to our wireless set, hidden in his own quarters, and invited to find out the true situation. He agreed that the War was finished and handed over command of the camp to the British CO who immediately put him under close arrest. The Sergeant Major was arrested too, but I believe the Japanese guards simply drifted off and were rounded up later on.

Our actual rescuer was a single American paratrooper who walked into the camp one morning. He was a most impressive sight in well-pressed jungle green uniform, polished boots and a complete armoury of weapons. He carried a sub-machine gun, had two pistols stuck into his belt, and several knives, a most astonishing spectacle to a bunch of very thin men in Jap happies or tattered shorts.

This soldier told us that we were to expect a large number of Siamese lorries in the near future to take us all to Bangkok. He also told us about the Japanese machine gunners surrounding the camp, who had all been disarmed and made PoW. The lorries arrived, loaded with Red Cross parcels, which were quickly shared out, and we tasted forgotten luxuries like Spam and corned beef, even peanut butter which I had not tasted before.

All these events took many days and it was only at the end of August that the men had a chance to communicate with the rest of the world. Barry now dashed off his first letter to Phyllis. As above, letters will be included in the date order in which they are written. This does not correspond with the dates on which they were received – mostly unrecorded – but is the only system available. Both Barry and Phyllis had vital things to communicate, but each was writing without having had the answers to important questions in their previous letters. There is a feverishness about their correspondence from now on, as if the patient endurance of the last three years has evaporated and been replaced, to their alarm, by an agony of anticipation.

30 August 1945, from Barry to Phyllis in pencil written on a page torn from a book of some sort (there is an elephant printed on one side)

Nakhon Nayok Camp, Thailand My darling wife, we have just ten minutes to write before a messenger bag for Bangkok. I am well and strong, have been so since the bad days of '43. Your letters have been arriving about a year late, and only 1 in 4 gets here. I hope for a long leave as soon as we get home. November perhaps, and after I have met my son and my mother and father I want to go right away from everything and everybody with you, and I'll try to make up to you for the years we have lost. I quite agree that Robin needs a sister (or brother) as soon as possible.

I've kept myself reasonably sane and reasonably happy by working on French and German and every kind of handicraft until the Japs made that impossible by taking away all paper, pencils etc; and, above all, by acting. I've played a number of straight girl parts in our PoW Rep Company and loved it. All my love my own dearest wife. I'll write a proper letter as soon as I can.

   Barry

In the top left corner a PS reads:

My future career will depend very much on post war conditions. Just now the army and everything connected with it stinks. But I must wait before deciding.

The first letter home after three and a half years.

Beside the elephant picture Barry has written in a box at right angles to the letter:

I've kept the Fayer picture. Battered but my daily inspiration.

From Nakhon Nayok the men were taken in lorries to a big transit camp near Bangkok. Here Barry wrote again:

2 September 1945, from Barry (in pencil, headed Bangkok airfield) to Phyllis
My own darling wife, We have already sent off one short airmail letter but I suspect that it may never reach you so I will assume this is my first letter as a free man.

I am well, very well, fit and strong and I have been so almost continuously since the black days of summer and autumn nineteen forty-three. I am more in love with you now than I have ever been since we first met. During the short time we lived together, and apart, in Britain after we were married I believed that I loved you as much as it was possible for any man to love a woman; but now I know that it is quite possible to surpass that. Your image has been in my mind continuously through all the hard times and the happy times we have met; and thinking about you and what we shall do together after the war has been my continuous inspiration in the days when it seemed hardly worthwhile trying to go on. Your portrait by Fayer has been with me in all my moves and is with me now, still smiling though slightly battered. The three polyphoto snaps of you and Robin are tucked into the frame. My own darling, believe me that I love you just as much as your letters tell me that you still love me.

I'll not tell you much of our history. It will keep and I have a very full diary buried which I may be able to recover and which will give a better picture of our doings than I could possibly write or tell. The short section casualty list will give a hint of what we did. It is by no means complete or official, it is only the casualties which I know of. I fear there may be many more.

My own worst time was July 43 when I was sent down to the base camp from our up country railway workers camp with dysentery and chronic malaria. We had no drugs at all and my weight fell to 5st 13lbs. It is about 9st now and I have rather a lean tough look and very brown. The Journalists who have met us are very disappointed as we look too fit to bear out the stories of starvation and ill-treatment which filtered out from the Thai Railway Camps. They complain that there are no living skeletons or beriberi cases to write about. The graves along the railway, about fifteen thousand allied, and many times that of Tamil coolies, will show what happened to our sick. We are the survivors.

Since the railway finished we have had better food and conditions. Although we still lived in a way that would have shocked a nineteenth century slave trader. Our conditions (since release) are still much the same but any day now a plane will carry us back to civilisation.

Section Casualty List sent in Barry's letter home, September 1945.

When I come home, probably in Oct or Nov, I hope to have a good long leave which we can spend together as a second honeymoon. I want to see Robin and my Mother and Father then go right away where we can disappear from any circles that know us. A time in London perhaps, then away in the country somewhere. I am very sick of my fellow men, and I've a terrible distaste for orders or authority in any form and even stronger distaste for any personal responsibility. This will disappear quite soon I hope. Whether I stay in the army or not must depend on a later decision. When I am mentally fitter than I now am to make it. Just now an army career fills me with horror.

Your letters have reached me; about ¼ of them and have been a great help and comfort. They come about 1–2 years late which makes you seem very remote. Our future moves, after Rangoon are not yet disclosed. I feel just as you do about a sister or brother for Robin. This letter is stiff and formal. I can't help it; you are almost a stranger to me. But a very beloved stranger. Your husband Barry

In his memoirs, Barry recalls:

From Bangkok we were flown out in Dakotas of the United States Air Force, which took us to Rangoon. It was my first experience of flying, as it was for most of us. The flight was uncomfortable on hard metal seats and very noisy.

Our flight took us to a big military hospital in Rangoon, where we were very thoroughly checked for any remaining diseases, weighed and measured and treated with a comfortable dose of TLC.

Trying to bridge the void
From Rangoon Barry wrote to Phyllis again on 4 September, searching for the way ahead, trying to revive in his mind the wife he left behind. The desire to reconnect was so strong that, still without having received any letters from home, he wrote most days to Phyllis or his parents.

4 September 1945, Barry (pencil on airmail form, Rangoon) to Phyllis
PS I've written to Dad as well. Reply to ex P. W. Mail Bombay.
My Darling, I've written twice already and I hope that one at least of the letters will reach you, so I'll not repeat what I said in them.

We reached Rangoon yesterday afternoon. Having flown from Bangkok by Dakota transport planes. Just over 2 hours that trip took but it was like stepping over a threshold out of a muddy lane into a lighted ballroom.

At Bangkok we still slept cheek by jowl in coolie quarters on the floor with no bedding. Admittedly better than Jap quarters, but not good. Last nite I slept in a bed with sheets and a pillow, in a pair of hospital pyjamas, with a sister and an orderly mothering me. We have all been sent to a big hospital tho' most of us are quite fit now and I am one of two occupying a small private ward. I was medically examined and marked fit and for immediate discharge, which means that at any time after a few days I shall be waiting for a ship to take me home. One party left yesterday and it appears to be just possible that I may be with you in five or six weeks from now.

We are waiting now for a second medical exam and then a clothing issue. We are all wearing our pyjamas still as it is quite distasteful to get back in the filthy rags we wore until yesterday.

Since capitulation I've had a bunch of letters from you and my Mother and Father and also from Kurt Abrahamsohn and Mr Kirkman of Rose Hill School. All 1943.

Formerly we longed for letters and to get one made us happy for weeks, but now that we are free it is quite utterly inadequate and makes our separation seem harder still to bear. But I am sure it is not for long now.

I will tell you in outline what my plans are for the leave which I hope to get when we come home. This is an idea only and you must not hesitate to make any plans which you prefer because from now on I want to avoid all responsibility and all such onerous duties as demanding as what to do tomorrow. (For a time at least).

I want to meet you in town and stay just a day or two in luxury. I hear the Park House hotel well spoken of. Then go to meet my son and Mother and Father if possible all together at Wye; that may be difficult. Stay there a short time and then disappear from the haunts of men, just our two selves. If we can get hold of a car so much the better but I fear that both cars and petrol will be quite impossible. Later we might perhaps stay at Missenden for a bit to give me an opportunity of getting to know my son Robin and your people.

I don't think you will find much change in me. I am four years older, but then so are you. I am a little thinner, just 9st, but then I went down to 5st 13 in 1943 and I find 9st just right. Face a bit lined and skin rather coarsened from sun and bad soap. Hair very blonde on top. Very brown [body] except for a small triangle in the middle.

I've managed to keep quite happy since 1943 until the last few months by working on French & German and plenty of sewing and cobbling. I made 47 pairs of shorts and about 18 sandals. And best of all by acting. I played straight girls, rather tarty, in the Chungkai Rep Company with a pro actor producer. The best fun I've ever had (nearly!) 'Myra' in 'Hayfever'. 'Anne' in 'Outward Bound'. 'Sarah' in 'Major Barbara' and a panto Fairy Godmother. Many others and chorus. Darling I've been waiting all the time to tell you how I love you and I've left it too late. But I do tho from such a stranger I can hardly write it.

Barry

In the Rangoon hospital they spent a few days getting used to civilized behaviour, in particular not walking about naked as they often had done in the camps. After a day or so Barry wrote to Barbara again.

7 September 1945, Barry (Rangoon/Bombay) to Barbara
My darling Mother, altho this is headed Bombay, we are still in Rangoon at the Central Hospital waiting ships to take us home. I've written to Phyllis and to dad (and you) and this is to you (and Dad).

I sent casualty lists of My Section in both letters, a total of 15 dead and 5 presumed dead. Since then there are three more reported Dead and four missing but as it's not really certain I'll hold the names until I have confirmation.

One of your letters to me was the first I received. I was in Chungkai hospital just recovering from a bout of general no goodness in July 43. The letter was dated May 42 so it wasn't exactly hot but it was the first news I'd had from home and made such a difference.

I've heard nothing of Roger at all. I don't even know if he had news of Joyce's death. Derek Tyer who is here has written to him and we hope to hear of him at Bombay or Calcutta.

On our way home we may be able to do some shopping in India and I thought that you and Phyllis would probably need clothes ...

I've been very proud to hear about your writing. But the news has been so disjointed and out of date that I really don't quite know just what you have written and published. I hope to get signed copies very soon.

Barry already had a signed copy of her first children's book, *The Talking House*. During the war she had been busy publishing a second book of verse, her second children's book, *The Three Rings*, and writing a third story, *The Herewegoes*, about children escaping by boat from Singapore.

Phyllis wrote that the annexe at Missenden has been made into a 'flat' for us. Of course we hope to stay there for a bit when I come back. But I do so hope we'll be able to stay at Wye or Wilks. I'm sure you can manage it because I don't want to make a precedent of always having family gatherings at the White House. My in-laws are nice people but I think my own parents are much nicer and I think you're both better for Robin too.

All my love, Barton

This letter was postmarked Wye, 8 Sept and may have been the first direct news from Barry, alive and free, to reach Britain, but it was forwarded to his parents in San Francisco. Barry's letters show that he has not yet had any recent news from home.

9 September 1945, Barry (Rangoon) to Phyllis
My own darling, still in Rangoon but hoping for a ship in a week or two.

The town presents few attractions. One dancing club which I've not yet visited and parties at the various messes which always consist of a large number of men fighting for a very few girls. I have not yet attended one. I've made friends with the ward sister and help her by acting as clerk in the office. I do all the admin side now which leaves the MO and sister free to look after the sick instead of making out nominal rolls and bed states.

I find the occupation helps to pass the time and also brings a few invitations to a civilised tea or evening drink in the Sisters Mess.

We read the newspapers and magazines with astonishment. The jokes go by us four times out of five. The photos in the *Tatler* all seem to be of children or near children. The gutter press, of which I have several shining examples, is quite shockingly bad. Americanised in the worst way and utterly trivial and irrelevant.

We had one copy of the *Telegraph* which seemed to preserve a reasonably sane and balanced outlook. We've had none of the more reputable labour and liberal papers but I hope that some have managed to keep clear of the blight which appears to have descended on the others.

This is a terrible letter. It's the reaction of coming out and expecting to step into a demi-paradise and finding that the war has left scars everywhere. Perhaps my wife and my son will still be as I remember them. I think they will and that will make up for many disappointments.

We have been told roughly how our pay stands including information about gratuities and about refunds of money stopped from our accounts as PoWs but never paid over by the Nips. I think that the government is going to treat us really handsomely tho money seems not to have much use or meaning now.

Lord Louis [Mountbatten] is to visit the neighbourhood tomorrow but I think he is not coming to our hospital. Still I hope to see him. He is the big name out here and our hopes of speedy repatriation will depend on him.

It's fairly late now, after lights out, tho I have a lamp in my office. I've made out my two night reports and the night sister and orderly have come on duty so I'll soon be off to bed. I don't dream about you because I don't dream at all. I just lie awake until the small hours and think about our next meeting. Sometimes one way sometimes another always quite unbelievably happy. I think I can feel now as you used to feel when you sat up late at the White House writing to me. I'm alone now which I've not been for three years. And one's thoughts move much more freely when you're alone. I'm quite frightened at how much I love you. If you ever went away or stopped loving me or died I think I'd just have to pack in. There would still be Robin but that's not enough.

I'm getting morbid with sleepiness but I do love you so my darling. Barry

It is only after writing this letter, that Barry received the first news of other members of his family. He finds out that:

My father and mother had been sent to San Francisco to take charge of the Malay language propaganda broadcasts beamed at South East Asia. Several ex PoWs have since told me that they had heard these broadcasts and had

John Custance Baker in 1945.

recognised my mother's voice. My youngest brother, John, whom I remembered as an undersized pigeon-chested asthmatic schoolboy had become an RAF hero with a DFC and bar, and had died in an air accident at Calgary in Canada almost at the end of the War.

Barry kept a box file of John's medals, photos, letters and papers. On the back is a scrap of paper on which Barry has written a verse of a well-known poem of the time by John Pudney.

Do not despair
For Johnny head-in-air.
He sleeps as sound
As Johnny underground.

Chapter 32

Britain: September 1945

The telegram

It was now September 1945 and in Britain Phyllis is still waiting to hear if Barry had survived. Other wives and mothers have heard.

> *7 September 1945, from Mrs E. Shaw (Manchester), mother of Driver Percy Shaw, to Phyllis*
> Dear Mrs Baker, Just a line to let you know that we have received official news of our son Driver P. Shaw 2340027 that he is now in Allied hands what a blessed relief as we know that everything possible for their comfort and to get them fit again will be done. Have you had any luck yet I sincerely hope so and that you and Captain Baker will soon be reunited.
>   Yours sincerely, E. Shaw

On 10 September the long-dreamt-of telegram finally arrived. Phyllis phoned her father, who cabled Barry's parents in San Francisco, who then cabled Barry (both cables are missing). Phyllis then wrote to Barry on 10 September (this letter is

Percy Shaw in 1941.

also missing and may never have arrived). We do have Barry's cabled reply to his father, Alan.

11 September 1945, cable from Barry to his father Alan Baker (received 12 September 1945)

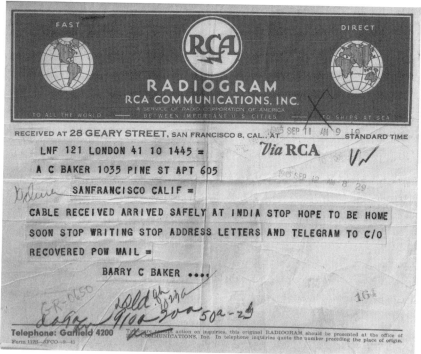

RADIOGRAM
RCA COMMUNICATIONS, INC.

RECEIVED AT 28 GEARY STREET, SAN FRANCISCO 8, CAL., AT SEP 11 AM 9 19 STANDARD TIME

LNF 121 LONDON 41 10 1445 =   *Via RCA*

A C BAKER 1035 PINE ST APT 605

SANFRANCISCO CALIF =

CABLE RECEIVED ARRIVED SAFELY AT INDIA STOP HOPE TO BE HOME

SOON STOP WRITING STOP ADDRESS LETTERS AND TELEGRAM TO C/O

RECOVERED POW MAIL =

BARRY C BAKER ....

Telephone: Garfield 4200

Only those who have experienced such relief can imagine what Phyllis, Barbara, Alan, the rest of his family, and so many other waiting families, were feeling as they took in this glorious news.

On 13 September the letter Barry wrote on 2 September from Bangkok finally reached Phyllis, who was still living in the annexe of the White House. She wrote again.

13 September 1945, from Phyllis (the White House) to Barry
My dearest darling, The letter you wrote at Bangkok airfield reached me this morning. Thank God you are fairly fit now. My darling, I am very much afraid my first letter (written Aug 22nd) may not get to you. In which case the one I wrote on Monday night (Sept. 10th) will be the first [both are missing]. And it didn't tell you half the things it should have done – nor say nearly strongly enough the most important thing of all – namely, that, like you, I love you more – far more – than when you went away, although then I didn't believe that was possible. As for what we do on your return, it will be just as you wish except that by now you will no doubt know that your parents

are in San Francisco. However, it may not be so very long before they come home. (Young) Alan and Hannah came over yesterday – they are expecting their first baby next April ... My darling, I feel I must tell you again, in case other letters have gone astray, that your dear brother John was killed last May – he, his pilot, & his beloved 'Mozzy' all went together. They had all survived 118 operational flights, & John had 2 DFC's. He also had everybody's love who met him. He was a great comfort to me, my darling.

In my first letter I told you that Daddy bought a house near The White House, which we could rent from him – at that time we had thought it would be very much longer before the Far East war was over. So now Robin & I are moving in – but I'm leaving most things to be settled 'when Daddy comes home'. My own dear one, there is one point I mentioned in my first letter that I must raise again. Robin is just waiting & longing for your return. Once you have come, it won't be possible to go away without him, without making him bitterly jealous. Could you bear not to see him for a fortnight? I have told him I shall go to 'fetch' Daddy, & it will take me about two weeks. Meanwhile he will stay with Hannah ...

Aunt Ada is most anxious for me to go to Folkestone to see her. I was wondering how I could manage this when Robin remarked 'why not wait until Daddy comes home, then he can look after me, while you go, Mummy!' Dear one, I do hope you will agree to my suggestion, for you can have no idea of how much time & attention a young child takes, & just at first I want to forget I'm a mother and just be a wife – or lover – for a while. Last night I got out all your clothes & looked them over. Soon, if you write often enough, I shall begin to feel human again. I have refused to wear my trousseau things while you were away, so now I can come to you with a little bridal array for our honeymoon (for a nation we must be one of the shabbiest at the moment). Oh dearheart nothing really matters anyway, except that you are alive, & you love me.

Your own longing, loving wife.

Phyllis also put a notice in *The Times* and wrote immediately to Barbara and Alan.

13 September 1945, from Phyllis (the White House) to Barbara and Alan
My dearest Barbara and Alan, I have this morning had my first letter from Barton, written on Sep 2nd at Bangkok airfield ...

The whole letter is quite cheerful but grave. As if having laughed at the Japs and helped the men to laugh at everything, he was quite drained of any further ability to even smile, at the moment. Don't worry, Alan, that I shall try to persuade him to give up the Army. I had all sorts of wild plans, but it was only because these were only 'plans' & not of any real practical application, that I indulged in them. I'm with Barton whatever he may decide, but so far as I am concerned, all I mind is that we shall be together ...

He admits there were days 'when it seemed hardly worth while trying to go on' but for the hope 'of what we shall do together after the war' ...

Before she finished her letter, another letter arrived from Barry, the one from Nakhon Nayok Camp written on 30 August 1945. She quoted it to Barbara and Alan, finishing:

(same letter) Friday morning
There is a P. S. 'My future career will depend very much on postwar condition. Just now the army stinks. But I must wait before deciding.'
  Daddy is waiting to take this.
  All my love, Phyllis.

Although Phyllis frequently talked about her father, we have few letters where his own voice can be heard. He writes to Barry's parents:

14 September 1945, from James Bacon (the White House) to Alan and Barbara
Dear Alan and Barbara, We are all over-joyed at the news of Barry's release and that he seems in reasonably good health. To you it must be even more joyous. Please forgive me for not adding a personal word to the cable I sent giving the contents of one from Barry. The fact is that the news and the wording of Barry's cable were 'phoned up to me by Phyllis with an urgent request to send it to you as priority and I shared her view so fully that I despatched it forthwith and only after it had gone did I realize my failure to add a word of congratulation or even a name. However, the news was the thing ...
  I am fairly fit but Lily doesn't seem very well. Perhaps the end of the war and the good news will help her.
  Love, Jim

14 September 1945, from Phyllis (the White House) to Barry
My own dear one, The first letter you wrote from camp got here this morning. Slowly you are becoming more real and human to me, though it still seems too good to be true. For a long time after you had gone, I could imagine what it was like to lay my head on your shoulder and forget every little worry. But for so long now that has seemed more like an impossible dream of heaven than anything else. No one could have had kinder friends or family than I have – but that still couldn't make up for my own lover. Oh my darling, there is only one person in the whole world to whom I can really say any (& every) thing that comes into my mind, without reservation. You must be longing to hear about and see your son. But for me at the moment you are not Robin's longed-for Daddy – you are my man. I keep waking in the night, and saying to myself 'It's really true – the time will pass somehow, and once more I'll be able to love him – not only with my mind and soul, trying to keep up the standard he expects of me, but with my heart and body too, as much as ever any woman loved her man.' It has made me so happy that in

both the letters I have had from you so far, you have mentioned a brother or a sister for Robin ...

About your son – he is a dear little boy, but has one very marked characteristic. Even in an age of 'asking' children, he is outstanding for the quantity and quality of his queries. Daddy says if he doesn't turn out a scientist he ought to! He is a loving little boy, and any loving messages you send him he will be thrilled with. As for an actual letter, printed in big capitals – it would thrill him. But my darling, he is so quick, so loving, and so intelligent that you will have to go very carefully with him. He is prepared to adore you, but will doubtless show off appallingly at first, so that you feel he needs disciplining. What he really needs, I think, is lots & lots of love and a steady home background. Also a puppy. Long promised 'when Daddy comes home!' There is a work-shed in our new house and whenever I find anything lacking he assures me 'Daddy and I will make you that when he comes home, Mummy!' He also is longing for a baby brother or sister, though he knows it will take a long time to grow inside me.

I was so pleased to hear about the acting, my dearest. Just another big interest we now have in common. But didn't you have to sacrifice your huge moustache? (Yes – a rescued survivor told me about that!) As for your career – we'll leave that till you come. You know I'm with you whatever you decide. But I'd like to know if you've given farming any serious thoughts? ... Then we might achieve those 8 children I hanker for! ...

Your own – very own – wife, Phyllis

15 September 1945, from Barbara (San Francisco) to Barry
My darling Barton, When I opened the front door after we'd been away for two days, there was a cable lying on the floor. It told us that you'd been taken to India. That means that you were getting food & beds & letters, & medicine if you needed it, & were able to walk about & read and listen to the wireless, and – oh darling – it meant that all the things we have not dared to think about, & yet, at the same time, have been unable not to think about, were ended. You are free & soon you'll be at home.

Perhaps you have already had letters from us. We did not write from America until the war was over because dad thought it wiser for your sake that we should not do so as the work he was doing was for the war. Now perhaps you will hear some of the broadcasts which are in Malay. When the Japanese surrendered we wrote to you through the American Red Cross & ordinarily through the post.

Even if our letters have not arrived yet you will have heard from Phyllis. We had a long letter from her today, a letter written before she knew that you had been set free. She has been so brave darling through these long years but nothing can match the way you and the others who were captured have behaved under conditions that are impossible for us to imagine. Some of our letters will have told you the main family happenings ... & that our John died when the Mosquito he was navigating crashed at Calgary in Canada . . . All these things have been told you many times so I will not go into them more fully.

It seems that we may still be in America when you get home. So far we have not been told when Dad's job will close down which means, I suppose, that it is still thought to be doing useful work which is nice to know, but even so, our thoughts are generally in Britain where we will certainly be far less comfortable but we would have our family within calling distance . . .

Ever your loving mother, Barbara. Dad is writing too.

15 September 1945, from Phyllis (Mapleton) to Barry. Letter numbered 4
My own darling, This is the fourth letter I have written since I got your cable. I shall number them, so that you'll know if there are any missing. Also, from now on I shall address them from 'Mapleton'. The furniture has gone now, and Robin and I will start sleeping up there tomorrow night . . . About this house 'Mapleton', my darling. I do so hope you won't think it too near my folks. But houses are almost unobtainable, except to buy for 1–200% their real value. Mother was very ill earlier this year (heart-trouble) and so I decided to try to settle near her, till you came home. I house-hunted desperately for months. Then this house came on the market, to be auctioned. They put the reserve price at the auction high, the bidding didn't reach it, and it was withdrawn. Afterwards, Daddy made an offer, & bought it. That was Aug 9th. On the 10th came the first murmur of Surrender from the Japs, right out of the blue . . .

That's all I'll say about the house in this letter as otherwise there won't be room to try and tell you how very very much I love you. It was unbelievably lovely to get your first long letter from Bangkok airfield. You have, even if belatedly, had one or two letters from me. But that was the first love-letter I've had for 3½ years – & I was starving for it. And now I am so hoping there will be another one tomorrow. Dear darling husband, I find it hard to believe it's really true. That it won't be many weeks before I can put my head on your shoulder.

Your very very loving wife, Phyllis.

16 September 1945, from Phyllis (Mapleton) to Barry. Letter numbered 5
Dearest husband, There is so much to tell you and none of it seems important enough to say, except that I love you with all my being, and just ache to be in your arms again. All that has happened since Feb. 1942 now belongs to an odd spot in my existence, and has no real connection with my proper life – as your wife – except so far as Robin is concerned . . .

10.20pm. At that point I suddenly felt so sleepy I gave up, as I knew I should only write non-sense. My darling, the relief of hearing from you has been so great, so very great, that I just can't sleep at all. I keep waking up to consider whether I'm dreaming, or it's really true the long nightmare is over. This time now is a bad one to write to you, for I find it more difficult to write as decorously as one 'almost a stranger" should to another. You will wonder that I say so little of Robin. I have got out of the habit of considering him objectively, and fear to give you false impressions ...

Dear one, this letter just won't go. I've not told you much yet about the house, nothing at all about the Section wives & mothers, and very little of our families and friends. And I don't want to. Sometime, in the long winter evenings ahead, you may ask odd questions about friends and I'll answer them – but just now, no! Yet if I just go on saying I love you and I'm going to bed tonight in the hope of sleeping soundly, to make the time pass before the Post comes in the morning, and I'm hoping against hope there will be a letter from you, will you be bored?

You will by now, I hope, have had my cable letter telling you your people are in San Francisco. But as soon as I got your cable, Daddy passed it on at the highest priority rates. I got this typical reply 'Wonderful message gratefully received. Knowledge your happiness adds to our intense joy'. So like your dear mother. It has been of the greatest comfort to me, my dearest, when I dared to let my mind rest on what you must be undergoing, to feel that no son of your mother's could fail to win a moral victory, whatever might be your physical failings.

Letters and telegrams have been coming in to me ever since I got your cable. I put a notice in *The Times* (Sept. 13th), and the first result was a note from the vicar! [Several other people] and Aunt Ada all wrote & phoned at once (Aunt Ada is wondering just how soon she'll be able to see you!!). I am trying hard to beg or borrow a car (ours fell to pieces) for the beginning of your leave. There is a small farm in the Lake District I wot [*sic*] of – or what about the Wensley Dale Heifer?!?

My truest, dearest love. Your wife Phyllis.

18 September 1945, from Phyllis (Mapleton) to Barry. Letter numbered 6
My own dear darling, If when you get this you are with a crowd of people, please put it away to be read for another time. For I feel so full of love & longing for you, that I may be very indiscreet, though I'll try not to be. For I'm a disappointed woman. A letter last Monday (from Bangkok) one on Friday (from the camp) & none since. Having had nothing but 4 Field cards from you for 3½ years, it is quite absurd of me to be so on edge for letters after getting two in one week. But indeed, my darling, I think those two must have gone to my head. Just think, yesterday Robin & I officially took up 'residence' here, and although we have beds to sleep on, the rest is absolute chaos. You may be here at any time, should you fly (& I rush to the phone the minute it rings) & yet I have to waste time walking to the village, yesterday & today, to ask if there was any airmail for me on the afternoon post! Quite, quite ridiculous. And now, when I ought to be answering some of the dozens of congratulatory letters & telegrams, I just must write again to you. Yesterday I didn't. I got into bed, very very tired, at about 9.15pm, &

started to write to Mrs Abrahamsohn. I fell asleep almost at once, & only roused sufficiently to put away my pen and turn off the light. So tonight I am starting with you. Though I ought to have written to Mrs Garrod days ago. I do trust Bob is alright.

Dear one, I am not mentioning your future career – that can wait. Don't worry about our having this house, either – that we can leave at any time. Suffice it, you are coming home, & there is here a home to come to. Of our very own, with a front door we can shut on the rest of the world. And a wife and son who think you are the acme of perfection ...

Dear husband – dearest dearest husband – I just don't know how I'll get through the next few weeks. Surely surely it can't be longer, if I can believe your own account of your health. Have I ever told you that Robin and I are both fairly fit? I say 'fairly' as I think Robin still has to catch up a bit on what he lost in having his adenoids and tonsils out (Aug 2nd) and I need you. Now I am going up to bed, to give thanks for your safety, & pray for a dreamless night & a letter in the morning. I copied out all that was not meant 'only for me' of your letters, & forwarded it to your parents.

Dear darling, I've also said nothing of all you have endured (I've heard you referred to as 'He's the man the Japs can't do anything about – he just laughs in their faces'). Words are too inadequate. But I love – and admire – you with all my heart and soul.

Your loving wife Phyllis

20 September 1945, from Phyllis (Mapleton) to Barry. Letter numbered 7
My own dear boy, Your air letter from Rangoon dated September 4th just received. My darling, how well I know what you are feeling over letters for I am just the same. Your plans for leave won't quite work out, I fear, as your parents are abroad. And Park Lane may be beyond us. There is little to be had in the way of luxury now. But if I really knew several weeks beforehand just when you were coming, I might be able to get a small room somewhere for 2 nights. It's like looking for a needle in a haystack, trying to get rooms in town. My own plans, like yours, were suggestions to be offered for approval. I am hoping by now you will have got some of my letters, & will know what I suggested about Robin ... My darling, I'm hoping you'll feel just like vegetating for a bit, pretending you are a gentleman with a private income, whose only duties are the improvement of his own property and estate. We shall have to watch our budget a bit – living is fiendishly expensive. But there is a bit put away, so we can embark on Pup No. 2 [a baby] as soon as we wish. As for cars – they are almost impossible, but I've not given up trying to borrow one ...

Darling, I love you. I'll write another letter straight away. Your Phyllis.

20 September 1945, from Phyllis (Mapleton) to Barry. Letter numbered 8
Dearest darling, this is really just a continuation of letter No. 7. To tell you something of the home that is waiting for you to make ... I am <u>so</u> hoping you

will approve of the furniture I have bought ... This is all very problematical, as I am hoping you are already on your way home, having had <u>at least</u> one letter from me, to make you feel a little less of a stranger to me.

Dear darling ... I'm in bed in no fit mood to write to a 'stranger'. Come to me quickly, my dear one, for where I once thought to hear news of your safety and well-being would bring me peaceful nights, I find myself in such a fever of impatience that I sleep as badly as ever.

Darling, the 'section' casualty list you sent me in your letter from Bangkok. I have been in touch with the wives and/or mothers of almost all those men ... Could you, during the voyage home, write letters to the next-of-kin, to be posted after you get back? Say all you can about the man, and above all, if they ever had a chance to leave a last message, give it. I have all the addresses here.

(same letter) 21 September 1945, 11.00pm
My pen ran out at that point last night. This morning I had to be out bright and early, as I was due for the 'perm' I have been saving up for so long. To arrange for that was one of the first things I did after your cable came! My hair is very much darker than it used to be. Hardly what you would call blonde at all. I hope you won't find much change in me – at any rate, for the worse. I look fairly much the same, only older, and fatter. I'll never again be quite as small as I was when we were married, for I think my pelvis must have widened when Robin was born.

It's no good – I'm half asleep now, and all I can think of is will there be a letter from you in the morning, and how soon will you be home. Also will you have had a letter from me yet, & if so, do I still seem so remote. I almost think I shall insist on being woo'd and won all over again!

All my love, my darling Phyllis.

Barry has still only received one of Phyllis's letters. He writes:

23 September 1945, from Barry (aboard the SS Orduña*) to Phyllis*
On my way at last, dear wife, and only a few days until we're together again. We are two days out of Rangoon and hope to reach Colombo the day after tomorrow.

I can only give you a rather doubtful prophecy of our arrival. It's said, Liverpool on 15 Oct, one day at a dispersal camp then on leave and a medical board after a fortnight. You will be able to get the date more exactly from the shipping lists if they are now published ...

You'll have to bring a selection of clothes up to town for me as I shall have absolutely nothing except a battledress and a toothbrush.

I'll telegraph or ring as soon as I arrive and fix up details.

I had your letter with news of my Mother and Father and of John.

We are fairly well off in this ship. She's old but quite comfortable and the accommodation is not quite as crowded as it might be. At least I have a cabin tho it is double bunked making 4 places instead of two.

I've put no address on this letter as I don't know of any one that will find me. But please write if there is any way of getting a letter here.

I am getting so near to you now that I can't say any of the things I want to say. But in three weeks time I'll be able to show you how deeply I love you and these unsatisfactory letters will be finished. I hope for ever.

I am told we ex PoWs are to have 250 clothes coupons and double rations for a bit. Nice but undeserved because since '43 we've really had quite fair rations and probably more meat than you. Still I've no doubt we'll be able to find room for any extras.

Unless the Bay and the Channel set me right back I think you'll find me as fit and well physically as I've ever been, and I hope that being with you will soon cure any distemper of the mind.

My dear I love you so much. Barry

27 September 1945, Thursday, from Phyllis (Mapleton) to Barry. Letter numbered 10 (9 is missing)
My own darling, Such a sad little letter from you in the post yesterday [dated 9 September, p. 201]. I wanted to answer it at once, but had a great rush to get off to town. Oh! I do so hope you have had letters from us by now. To answer your letter first – it is so like you, my darling, to help in the hospital. And I'm glad it brings you a little social company too. Secondly about the 'gutter press', I don't know whether it really is all that much worse than it used to be. But life has been so hard for years, that what made one smile tolerantly before, irritates and disgusts one now. Here I take the *News Chronicle* (Liberal paper) every day & Daddy has *The Times* down the road. Oh my dear one, how I do pray that you will find Robin and me as you imagine us. Only my dear I so fear that in the longings of absence and separation you will have forgotten the small things that used to annoy you, & endowed us with perfection. In one thing I do not see how I can fail you – in loving you. For to me you are almost my raison d'être – Robin is a part of you – the part that has kept me sane & reasonably happy these weary years.

Yesterday I met Yvonne and Enid for lunch. They both demanded to have all of your letters that were of general interest read to them. Also they send their love. Like everyone else who knows them, they were delighted to hear of your parents impending return from America. Then, after a 5pm visit to the dentists, I went to Folkestone to see Aunt Ada. I got there 8.30pm. We talked till 12 midnight. I left at 8.30am for London. She has mentally bullied me till I felt obliged to go, though I fear she was hurt by the brevity of the visit. I hated leaving here at all, when any time the phone might go … However, as you can guess, her wish to see me was generous, in that she has given me many most useful & unobtainable things for our home. She has also said quite openly that she will leave us alone till you are quite fit, & then she expects to be asked to stay. I said she should (though we may not agree on when you are fit to stand her!) ... In the paper it said 6 ships are expected on the Oct 9th. Less than a fortnight now – it's incredible. And then when I reached home there was the news that Phil had a baby girl this morning. What with Aunt Ada, travelling, moving house, Phil & your cable, I scarcely know if I'm here or there – for Paul and Margaret are meant to come here for the next two weekends while Phil is in the nursing home. I dunno. I'll survive somehow, & anyway nothing really matters except that you are coming home to me. I only resent all these interruptions to the all-important job of getting ready for you – literally, mentally morally & physically.

Your own Phyllis.

28 September 1945, from Barry (aboard the SS Orduña, *two days out of Colombo) to Phyllis*

My own Darling. I've written you two letters already since we came to Rangoon and two before that, but I've not felt at all able to say the things I wanted to. I've felt shy and constrained but now that I'm getting daily nearer to you perhaps it will be easier. When I wrote to you from Catterick or Salisbury [before the war] I had a recent image of you in my mind and could talk to you as a person whom I'd just seen and would be seeing again very soon. It was almost like an interrupted conversation. But now you're some-one out of the dim and distant past whose face and even whose voice I can hardly remember. I can remember more easily what you feel like to touch and to kiss. Such sensations have not come my way since I saw you and my memory of them is unconfused. But I've seen so many different people men and women, and heard so many different voices some ugly some pretty that the memory of your looks and voice are dimmed and almost forgotten to me. I know I thought you beautiful: I know I loved the sound of your voice. But what you looked and sounded like, I can't remember. That I loved you I know and that I still love you I know even more surely. I say your name aloud, Phyllis, Phyl, Philly, Fillet, to try to bring back a picture of you. I look at the Fayer portrait. I read your letters and sometimes I can get a glimpse of the real you I knew years ago, but when I meet you in about 3 weeks time it will still be as a stranger. That is why I want to see you first right away from all our family and friends. Otherwise I might be tempted to play a part, 'The loving husband returns to the arms of his wife'. What I really feel far more like is just before my first visit to you at Grange Park, soon after we met at Cambridge.

The excitement of newness is on me and I don't want to hurt your parents or mine by appearing shy or uncomfortable with you. Just a day or two or longer, all on our own will enable me to adjust myself.

This is all selfish: all about my feelings and no thought of yours. I've hoped that being in the places where I have lived and with people who all know me

I may not be quite such a stranger to you as you are to me. But whatever happens I've little fear for our future happiness. I love you so much, so deeply and so quite certainly and I feel from your letters that perhaps you love me as much. If we have that nothing else matters much.

We were married for nearly two years before I went away and all that time I cannot remember any quarrel or difficulty between us which amounted to more than a momentary difference of opinion, or one which lasted more than a few minutes.

My time as a PoW has taught me to accept most things without too much difficulty and your time at home has probably developed a good degree of tolerance in you which I am convinced is the highest virtue. We cannot help being happy together.

I started this letter hoping that at last I might be able to put down on paper all the love I've felt for you in these years of separation but I find myself wandering into other channels. I'm thirty now but I feel just as I did when I was 22 and 23. Shy at times then bold and adventurous but always so much in love. I've been in love with you for over eight years now not just the settled happy love of a young married couple but like young lovers meeting rarely and under difficulties; looking forward frantically to the next time I should see you. It's like that now, but magnified a thousand times.

I used to dream at one time in '44 that you and Robin had been killed. For several months that dream came and I'd wake up frantic. I got almost afraid to go to sleep at times because although I knew it was a dream I still felt all the time that it might be true. It nearly drove me crazy. I've not had that dream for a year now but it was still a grand relief to get an up to date letter from you and a cable at Colombo. This will catch the post at Suez. I may see you before I write another letter.

All my love, my dearest wife, always Barry

Undated, [8 October] 1945, from Phyllis (Mapleton) to Barry. No number
My own dear darling, I'm a disappointed woman! The newspapers said the *Orduña* was docking on Sat 13th, & I planned accordingly. I'd got down to where I could count the days on one hand – & now it's put off for a week! … I've tried every hotel in London, with no success. And have been only too glad to have Yvonne get us a room at the Russell Square Hotel, through 'influence'. We can dine out.

My darling, your long letter written 2 days out of Colombo came this morning. So we both feel a little the same way, don't we? Good. Let's make the most of it. We'll have a <u>real</u> second honeymoon, with all the 'excitement of newness' properly there. And with a proper bashfulness on your side and shyness on mine! <u>Only</u> – and I <u>must</u> write this now for I shall hate telling you when we meet, I'm 'due' [for her period] at that time. That's partly what has made the upset over the delay so hard to bear …

What a letter for one who is feeling a trifle bashful to get! But my darling, I too want to meet you away from all who know us, for the same reason. We mustn't act to each other, whatever happens. And also I've no fear for our future, so long as we are together. To my mind, one of the strongest reasons for quitting the army is that. Sooner or later there would have to be a foreign tour, & then I'd be torn between you and the children – & they would suffer.

In case you can do anything about it at your reception camp – you have a car, a Morris 8, no DMM 303. Get all the petrol coupons you can – and find out, if you can't get them without the registration book, where you have to go. We have a room booked for 19th, 20th, 21st in London, then we are off on the Great North Road for Yorkshire &/or the Lakes. Unless you have other ideas, of course. Anyway, we can have that fortnight all to ourselves, before you become the head of the family, & I a busy housewife!

Now I must go to bed. I've a slight sick headache – due to excessive anticipation & subsequent reaction, I fear. And my dear one – I'm not beautiful – not even really good looking. Love me just the same, please, but don't expect me to come up to the Fayer portrait. I don't.

This is a poor letter. But the nearer you come, the dumber I feel. But I do love you so much.

Your wife Phyllis.

8 October 1945, from Barry (aboard the SS Orduña, *Suez Canal) to Phyllis*
My, Darling, I posted a letter and a cable [missing] to you at Suez where we stopped for kit. I had there two letters forwarded by you from Mum and Dad and also a letter from yourself in which you seemed very unhappy and worried about the lack of mail from me. Deliveries must be rather disorganized I suppose but surely by now you'll have had at least one of the letters I've written.

This I hope will be posted at Port Said where we are to stop for a few hours only, then straight home.

We are told that we go to Liverpool; that we reach there probably on the 19th: that we are likely to be free to go home on the 20th or 21st. How and where we arrange to meet I must leave entirely to you to decide as I've no idea of conditions at home ... I believe you are not allowed actually to meet the ship and it is obviously sensible for you to stay in the South and for me to come to you. On the other hand if other people have wives and mothers to meet them, and I don't, I'll be terribly disappointed ...

My darling this is terribly vague but I can't decide anything until I know what is to happen to us. I'm sure that I shall fit in very happily with any arrangements you may make.

People at home seem to expect us to arrive looking like wrecks of men. Had we been released in 43 or early 44 this would have been so. But now we are all very fit tough brown and only a little underweight. Goodbye my darling. I'll see you soon after this arrives.

Love Barry.

Phyllis, already in a state of frustration and excitement, began to hear from relatives whose men have already returned. Mrs Ivy Graham, mother of George Albert Graham, writes, 'I hope your husband has also got back to you ... My son has told me that he owes his life to your husband. How he took care of him ...' Phyllis continued to correspond with the others who, like her, are still waiting. Ships full of ex-PoWs sailed both east and west halfway round the world, and planes hopped from country to country, so that even those who had received good news were still in limbo as late as October 1945. Authoritative information was rare and relatives depended on each other for support. Ronald Murrell's mother wrote:

11 October 1945, from Mrs Murrell (London), mother of Signalman Ronald Murrell, to Phyllis
Dear Mrs Baker. Thanks for your letter I was so pleased to hear that you were able to get a house, altho I can manage [*sic*] the work & planning it all means.

The reason I write is, because you so kindly asked about Mrs Harrison & her son. I have sad news of both. Mrs Harrison passed away on July 4th & just as Japan gave in, news came through that Ernie [Lance Corporal Ernest Harrison] was lost at sea Nov 44. I have heard from my son since, confirming it, as my son was a great friend & they have been together since before the war. My son saw Harrison last when they were at Manila on the way to Japan but has been enquiring & has met a man who was on the same boat going from Manila. It is very sad. My son mentions your husband in his letters. He is quite pleased with his medical & so am I. Everything is OK except he must have strained his inside while working on that railway & there is a Hernia on the left side but he is young & and an operation will put that right.

Thank God for the return of our loved ones, there are so many with sad news.

I am thinking about you as the Captain may arrive today.

I hardly know when to expect my son as his letters are a month & a fortnight old & he did not know which route he was coming. He is not in hospital so his trouble cannot be very bad. Dennis Lovell is expected back today.

Now, I must wish you and yours good health and happiness together, after this awful separation & strain.

Thanking you for your kind enquiries.

Faithfully Yours. M. E. Murrell

Murrell may have been on the *Osaka Maru*. This was shipwrecked by a typhoon off the coast of Formosa (Taiwan), but many of the PoWs were picked up by another Japanese ship and eventually reached Japan. Leonard Russell was probably on the same ship.

Undated, from Mrs Russell (Nottingham), wife of Signalman Leonard Russell, to Phyllis

Dear Mrs Baker, Just a line to let you know I have received the good news that my husband is now in Australia. It is such a great relief after so many years of waiting. I hope you have also had good news of your husband I wish to thank you for what you did for me in the past years.

Yours Truly Mrs Russell

Leonard Russell in about 1941.

Chapter 33

Britain: Autumn 1945

Second honeymoon

It is tantalizing that the correspondence between Barry and Phyllis ends with the letter of 8 October. We can only imagine the meeting between husband and wife. In later years they would laugh about one of their first conversations: Barry asked, 'Do you have any rice? I know some very good recipes.' The relatives of the returning Far Eastern prisoners received a lot of advice about the men's diet. The Red Cross journal *Far East* offered a menu plan of six small meals a day, with milk a major feature.

Phyllis remembered being instructed to hide any rice as this would be anathema to their men. For many men this advice was correct but, as Barry said elsewhere, 'our wives had been advised not to give us rice to eat as we would associate it with the PoW camps. This was quite wrong as rice in quantity had been our measure of a good or bad day. I still prefer it to other cereals.' There were other funny moments, such as the neighbours seeing Barry mowing the lawn wearing nothing but a 'Jap happy'.

We have Barry's memoirs, of course, but they are brief about the couple's reunion:

> We landed, I think, at Tilbury Docks and then went by train to a London station where a welcoming committee was waiting for us. I saw Phyllis alone on the platform and we enjoyed a very emotional reunion. My parents were

From Red Cross journal *Far East*, September 1945. Advice to families about how to feed their returning PoWs (British Red Cross Museum and Archives).

still in San Francisco, but James and Lilian Bacon had taken charge of Robin, now nearly 5 years old, and Phyllis had been given a fine little motorcar, a Morris 8 saloon whose number I can still remember as DMM 303. She had packed a suitcase of my pre-War clothes so that we were able to set off on my fortnight's leave without any delays or formalities.

We spent one night at a London hotel and then pointed the car towards Yorkshire on the Great North Road, and almost without planning found ourselves at the Wensleydale Heifer Hotel in West Witton, where we had spent many happy weekends during my Catterick period.

Robin cannot remember his actual reunion with his father, although he was told that his first question on meeting his father was, 'where is the puppy?' – long promised for 'when Daddy comes home'.

Barry remembers those first months home:

After our happy second honeymoon at the Wensleydale Heifer we came back and settled briefly in a small, furnished house called Mapleton, near the White House. My fortnight's disembarkation leave was extended to a month or two ex-PoW leave, and I set about getting acquainted with Robin. As a PoW I had formed ambitions about more children, dogs, and horses. The first was already well forward and for the second we decided to buy the most [*sic*] dog that was available and acquired a very handsome brindled Great Dane puppy which we named Beves after my tutor at King's whom he resembled.

Robin and Beves.

Robin with Beves the Dane were about the same height and became friends. He was a very quiet and gentle dog unlike my mother's Dane in Kelantan, which used to eat goats. Beves loved to lie stretched out on the hearthrug in front of an open fire at Mapleton where he easily covered the whole of the space available. He enjoyed the usual Great Dane trick of greeting anyone, family or stranger, by standing up on his back legs with his paws on their shoulders and licking them from ear to ear. He gave us a lot of pleasure.

Who else came home?

The story of Barry and Phyllis's war did not end with their reunion. On the ship home Barry had started the difficult task of writing to relatives of the men who had died. This was complicated by the length of time since their deaths, uncertainty about what the relatives knew of their conditions and even greater uncertainty about the fate of those who had disappeared to Borneo, Java, Japan or elsewhere.

Once their honeymoon was over both Barry and Phyllis spent the next three months getting in touch with the remaining men in his unit to piece together what had happened to each of them and to offer comfort to the bereaved. This was a complex task as 27 Line Section, like all the Pacific region PoWs, were spread across the globe. The Repatriation of Allied Prisoners of War and Internees (RAPWI) organization commandeered any form of transport they could lay their hands on and used all possible routes. At least one of the men, Sergeant Pawson (who directed those Eightsome Reels on the Liverpool Docks in 1941), stopped off in America and stayed there, though Barry has recorded him as having died. Piecing together the snippets of information correctly must have been an exhausting process for everyone. For instance, some relatives, such as Marjorie Parker, went through a prolonged period of alternating hope and despair between July and November 1945.

26 July 1945, from Marjorie Parker (Glossop), wife of Driver Ernest Parker, to Phyllis

Dear Mrs Baker, I received news from the war office last evening that it has been ascertained through interrogation of ex-PoW from Far East that my Husband was last seen on a raft following the sinking of a Japanese transport vessel which was sunk off the island of Luzon on 21.9.44

Names of men who embarked & any survivors are being awaited from the Japanese. So in the meantime I shall have to keep hoping. Three of the Glossop boys who were PoW in Japan have been dead 2 years & news has only just arrived.

I sincerely hope that you have not had any bad news.

Yours sincerely, Marjorie Parker

Jim Bridge and George Hobson died in the summer of 1943 (see pp. 122, 125). The third boy, Andy Minshull, died towards the end of the speedo on

16 September 1943 near Bankao (south of Tha Kilen) of dysentery (among the notes it says of him – 'good kid').

Monday ? 1945, from Marjorie Parker (Glossop), wife of Driver Ernest Parker, to Phyllis
Dear Mrs Baker, I have just received news that my Husband was picked up & is on the island of Formosa, I am now awaiting a cable from him. Pleased to hear your husband is safe.
Yours Sincerely, Marjorie Parker.

27 November 1945, from Marjorie Parker (Glossop), wife of Driver Ernest Parker, to Phyllis
Dear Mrs Baker, At last, after waiting for 5 months to hear from my Husband, who was reported to have been picked up on 21.9.44 by the Japs & put on Formosa, I have had news from the War Office. They state that he died on 26.9.44 whilst on Formosa but the cause of his death is not yet known.

All the Glossop boys have now been reported dead, that is the total 100% who went out there.

I hope by now you have your Husband home and that he is well. You have a happy life to look forward to.
Yours sincerely, Marjorie Parker.

Ernest and Marjorie Parker on their wedding day on 31 May 1941.

Marjorie and Ernest had had a fortnight of married life before he was posted to the Far East and never returned.

Others, in heartrendingly pathetic need, wrote to Phyllis hoping she could countermand fate.

Undated, late 1945, Mr & Mrs F. Tomkinson (Manchester), parents of Signalman David Tomkinson, to Phyllis

Dear Mrs Baker, Please Excuse me Writing you once again But we are getting so Worried about our Boy Signalman David Lloyd Tomkinson no 2346404 of the Royal Corps of Signals. Dear We are in the Eventide of our lives and our Boy was our youngest (our Baby) It is terribly hard for us to keep up we Have to have Faith and Prey that God will Bring our Loved one home to us once again It is Hard we shall be 60 on our next Birthday But the Cruel Hand of War Cares not for the old or very young I do Hope and Prey that you have Heard good news of your Dear Husband I am sure It been a great trial to you Knowing as we know How terrible it is for them to keep up amongst those vile and cruel People. Never Mind Dear Have Faith and Prey that God will care & Guide them. Though the night be Dark and they are Far from Home he will lead them on. Well Dear we Have Received news from the War Office stating that our Boy Died on the 2nd March 1945. But We cannot Believe what they say. They state that the Japanese say that he died on this Date But Don't Know what Camp or the circumstances of his Death they dont Even say that he Died in Borneo a Terrible shock to us seeing that only two months ago We Received a Card from him saying he was Fit and Well and told us to Keep Smiling Love from David. We are so upset about this news and we feel that By writing to you, you might be able to get in touch With someone who might help us to trace our Loved one for now we still Believe our Darling Lives and our Preyers to God will be surely answered With Faith and Prayer we are sure God will not let us Down Well Dear will you Do your Best for us we are Broken Harted and think it is a shame that the War Office should be trifling with us in this manner Cold and callous as they are Surely they could have Kept this Bad News untill they were Definateley sure of all Circumstances

In closing may God Give you strength to Carry through untill your loved one Returns yours Sincereley

Mr and Mrs F. Tomkinson

David Tomkinson was one of the unlucky men sent to Sandakan in Borneo. All the men in Sandakan Camp after 1943, except for six Australians, perished, many on an endless march across the country. Very often the cause and place of death were unrecorded. The grim news from Borneo was slow to filter through to England. Most of the victims were Australian, but four men from 27 Line Section ended up there. Another was Arthur Newton, whose grandparents waited uncomplainingly until all hope had faded.

2 December 1945, from Mrs Lane (Portsmouth), grandmother of Signalman Arthur Newton, to Barry
Dear Major Baker (Capt), This is just to line to say that I received your letter, concerning my dear Grandson Signalman A Newton, and his number was 2361041. 27 Line Section. And I am very distressed, when I write to tell you that the news came through about a fortnight ago to tell me that my Grandson had died in Sandakan Camp Borneo, on April 14th 1945. It was a very cruel Blow to me as I have been very anxiously waiting for him to come Home in one of the Ships from the Far East. And I am afraid I should not have known now, only Mr King suggested to me that I should write to the War Office and I did so with the result that has nearly broken my Heart. I wrote to him every fortnight a Japanese P.C. too but I have only had three cards from him in 3½ years Goodness knows what he has gone through in those dirty Japanese hands, poor Boy It makes my Heart acke to think of it all. Well dear Maj Baker I feel too sad to write any more at present.
So I will close by remaining
Your Sincere Friend, Mrs. A. Lane

Two more of 27 Line Section, Andrew Graham (on 15 June 1945) and Stanley Blackburn (on 21 November 1944) also died in Borneo.
The Wakelings received a card from their son written from a sanatorium in June 1944, arriving in January 1945. They wrote increasingly concerned letters to Phyllis. By November they were among the unfortunates who have heard nothing. They know what this must mean but by this stage were desperate for even bad news.

5 November 1945, from Mrs Wakeling (Colchester), mother of Signalman C. Wakeling ('Ginger'), to Phyllis
Dear Mrs Baker, I am sorry to trouble you, but I wonder if you could try & find out any information about my son, we have not heard a word about him, & as they are nearly all home, makes us wonder if anything has happened to him.
I wrote to the Red Cross a month ago & they had no news of him, they told me the War Office would inform me as soon as anything came through, but time is getting on, & we don't hear anything one way or the other.
His last card from him in January was addressed Sanatorium, & we have not heard anything since. He was at No 1 Camp Thailand before he went to Sanatorium. His last card was written 4.6.44
I would write to the War Office, but my husband does not think it worth while, as they would soon inform us if they knew. I thought perhaps you might get in contact with some of the men who were there and might know something about him.
I hope you will forgive me for troubling you, you know the anxiety at not knowing anything We have given up hopes that he is alive, although we still keep hoping some news of some sort will soon be sent to us.

Hope your husband has arrived home safe. Thanking you for your help in the past.

Yours Sincerely R. W. Wakeling

P.S. I enclose an envelope for reply.

Wakeling must have recovered sufficiently to have had the misfortune to be on one of the railway repair parties sent far up country towards the end of the war. He is recorded as having died in Burma on 27 May 1945. We know from Barry's notes that he or Phyllis wrote to Mrs Wakeling on 7 November 1945 and again on 2 January 1946 long after his PoW leave had ended.

The generosity and gratitude of even those who had received bad news was remarkable. Barry wrote to Mr Watson, the brother-in-law of Sergeant Gordon Hunt, who died in 1942 and was much admired by Potter. Mrs Hunt replied:

23 November 1945, from Mrs Hunt (London), mother of Sergeant Gordon Hunt, to Barry

Dear Captain Baker, I would like to know how very much I appreciate your kind letter to my son-in-law Mr Watson. I feel all you say of Gordon is true for it sounds just like him. We have many happy memories of him.

My daughter and her husband join me in thanking both you and your wife for all your kindness and in wishing you all the very best for the future.

Yours very sincerely, Bertha Hunt.

Not all communications were sad:

Undated, from Signalman L. C. Russell (Nottingham) to Phyllis

Dear Mrs Baker, I take this opportunity to thank you for your kind letters to my wife. I have got home safely from Japan, and I am trying to settle down once again. I would like to know if Captain Baker has come through O.K. If so would he care to drop me a line, I have not seen any of his old section for a long time and would like to know how many got through. Hoping that everything is OK & you are happy again.

Yours Sincerely L C Russell.

The most wonderful letters are, like the one above, from the men themselves who have returned home safely and are concerned to find out what had happened to 27 Line Section. They contain a lot of sad news, but each displays affection for their fellows and their former officer and most seem to radiate reassurance that they will make something positive of their lives.

Several of the men give versions of the unluckiest story of them all, that of Lance Sergeant Arnott. John Arnott was liberated in Java, but then died of a cerebral haemorrhage while playing in a football match in Singapore on the way home.

Undated, from Lance Corporal Peter Sampson (Glasgow) to Barry

Capt. Baker, Dear Sir, I would just like to let you know that I'm back home safe and sound, and I sincerely hope that you are keeping alright yourself.

John Arnott in 1941.

Would you please give your wife my thanks for all that she has done these past years to try and lessen the anxiety and worry of both my wife and mother. I appreciate the sincerity and thoughtfulness behind her efforts, and would just like to take this opportunity of thanking her on behalf of us all.

Well Sir, I don't expect I'll ever run into you again. I hope to be de-mobbed soon, whereas you I expect will be remaining in the Army. In any case I wish you all the best of luck and hope it is not long before you receive your two pips and a crown.

Thanking you for your help at different times whilst in your section.

Yours Sincerely, Peter Sampson

PS Did you know that Sgt. Arnott died in Java [Singapore] from con-cussion due to a kick on the head whilst playing football?

Ln Cpl. Graham died in Borneo.

It is sometimes difficult to grasp quite how scattered the prisoners were both during their captivity and after liberation. Lawrence Whitton's letter below gives a very good flavour of this driftwood existence.

22 November 1945, from Driver Lawrence Whitton (Manchester) to Phyllis
Dear Mr and Mrs C. Baker [he has assumed that Mrs Baker is Barry's mother], I take great pleasure in writing to you especially Mrs Baker for keeping in contact with my wife and parents.

Please forgive my people for not writing to you immediately as they are too excited at my homecoming and also my youngest brother came home from Italy just a few days after I arrived home so now everyone quite happy. My eldest brother had only just gone back to Italy just before I came home so I shall have to wait until February before I see him I cabled him soonever [*sic*] I got home and I also wrote to him the following day and I got a reply from him yesterday.

The last time I saw Capt Baker was at Chunki [Chungkai] in Thailand in about June 1944 I don't know where he went from there. I left Chunki and went to Nompladuc [Nong Pladuk], which is just a little lower down than Chunki we stayed for a few weeks there before proceeding down to Singapore (Havelock Road). And at Havelock Road I met the boys who were left of 27 Line Section. From Havelock Road we boarded the 4,000 ton ship *Osaka Maru* which was to take us to Japan and what a voyage, but I'll skip all that.

We spent 21 days lying off Manila, and then we made a dash across to Formosa but we were caught in a typhoon and were finally shipwrecked off the southern tip of Formosa. We were picked up by Jap destroyers and they landed us in the north of Formosa were we boarded another ship for Japan arriving there the same day that the British retook Paris [25 August], we arrived at a place called Mugi and from there we went to AMAGASAKI which lies between OSAKA and KOBI here I stayed for about nine months working on a big lathe. Then we moved up to TOYAMA which is in the NAGOYA area. At the last place we worked on the docks unloading ships, but I did very little work here for I went down with Malaria and an ulcer on my foot.

We were relieved at TOYAMA by the American troops.

We were taken down to Yokohama were we boarded a destroyer which then took us to Tokio Bay, and we flew Tokio to OKINAWA stayed a day at OKINAWA then flew to Manila were we spent 21 days recuperating Then we sailed to Victoria B.C. Canada were we stayed another 7 days, then we travelled across to Halifax by Southern Pacific Railway passing through the Rockies At Halifax we boarded a ship for home (*Ile de France*) arriving at Southampton on the 31st October. Proceeded to Amersham Bucks. for a day.

My people were all waiting for me at London Rd. Manchester and had been for three days. I came Warrington way and arrived home whilst everyone were at Manchester so I took a taxi and went to pick them up. And what a meeting it was. I hope I don't have to go through it again ever.

Well Mrs Baker it is all over with now and I am fit and well my pals say I look better than I did the day I left Britain.

I hope Capt Baker has arrived home safe and well and please give him best regards, and tell him I would like to know who are left of 27 Line Section, I learned a few days ago that Cpl Harrison and Cpl Earnshaw & driver Woodend all went down with the boat just off Manila.

I will close now sending you sincere and best regards from my wife, myself & my parents. L. Whitton

Barry replied immediately, sending a list of the men he had still not traced for certain, and received this in return:

28 November 1945, from Driver Lawrence Whitton (Manchester) to Barry
Dear Sir, I am highly delighted to receive your letter this morning and glad to know that you are home and quite well.

I can give you some information about some of the boys from 27/LS Charlie Knee is alright I had him down at my parents home for a week-end and the following people I met in Hobart, Nova Scotia, Sgt Pawson E., L/Cpl McNicholl, Ronny Murrell, Cpl McWhirter, Davey Sinclair.

Sigm Russel & Driver Jardine I last saw these two at Amagasaki which lies in between Osaka and Kobi in Japan, and they were well then in July 1945.

I heard that Tom Potter was one of the first to get released at Manila and also that Dvr Parker survived the attack on the convoy but later died at Manila from Dysentry. The person who told me about these two persons also told me about Cpl Earnshaw & L/Cpl Harrison & Driver Woodend losing their lives off Manila.

I've never heard or seen anything until I received your letter about:- Sgt Arnott, L/Cpl Graham A.S., Sigm Lovell, Sigm Newton I cannot help with Blackburn, Gilbert, Dvr Lyons. I have not seen them since Singapore.

My mother and I went to a Red Cross meeting at Manchester and I was surprised at the number of people there who had not had any news from either their sons, brothers or husbands. There were one or two people asking me about M. Section 1 Coy 11th Div. But I could not help them at all.

Well Sir, it is 10am now and I have a appointment with the town council at 11am about a house. We are living with my Mother-in-law and I want to get on my own so I must keep this appointment.

I will close now wishing you the best of luck and please give Mrs Baker my kindest regards and I hope you will write again sometime.

Yours Sincerely, L. Whitton

P.S. Sigm C. Knee, 240 Stockport Road, Cheadle Heath, Stockport

With sixty-eight men to trace, Barry and Phyllis must have spent much of the time at their desks. This in spite of the fact that they were now living in the house that Phyllis had moved into only a month before and which was in dire need of renovation. It was also during this period of PoW leave, while Barry was recovering and getting to know Robin, that he had to decide whether to stay in the army or find a different career. He was given a temporary promotion to Major and local desk job, recalling later: 'The job was nothing, a gentle re-introduction to Army life. I believe I was responsible for the smooth operation of the telephone switch board and the operators, which would have worked just as well without me.'

Meanwhile, the letter flow continued. Dennis Lovell and Douglas Jones also write to thank Phyllis, to rejoice with Barry and to list and remember the members of 27Line Section who did not make it. Jones lists the ones others have mentioned and adds: 'News ... from Gibby Douglas, who by the way, is in good health and living life to the full . . . I am in correspondence with Dvr Appleton and L/C Hann and I know that Hannam is O.K.'

Gibby Douglas, who in the worst of times helped to carry Barry, now wrote generously to Phyllis. It is letters like this, which must have given Barry a better idea of the life Phyllis had been living in his absence and how much she had been involved with his men and their families. It probably also made him realize what a wonderful 'army wife' she could be.

23 November 1945, from Driver Gilbert Douglas (Glasgow) to Phyllis
Dear Mrs Custance-Baker, somehow I find it difficult to commence this, my first letter to you, because frankly I don't know how to put into words the gratitude I wish to pass on to you for the way in which you have kept my wife and all the others informed on each detail of news. And this, at a time when you must have been just as worried as they, to whom you were trying to give comfort.

My vocabulary proves to be very meagre when it comes to anything like this so I'll drop back into my more familiar but none the less sincere Scots and say that old toast which we usually reserve for those in the top flight, 'Here's tae ye'!' 'Wha's like ye?' 'De'il the gin!'

My wife has kept your letters to her, so that she could show them to me when I turned up and after looking through them I fully understood her admiration for 'Captain Baker's wife'.

The work you must have had in collecting all the details about us must have given you a great amount of trouble but I can assure you that if you could realise just how much pleasure and how often you have allayed the fears of the wives and mothers of the boys of 27 you will feel that it has been worth while.

Knowing that you will be too busy to read a long winded letter, I'll finish off but before I do let me say that my wife, my boy and myself join together in hoping that you, your son and your husband, have as much happiness as you have been instrumental in bringing to us.

Yours Sincerely, G. B. Douglas.

Barry responded almost immediately to Gibby Douglas, who replied:

28 November 1945, from Driver Gilbert Douglas (Glasgow) to Barry
Dear Cpt. Baker, It's good to know you are home and in the best of spirit. Re. your request for information in regard to men of 27 the following may be of some assistance to you.

To my certain knowledge these men have arrived home and are in good health:- Walls, Johnstone, Farrell, Sampson, Canning, Taylor. The last mentioned is I believe trying to collect data to forward to you.

L. Kennedy, one of the original members of 27 [who must have been detached from the Unit before capture] paid me a visit from Stranraer and

John Lyons and his father in about 1940.

according to him McNicholl and McWhirter have arrived safely, but unfortunately also told me that Arnott had died in Borneo [actually Singapore].

This can be verified if you care to write to McWhirter. In addition, Graham, that is L/Cpl Graham, also died in Borneo in January of this year.

As for Lyons, McDonald and Jardine, my wife has received letters from the wives of the first two to say they are home, and we gather that Jardine has arrived or is on his way from Australia.

Sorry I can't add to this, but you can be assured if anything else turns up I'll let you know.

Please pass on our regards to your wife and boy and I would esteem it a great favour if you would keep me informed about the section.

Sincerely yours, G. B. Douglas

P. S. I'll pass your note round the boys, maybe they can help.

Neil and Margaret McDonald in 1941.

6 December 1945, from Signalman Jack Taylor (Glasgow) to Barry
Dear Sir, Thanks very much for you letter of 29th Nov. which arrived yesterday. I am very pleased that you have got safely home and hope you are fit and well. Poor old 27 Section got its share. I understand that Jardine is home, & Kittwood I saw in hospital in Rangoon, along with Carter & Neil McDonald. Dawson was also there. Murrell I was told went down on the way to Japan with Harrison but I have no confirmation of this. L/C Sampson, Cpl Stewart, & L/C Johnston came home with me and I met Canning who had already seen Douglas at home. My travels took me up into Indo China & I was freed on our return to Saigon in preparation for a further trip on airfield work.

Please convey to Mrs Baker my thanks for all she did in endeavouring to get some news for Mrs Taylor during that period of anxious waiting.

Yours sincerely, J. A. Taylor

Luckily, Jack Taylor had been misinformed about Murrell, who was not on the same ship as his friend Harrison. On the same day as Taylor wrote to Barry, Murrell also wrote. Dawson's homecoming will have comforted his father but been sad for him, as his mother had died since he disappeared.

6 December 1945, from Signalman Ronald Murrell (London) to Barry
Dear Sir, During the past few weeks I have been in the company of Sig. Lovell almost daily, and several days ago he passed on your letter of the 25th Nov. and asked me if I could supply you with any information of the men you had mentioned in it.

Jack 'Cowboy Ted' Taylor in 1941.

Charlie Johnstone in about 1941.

Sgt. Pawson was fit and well when I last saw him in Manila Oct 1945. I believe he went on to visit people in the U.S.A.

McNichol, McWhirter, Sinclair, Knee and Whitton were all on the same [repatriation] ship as myself and were all in good health when we arrived in Britain.

The last I saw of Jardine was three months before V.J. when he was as fit as could be expected.

Drv. Parker was on one of the ships that went down off Manila. He was saved, and on arrival at Formosa he went down with dysentery from which he died. This report was given to me by Sig Alcorn [?], Malaya Command, who was also on the ship. My two friends Cpls Harrison and Earnshaw were also on this ship and lost their lives when she went down.

I was present at the funerals of Sig. Bamford, Jennings and Goddard all of whom died in Thailand.

Of the others in your list I can confirm many, but only from hearsay.

I have also heard that L/Cpl Johnson and Walls are OK.

This is about all the information I can give you at present, But may be able to forward some additional news after enquiries through my friends.

I shall close now wishing you the best of health in the future.

Yours Sincerely, Ronald W. Murrell

The reality of coming home

Coming home, the great dream of all Far Eastern PoWs for three and a half years, was for many of them difficult to handle when it came. Even for Phyllis and Barry there were some tensions in the unaccustomed family life, and Phyllis did remember that Barry found having Robin always at his heels a strain on his patience at times. On the whole, though, Barry felt looked after: 'Stories about the Siam Burma railway were appearing in the newspapers and we surviving ex-PoWs were treated very tenderly.'

While this may have been true for Barry, sadly it was not true for all Far East PoWs. They were discouraged from talking about their experiences and sometimes looked down on for never having fought. Even when they were treated tenderly, not all of them were able to respond. Unrelenting hunger, sickness, fear, inhuman conditions and exhaustion; enforced closeness with vast numbers of men and total loss of privacy; the dependence on mates whose lives could be snuffed out any day; survivor guilt and prisoner humiliation; these were some of the many factors that strained returning PoWs, often beyond recall.

Many surviving men were never able to live a normal life again. Mental problems, repeated illnesses, suicide rates and alcoholism were all more frequent in Far Eastern PoWs than in other similar groups. The total absence of communication for three and a half years resulted in broken relationships, including men coming home to wives who had remarried. Married PoWs often could not settle comfortably into their roles as husband and father. Some of them returned to sons or daughters they had never met, or only seen as a babies, and who rejected or feared the strange men who entered their lives. The children, in turn, often found their change of status, from being their mother's major concern to her secondary one, painful or frightening.

At a very practical level, clothes chafed and shoes hurt feet that were accustomed to walking bare. Beds felt strangely soft and nightmares meant broken nights for the whole family. Western foods were too rich to digest and tropical parasites made digestion a continuing problem. Chronic malaria was poorly understood by western doctors. Yet returning PoWs were encouraged to put the past behind them and get on with life. Many succeeded quite well, but those who did need help rarely received it.

Like Barry, most army officers will have seen it as part of their duty to be in touch with the families of the men for whom they were responsible, in particular with those who had lost a son or husband. Revisiting the events of the last three and a half years, trying to recall details of all the men who died, mostly in grim conditions, and then writing positive things to grieving relatives, will have been tough. Yet we now know that being able to 'tell the story' of a trauma helps the memory to process and accept it. Those men who locked their PoW experience away often suffered more when it was brought suddenly to mind by an unexpected event later in life. Barry and Phyllis, by exchanging information about the men and their families over the previous four years, will have had a chance to join up their experiences and perhaps suffered less than others from the loss of those years apart.

Barry also brought Pat Stephenson and John Perret from his kongsi into the family circle. This may have eased the transition from the all-male friendship groups to family life. Pat, in particular, became a close family friend and godfather to their first post-war baby.

There are no records of how he reached his final decision, but by the winter of 1946 Barry was on PoW retraining, stationed once again at Catterick Camp. The fact of Phyllis's early pregnancy may have hastened his decision.

Aboard the steamer on the way home from Rangoon a few of us, young marrieds, had made a pool as to which of us would be the first to become a new father after our return to Britain. Phyllis and I did our best to be the winners of this wager and after getting in touch with some of the other contestants I formed the opinion that we were a few days ahead of the field, but sadly she suffered a third month miscarriage.

By March 1946 Barry, in a letter to his mother, gives a glimpse of life after his return.

8 March 1946, from Barry (Catterick Camp) to Barbara
My Dear Mother, your letter arrived just too late to catch Phyllis but I sent it after her ...

Phyllis and Robin's visit here for our long Weekend was a great success. Brat and I had two tobogganing trips and he seems quite happy to do long fast runs on his own. We tried going together once but upset which amused him enormously but left me with a very wet seat to my pants ...

My dancing seems not to have suffered too badly from lack of practice but is definitely rusty in places.

We were highly amused to hear that the wife of a certain Major Scott on our ex p.w. course has quite unintentionally started a baby. She's 42 and has children of 16 and 11. This means that they will win the silver cup offered by one of our course for the first baby. A cup which we had really had in our pockets.

Incidentally Phyllis seems to have almost got over her disappointment which is a great relief.

I have been lent a first class S.M.L.E [.303 rifle] for Bisley this year but I rather feel I may be in Germany and unable to attend.

I wish I were at Wye to help you settle in.

Love, Barton

The possible posting to Germany shows that Barry was sufficiently recovered from his imprisonment to have made a firm decision to stay in the army and for the army to be making plans for him again.

Like all Far East PoWs, Barry did suffer long-term consequences of his imprisonment, particularly from his work in the grim conditions and with desperate, incurably sick patients in the hospital wards in Chungkai PoW camp. He was a wonderful, sympathetic and practical husband and father, dealing efficiently with all the mess and accidents of childhood; he also tolerated pain to an extraordinary degree, though never disdaining painkillers when available. Yet, as he grew older, he became increasingly unable to face contact with sickness or disability in others. He made no excuses, he simply said sorry, I'm not going to see whoever it might be, in hospital or at home. He also, like many other ex-Far East PoWs, found it necessary to be busy every minute of his life. So days were planned down to individual TV programmes, and no task was ever left undone.

Part Five

The End of the Story

Barry on his eightieth birthday, with three of his children and all eleven grandchildren wearing kimonos he had made.

Phyllis and grandchild in 1984.

Chapter 34

Britain: 1946 to 2009

Phyllis and Barry

Phyllis and Barry, with their supportive and comparatively wealthy families, their frankness and desire to communicate openly, fared better than most.

After a further miscarriage Phyllis finally produced a sister for Robin in 1947. We have some ciné films of family gatherings at the White House in the couple of years after the war. There was an explosion of babies, as all four of James' and Lilian's children and Barry's brother, Alan, have one or more children between 1945 and 1947. They romp in the sunken garden at the White House, showing a cheerful disrespect for their grandparents. Robin is seen being taught archery by Barry with bows and arrows no doubt made by Barry himself.

The sister was followed by two brothers, at which point Barry and Phyllis decided that perhaps eight would be over-ambitious. Neither of them wasted a moment of their lives. Their children canoed in home-made canoes, went under-water fishing in the sea with home-made harpoons and home-made underwater cameras, swam at home in a home-made swimming pool with home-made solar heating, went target rifle-shooting with home-made guns, drank home-made wine, skied on home-made skis, wearing stout clothing made by both Phyllis and Barry. Like many other Far East PoW children, they all learned to count to twenty in Japanese.

Barry was posted to Vienna in 1946 for eighteen months, then he gained a place at the Royal Military College at Shrivenham, where he studied Maths and Physics. In 1950 he joined MI10 (Technical Intelligence) for a couple of years. After this he was posted, with his young family, to Gibraltar and finally to Germany. In his forties he took early retirement and became an offbeat, even experimental, schoolmaster at King's College, Taunton. He and Phyllis bought a lovely Victorian house and they both worked tirelessly (putting in plumbing and central heating, turning a patch of field into a tennis court and eventually building a swimming pool) to turn it into the country oasis he had dreamed of during prison camp.

Phyllis pursued her love of drama wherever she found herself and after settling near Taunton in the late 1950s acted with the Taunton Thespians and helped to found the Brewhouse Theatre there. She continued to feel a deep sense of social responsibility and was vigorously active in support of local Liberal politics, the Citizens Advice Bureau, the British Federation of University Women, the Women's Institute, the Taunton Shelter group and the Taunton Youth Centre. She was a keen gardener and is fondly remembered bent double in a pair of green dungarees. At the age of sixty-nine she felt sufficiently unwell to see a doctor that same day. Very early the next morning she got out of bed and had a massive and fatal heart attack.

The shock to her family and all her friends was profound. She had been so incredibly active that none of us had had any warning. She had been the dynamo at the centre of our family and we were left forlorn without her. Our only consolation was that a year or so before this she had remarked, 'If I should fall under a bus tomorrow – it's been a good life.'

Barry – after many months of painful adjustment – rediscovered the activities that made life worthwhile for him. He made dining tables for his children, exotic kimonos for all his relatives and small chairs for all his grandchildren, his great-grandchildren, his friends' children and his children's friend's children (about eighty-six chairs in all). He went on skiing into his late eighties, he was cycling, target rifle-shooting (and winning) and busy in his workshop until the last two months of his life.

27 Line Section after 1945

'Well Sir, I don't expect I'll ever run into you again,' wrote Lance Corporal Peter Sampson at the end of 1945. And as far as we know, Barry never did meet up with any of the men of 27 Line Section again. In spite of this he made sure that we, his children, grew up to remember and respect these men.

We now know that out of the sixty-nine men forty-one survived. Eleven died on the railway; those not mentioned earlier are Signalman Samuel Goddard, who died of septicaemia and cardiac beriberi on 29 October 1943, and Signalman Stephen R. Carr, a victim of dysentery, on 3 November 1943 near Bankao (south of Tha Kilen).

About some of the men we know a great deal and of others very little. The information on the liberation questionnaires stored in the National Archives at Kew has been invaluable, but not all men filled in the forms. For instance, the bare information about Lieutenant Sutherland Brown's Malayan background was supplied by Terry Manttan and Jonathan Moffatt. Sutherland was clearly Barry's right hand man in the early stages, but Phyllis did not have an address for him as he would not have needed her help with the Clipper Mail service. In Lieutenant Garrod's case, Phyllis and Queenie Garrod had been in frequent communication and supported each other's efforts. It seems unlikely that Phyllis and Barry failed to communicate with the Garrods – as they did with almost all the other families after the war – but there are no post-war letters from them. Barry appears to have recorded Bob as having died (perhaps because he was liberated from Kanchanaburi and never arrived at Nakhon Nayok), yet he survived and filled in a liberation questionnaire. Bob is quoted in C. F. Blackater's book *Gods Without Reason*. Recently, in 2013, Sibylla Jane Flower told me that she interviewed Bob in the 1990s. He was then living in Canada and married to Pat; there is no more information about Queenie.

In 2010 I started to look for the men or their wives or children. It was not until November 2011 that we received an email from Michael Taylor about his great uncle George Hobson and his great aunt Ruth (see p. 184 above). George was one of the Glossop boys who all lost their lives on the railway. Michael had been across the world to visit their graves. He put us in touch with Christine Wood, daughter of Marjorie Garner, widow of another of the Glossop men, Ernest Parker, who had been on the *Hofuku Maru*. They too had been very active in remembering the missing PoWs.

Diane Carter, daughter of W. Harry Carter, was able to tell us about her father's memory of playing the piano in Raffles Bar at the moment of the fall of Singapore. Reg Hannam, son of Driver Reg Hannam, related to us his father's memory of the death of his friend Reg Holmes – the only man in the unit to die on active service. In 2005 Driver Hannam and his wife, Eileen, and son, Reg, visited the memorial at Kranji where his friend is remembered and also laid a poppy at the gravestone of Gordon Hunt.

Reg also directed us to Jack Earnshaw, nephew of Corporal Jack Earnshaw, another of those who survived Dunkirk and then was lost when the *Hofuku Maru* went down. The inheriting of names is one of the ways of offering these men a role in the next generation.

Gibby Douglas, who with another of the men from 27 Line Section helped Barry to travel 7km on their rest day, became active in support of Far East PoWs after the war and died in 1964.

In March 2013 I made contact with Steve Riley, the son of Geoff Riley. Geoff was not in 27 Line Section, but his memoirs tell the dramatic story of the 'hell-ships' and the Luzon raid at Cabanatuan. Everything he experienced would have been shared by Potter, another of the twenty-three surviving Britons (see p. 173) rescued in that raid. Late in 2014, I was contacted by the granddaughter of Lawrence Whitton, and we have been able to exchange information.

These contacts came slowly, and in January 2015, wanting to publish this book in the near future, I decided to send letters to the addresses in my mother's records. In February 2015 Joanne McQuillan, granddaughter of William (Jock) White RASC, a schoolfriend of Bobby McWhirter and James Stewart, emailed me. William's family were informed that the troopship on which he had sailed from Liverpool had been torpedoed and there were no survivors. A year or so later, hearing nothing to the contrary, his wife remarried. William had survived three and a half years as a Japanese POW and returned to find he had lost his wife and son to another man. The tragic effect on William, his children and his family is still evident now.

Over the post-war years dedicated men and women have worked to make sure that the names of the men who died on the railroad are all shown on permanent monuments erected since the war on the sites of the big downriver camps. Sadly, there are very few records of the innumerable men and women from the 'coolie gangs' who died alongside them. There are also monuments to those who died in other Japanese territories: the Kranji Memorial on Singapore Island, the Labuan

Reg Hannam at Gordon Hunt's gravestone at Kranji in 2005.

Memorial on Borneo and the Subic Bay Memorial for hellship deaths in the Philippines.

A list of the men of 27 Line Section can be seen in the Appendix.

The Kongsi

Barry stayed in touch with John Perret and Pat Stephenson, two of the three other members of his gang of four – his Kongsi – for the rest of their lives. He may well have stayed in touch with Joe Hepworth too, but there is no record of this. Of John Perret Barry writes:

> After the War John set about writing his book (on the characteristics in common between very large pure chemical molecules and the simplest living micro-organisms) and made good progress but some kind of brain affliction, a tumour perhaps, attacked him, [in the 1950s the family understanding was that he had had a nervous breakdown] so that his brainpower gradually faded until he found that his intellect had so much diminished that he was unable to complete the last and clinching chapters of his book. He later married Dorothy, and moved with her to Australia, where she nursed him through his continued decline until his death some years ago. At the recent (2002) handout of £10,000 to all ex-PoWs, Dorothy was able, with Pat Stephenson's help, to collect her late husband's portion.
>
> Pat Stephenson took up one of the special places available at Cambridge, St Catherine's, and took a good degree in some unrelated subject, English Literature and Economics, I believe. He then joined [Pye Ltd, which became] the Philips Electronics Company in some senior position and later moved into the Government Scientific Adviser's Department. He picked up a professorship somewhere on the way [Professor of Mechanical Engineering at Strathclyde University].

Barry and Pat continued to meet as their families grew up and latterly at least once a year at a Far Eastern PoW reunion, until Pat's death in 2005.

Last Days

In the last weeks before Barry died (of prostate cancer) he was on morphine. Whether because of the drugs or his open knowledge of his approaching death, he talked freely of his life generally and the war in particular. The memories he stirred up were extremely vivid and detailed. Very early one morning I went to his bedroom and found him clutching the duvet to his chest with both hands and staring ahead in terror. When I spoke, he did not at first know who I was. He started talking, describing the chaos of life outside his room and how the banging would start in a moment: the getting up, the noise, the encampment. It took me some moments to take in what he was describing: he thought he was back in the prison camp. Apart from this delusion, he was otherwise coherent and in a few minutes recognized me, but even then as I sat on his bed talking to him it took three-quarters of an hour to overcome his conviction that the horror of prison camp lay just outside the door.

During our long conversation, feeling my way at every sentence, I had to tell him that he had survived, that he had had a long, happy marriage, though Phyllis had died twenty years ago, that I was one of his four children. He agreed that our names – Robin, Jonathan, Stephen and Hilary – were familiar and that he knew us. I told him he had reached his nineties; that he had eleven grandchildren and five great-grandchildren, to all of whom he was a beloved legend. I find it impossible to describe the joy that this information, doled out bit by bit, gave him. He would murmur, 'Yes, yes' as he recognized names, and then, 'Glory be, glory be. Are you sure? No, no, THEY must be outside.'

He was desperate to believe, yet terrified of what awaited him should he be wrong. I pointed out the duvet in his hands. 'True, yes, yes. And you are my daughter. Are you sure? You mean I've had a life?'

In spite of all I could say he remained highly agitated. It was December, and until I could pull back the curtain and show the crack in the sky bringing dawn to the Somerset landscape outside, he continued to fear that I was the hallucination and the reality outside was a Japanese prison camp.

Finally he said, 'But I'm ill, aren't I?'

'Yes, I'm afraid you're very ill.'

'Am I going to die?'

'Yes. It is 2009, you are ninety-four and you have prostate cancer.'

With the most enormous relief and euphoria filling his voice he said, 'I'll settle for that.'

Postscript

On Christmas morning 2009 Barry was able to take some sips of champagne with a gathering of children and grandchildren around his bed. Two days later he died, in his bed at home, where he had lived for fifty years.

While Barry was among the fortunate ones, to survive the war and be fit enough to go on and lead a full life, both he and Phyllis deserve immense admiration for the success they made of their lives. As the letters demonstrate, this success was founded on concern for others, hard work and a willingness to search for, and if necessary to create, the fun in life.

Appendix

The Men of 27 Line Section

The editor would be very happy to hear from any members of the families of the men from 27 Line Section or the additional men listed below, although very limited information is available about the latter.

Key: Surname, rank & first name ('nickname' if any); pre-war occupation; family; letters (if we have them); date of death/survived.

Royal Signals 27 Line Section

Appleton, Driver Thomas; driver; wife & 2 daughters; letters; survived.

Arnott, L/Sgt John; telephone lineman; wife & son; letters; died August 1945.

Baker, Capt Lancelot Barton Hill Custance ('Barry'); Regular Army; wife & son; survived.

Bamford, Sigman William; waiter; aunt & parents, letters; died 30 September 1943.

Blackburn, Sigman Stan; Sheepbridge works; mother; letters; died 21 November 1944.

Bridge, Sigman Jim; pantographer; wife & 2 daughters; letters; died 5 June 1943.

Brown, 2nd Lieut Sutherland; wife; died 27 April 1942.

Canning, Driver Hugh; wife, daughter & 2 sons, sister, mother; letters; survived.

Carr, Sigman Stephen ('Steve'); telephone operator; mother; letters; died 3 November 1943.

Carter, Sigman Walter Henry ('Harry'); baker's roundsman; wife; letters; survived.

Dawson, Sigman William Eric ('Billy'); telephone hand; father (mother died); letters; survived.

Douglas, Driver Gilbert Black ('Gibby'); mail van driver; wife & son; letters; survived.

Earnshaw, Cpl Jack Kenneth Sunderland ('One Long Man'); apprentice compositor; father, fiancée; letters; died 21 September 1944.

Farrell, Sigman Henry ('Harry'); ?plumber; mother, sister; letters; survived.

Garrod, Lieut Robert Arthur ('Bob'); architect/surveyor; wife; letters; survived.

George, L/Sgt Cyril ('Ciggy'); draughtsman; fiancée, brother; letters; died 27 April 1942.

Gilbert, Sigman Clarence Victor ('Jim');warehouseman; mother; letter; survived.

Goddard, Sigman Samuel ('Sam'); parcel wrapper in bleach works; girlfriend, mother; letters; died 29 October 1943.

Graham, L/Cpl Andrew S. ('Andy'); GPO telephone section; mother; letters; died 15 June 1945.

Graham, Driver George Albert ('Judd'); cycle mechanic Halfords; mother, wife; letters; survived.

Grant, Driver James ('Jimmy'); carrier for father's firm; mother; letters; died 2 July 1943.

Grierson, Sigman J.; wife; letters; died 9 February 1943.

Hann, L/Cpl C.; survived.

Hannam, Driver Reginald T. ('Reg'); survived.

Harrison, L/Cpl Ernie G.; clerk in Gaslight and Coke Company; mother; letters; died 21 September 1944.

Hedges, Driver Reginald Albert Walter; delivery driver/Regular Army; parents; letters; survived.

Hobson, Sigman George; bleachworks anti-crease dept; wife; letters; died 8 August 1943.

Holmes, Driver Leonard E.; mother, brother or sister; letter; died 21 September 1944.

Holmes, Sigman Reginald S.; died 13 February 1942.

Hunt, Sgt Gordon Leonard; family printing business; mother, fiancée; letters; died 3 May 1942.

Jackson, Cpl Lewis ('Lew'); printer; mother, fiancée; letters; survived.

Jardine, Driver J. C. ('Big Jock'); postman; mother, wife, 1 daughter, 1 son; letters; survived.

Jennings, Sigman Reginald Edmund ('Reg'); PO engineer; mother; letters; died 18 July 1943.

Johnston, L/Cpl Charles ('Charlie'); steelworks labourer; wife, 4 daughters, 1 son; letters; survived.

Jones, Driver Douglas Henry ('Jeny'); stockroom leather factory; fiancée, mother, aunt; letters; survived.

Kittwood, Sigman William; GPO London; aunt, cousin; letters; survived.

Knee, Sigman Charlie; friend of L. Whitton; survived.

Lovell, Sigman Dennis ('Curly'); mother; letters; survived.

Lyons, Driver John Henry ('Harry') Lyons; bus conductor, Stockton; wife; letters; survived.

McCarthy, Sigman Daniel ('Mac'); electrician; mother, sister; letters; survived.

McDonald, Driver Neil George ('Neilly'); postman driver; wife; letters; survived.

McNicholl, L/Cpl Daniel ('Danny'); Electrical Engineering dept PO; mother; letters; survived.

McWhirter, Cpl Robert C. ('Bobby'); linesman in GPO; sister, fiancée; letters; survived.

Minshull, Sigman C. Andrew ('Andy'); joiner; died 16 September 1943.

Morris, Sigman Hugh B.; ?market gardening; survived.

Murrell, Sigman Ronald M. (?'Ginger'); solicitor's clerk, Moorgate; mother; letters; survived.

Nairn, Sigman H.; wife, 3 children; letter; died 21 November 1941.

Newton, Sigman Arthur H.; printer's apprentice; grandmother, friend; letters; died 14 April 1945.

O'Donnel, Sigman H. P.; died 27 May 1943.

Parker, Driver Ernest Bernard ('Ernie'); tyre fitter; wife; letters; died 26 September 1944.

Pawson, Sgt Eric W.; survived.

Pike, Driver W.; survived.

Plane, Driver John ('Jack'); butcher; mother; letter; survived.

Potter, Sigman Thomas; wife; letters; survived.

Povey, Sigman N. ('Nobby'); PO engineer; wife, daughter, sister; letters; survived.

Randle, Sigman Horace; timber selector; wife; letters; survived.

Russell, Sigman Leonard Charles ('Len'); wireman at GPO; wife, 2 sons; letters; survived.

Sampson, L/Cpl Peter ('Pat'); PO engineer; wife, mother; letters; survived.

Shaw, Driver Percy ('Pip', 'Perce'); van driver; mother; letters; survived.

Sinclair, Sigman David ('Davie'); sailed world, later GPO linesman; mother, brother; letters; survived.

Stewart, Cpl James; engineer for PO telephones; father; letters; survived.

Taylor, Sigman J. A. ('Jacky'); linesman in PO engineering dept; wife, mother, 1 son, 1 daughter; letters; survived.

Tomkinson, Sigman David Lloyd; electrician; parents, fiancée; letters; died 2 March 1945.

Wakeling, Sigman C. ('Ginger'); worked in jam factory; mother; letters; died 27 May 1945.

Walls, L/Cpl John J. ('Scotty', 'Jock'); sister, wife, son; letters; survived.

Walstow, Sigman A. E.; died 21 September 1944.

Whitton, Driver Lawrence ('Larry', 'Lol'); in brickmaking; mother, wife, daughter; letters; survived.

Wilson, Sigman Charlie ('Chuck'); bricklayer; mother; letters; died 30 October 1944.

Woodend, Driver J. Alf ('Dabber'); shipyard labourer; mother; letters; died 21 September 1944.

Additional men listed

Men added to Phyllis's dossier for the War Office, but not in 27 Line Section. Their fates are for the most part unknown.

Bartram, Corporal Jim ('Lofty'); 2 Co East Surrey Reg; mother; letter.

Black, Driver William G. ('Bill'); RASC; wife; letter.

Cassels, ?W. J.; A troop 49/48th LAA; wife; letter.

Gimson, Lieutenant George Stanley; Royal Artillery; mother; letters; survived.

Goldie, ?James; RASC; mother; letter.

Gunn, Gunner Alexander; 155 Lanarkshire Yeomanry, later Signals & Wireless; mother; letter.

Hewitt, Private William ('Muffin'); 2 company East Surrey Reg.; mentioned in Bartram letter.

Jennings, Company Sergeant Major Norman Edward; ?; stock exchange; wife & daughter; letters.

Kirkpatrick, Captain Scott McMurray ('Kirk'); Straits Volunteer Force; rubber estate manager; wife & son; letter, survived.

Lamont, Signalman Alex; Royal Signals; mother; letter.

MacArthur, Private James Neil; 2nd Bn Argyll and Sutherland Highlanders; piper; sister; letter.

McNicol, Signalman Alex; Royal Signals; mentioned in Lamont letter.

Monaghan, Signalman Hugh; Royal Signals; PO Linesman; girlfriend; no letter.

Murray, Signalman George Archibald Brown ('GAB'); Royal Signals; PO engineer; wife; letter.

O'Neill, Corporal James ('Sally'); Argyll and Sutherland Highlanders; Regular Army; mother; letter.

Peters, Signalman S.; Royal Signals; mother; letters.

Renfrew, Sergeant Arthur; RAOC; fiancée; letter.

Stewart, Lance Corporal (James) Albert; ?; Engineering dept of PO; father; letters; survived.

Taylor, Gunner James ('Jim'); 2/80 A/T reg. R. A.; father, letter.

Selected Bibliography

The books listed below are mostly the personal stories of individual Far East PoWs. They are often either the bravely preserved contemporary writings of these men or their courageous reminiscences gathered and relayed by children and grandchildren. Some came from Barry's own bookshelves – sometimes as a gift from the author. I have read and learned much from these histories, but I have not (with rare exceptions acknowledged in the text) used them directly. I have tried to remain as much as possible a transmitter of the writings of Phyllis, Barry, their relatives and the men and women of 27 Line Section.

Adams, K., ed. M. Adams, *Healing in Hell, The Memoirs of a Far Eastern PoW Medic*, Pen & Sword, Barnsley, 2001.

Adams, G. P. and H. Popham, *No Time for Geishas*, Leo Cooper, London, 1973, 2nd edition, 1974.

Alexander, S. A., *Sweet Kwai Run Softly*, Merriotts, Bristol, 1995, 2nd edition, 2006.

Ambrose, K., *The Suitcase in the Garage*, 1996 (unpublished ms).

Baker, W. A. C., *An Ordinary Englishman*, c.1990 (unpublished ms).

Baker, L. B. H. C., *Memoirs*, 2008 (unpublished ms).

Barratt, J. A. L., *His Majesty's Service, 1939–1945*, 1983 (unpublished ms).

Baynes, L. L., *The Other Side of Tenko*, Star, London, 1985.

Beattie, R., *The Death Railway: a Brief History*, Image Makers, Bangkok, 2005, 2nd edition, 2015.

Best, B. (ed.), *Secret Letters from the Railway. The Remarkable Record of Charles Steel – a Japanese PoW*, Pen & Sword, Barnsley, 2004.

Blackater, C. F., *Gods Without Reason*, Eyre & Spottiswoode, London, 1948.

Broad, R. and S. Fleming (eds), *Nella Last's War. The Second World War Diaries of 'Housewife 49'*, Profile, London, 2006.

Chalker, J., *Burma Railway. Images of War. The Original War Drawings of Japanese PoW Jack Chalker*, Mercer Books, Mells, Somerset, 2007.

Churchill, H., *Prisoners on the Kwai. Memoirs of Dr Harold Churchill*, Larks Press, Dereham, Norfolk, 2005.

Coast, J., *Railroad of Death*, Commodore Press, London, 1946.

Davies, P. N., *The Man Behind the Bridge. Colonel Toosey and the River Kwai*, Athlone, London, 1991.

Dewey, J. and S., *PoW Sketchbook. A Story of Survival through the diary and drawings of Will Wilder*, Pie Powder Press, Cholsey, Oxfordshire, 1985, 2nd edition, 1987, 3rd edition, 2014.

Dunlop, E. E., *The War Diaries of Weary Dunlop, Java and the Burma–Thailand Railway, 1942–1945*, Lennard, Wheathampstead, Hertfordshire, 1987.

Ebury, S., *Weary: The Life of Sir Edward Dunlop*, Penguin, London, 1995.

Eldredge, S. A., *Captive Audiences/Captive Performers: Music and Theatre as Strategies for Survival on the Thailand/Burma Railway 1942–1945*, http://digitalcommons.macalester.edu/thdabooks/1, 2014.

Furness, E., *Recollections* (vol. I), 1993 (unpublished ms).

Fyans, P., *Captivity, Slavery and Survival as a Far East PoW: The Conjuror on the Kwai*, Pen & Sword, Barnsley, 2011.

Gillies, M., *The Barbed-Wire University, The Real Lives of Allied Prisoners of War in the Second World War*, Aurum Press, London 2011, 2nd edition 2012.

Gillies, M., *Army Wives*, Aurum Press (forthcoming).

Godman, A., *The Will to Survive*, Spellmount, Staplehurst, Kent, 2012.

Hamilton, A. W., *Malay Pantuns*, Kelly & Walsh, Singapore, 1941, 3rd edition, Australasian Publishing, Sydney, 1951.

Hammond, E., ed. S. Colman and Y. Kasicka, *1941–1943. The War Diary of Edward Hammond*, Ixworth, Suffolk, c.1980.

Hardie, R., *The Burma–Siam Railway. The Secret Diary of Dr Robert Hardie 1942–45*, Imperial War Museum, London, 1983.

Horner, R. M., ed. S. M. McQuaid, *Singapore Diary: The Hidden Journal of Captain R. M. Horner*, Spellmount, Stroud, Gloucestershire, 2006.

Kandler, R., *The Prisoner List, A True Story of Defeat, Captivity and Salvation in the Far East: 1941–45*, Marsworth, Buckinghamshire, 2010.

Kinvig, C., *River Kwai Railway. The Story of the Burma–Siam Railroad*, Brassey's, 1992, 2nd edition, Conway, London, 2005.

Lomax, E., *The Railway Man*, Vintage, London, 1996.

Macarthur, B., *Surviving the Sword. Prisoners of the Japanese in the Far East, 1942–45*, Random House, New York, 2005.

McEwan, J., *Out of the Depths of Hell. A Soldier's Story of Life and Death in Japanese Hands*, Leo Cooper, London, 1999, Pen & Sword, 2005 and 2014.

McGowran, T., *Beyond the Bamboo Screen. Scottish Prisoners of War under the Japanese*, Cualann Press, Glasgow, 1999.

Milner, S. *Diary*, Imperial War Museum, 66/219/1, unpublished ms.

Mitchell, I., *Prisoners of the Emperor*, Pentland Press, Bishop Auckland, 1996.

Nellis, M., *Freeing the Demons: the PoW Recollections of WO2 A. E. Nellis*, 1996 and later (www.fareastern-heroes.org.uk).

Nicholson, V., *Millions Like Us. Women's Lives in War and Peace 1939–1949*, Viking, London, 2011.

Palmer, M., *Our Uncles Who Went to War*, 2010 (privately published).

Parkes, M., '... *A. A. Duncan is OK*', Kranji Publications, Hoylake, Merseyside, 2003.

Parkes, M. and G. Gill, *Captive Memories. Starvation, Disease, Survival*, Palatine, Lancaster, 2015.

Pavillard, S. S., *Bamboo Doctor*, Macmillan, London, 1970, 2nd edition Pan, 1962, 3rd edition, 1970.

Peachey, P. R., *Jeweller's Rouge. Survival by the River Kwai*, Springfield Leisure-Art Collection, Ventnor, Isle of Wight, 2002.

Peacock, B., *Prisoner on the Kwai*, Blackwood, Edinburgh, 1966.

Peters, G. P. G., *I Walked to the Station, around the World, and Walked Home Again*, Fulbourn Press, Cambridgeshire, 1987.

Poole, P. (ed), *Of Love and War. The Letters and Diaries of Captain Adrian Curlewis and his Family, 1939–1945*, Century, London, 1983.

Priestwood, G., *Through Japanese Barbed Wire. A Thousand-mile Trek from a Japanese Prison Camp*, Harrap, London, 1944.

Richards, R. and M. McEwan, *The Survival Factor*, Costello, Tunbridge Wells, Kent, 1989.

Riley, W. G., *Dishonourable Guest*, 1988 and 2012 (unpublished ms).

Seiker, F., *Lest We Forget. Life as a Japanese PoW*, Bevere Vivis, Worcester, 1995, 2nd edition 2002.

Shaw, M. and H. D. Millgate, *War's Forgotten Women. British Widows of the Second World War*, History Press, Stroud, Gloucestershire, 2011.

Silver, L. R., *Sandakan: A Conspiracy of Silence*, Sally Milner Publishing, Binda, New South Wales, 1998.

Stephenson, P., *Pat's Story* and *Notes on my Railway Odyssey*, c.2000 (unpublished mss).

Stewart, J., *To the River Kwai. Two Journeys – 1943, 1979*, Bloomsbury, London, 1988.

Summers, J., *The Colonel of Tamarkan. Philip Toosey and the Bridge on the River Kwai*, Simon & Schuster, London, 2005.

Summers, J., *Stranger in the House. Women's Stories of Men returning from the Second World War*, Simon & Schuster, London, 2008, 2nd edition Pocket Books, London, 2009.

Tamayama, K. (ed), *Building the Burma–Thailand Railway 1942–43. An Epic of World War II*, World War II Remembrance Group, Tokyo, 2004.

Tett, D., *A Postal History of the Prisoners of War and Civilian Internees in East Asia during the Second World War* (6 vols), 2002–2011.

Thompson, T., *The White Flag* (www.far-eastern-heroes.org.uk).

Turner, B. and T. Rennell , *When Daddy Came Home. How Family Life Changed Forever in 1945*, Pimlico, London, 1995.

Index

Members of the immediate family (*see* family tree p. xvi) are not indexed; they appear throughout the volume. The exceptions are John Custance Baker (who is of interest to aviation researchers) and Singapore residents Roger and Joyce Prentis.

1, 2 or 4 PoW Group or Camp, *see* Group 1 PoWs; Group 2 PoWs; Group 4 PoWs
211 kilo Camp [Nam Chon Yai], 119–21, 125
27 Line Section (RCOS), xiii, 1, 7–10, 15–17, 19, **21**, 25, 33–4, 36, 40, 46–7, 49–50, 56, 59, 61, 69–70, 75, 78, 80, 82, 84, 86, 89, 94, 95, 97, 106–108, 113, 115, 117–18, 129–30, 134–5, 142, 145, 147–8, 153–4, 159, 164, 166–7, 170, 174–5, 177, 186, 210, 221, 223–5, 227–9, 231, 238–40, 243–5
  dossier of, xiii, 153, 164–6, 170–2, 175, 177, 181–2, 184, 245
8th Australian Division, 10, 46

Abrahamsohn, Kurt, 99, **100**, 101, 129, 200, 211
Alcorn, Signalman, 232
Amagasaki Camp, 227–8
Ambrose, Kenneth, *see* Abrahamsohn, Kurt
Anti Tank Regiment, 2/80, 246
Appleton, Driver Thomas, 175, 229, 243
  Kathleen Mabel (wife), 175, 243
Argyll and Sutherland Highlanders, 46, 246
  2nd Battalion, 246
Arnott, Lance Sergeant John, 8, 9, 77, 170, 225–6, **226**, 228, 230, 243
  Margaret P. (wife), 9, 170, 243
Austwich, Miss, *see* Grant, Driver James 'Jimmy'; Miss Austwich (friend)

Baker, Barbara, books
  The Talking House, The Three Rings, The Herewegoes, 201
Baker, Flying Officer John Custance, 3, 41, 64, 67, 73, 87, 102, 115–16, 127–8, 144, 178, 180–1, **180**, 193, **203**, 206, 208, 212

Bamford, Signalman William, 167, 168, 232, 243
  Mrs (mother), 167
  Mrs Hanlon (aunt), 167, 243
Ban Pong, 79–80, 82, 124, 132
Bangkok, xiii, 79, 195–7, 199, 205–6, 209–10, 212
Bankao, 222, 238
Barrow-in-Furness, 154, 172
Bartram, Corporal Jim 'Lofty', 245
Battle of Britain, 7
BBC World Service, 134, 202
Bearsden, 164, 175
Beaver, Major D. J., 125
Birmingham, 96, 103, 136
Bisley, National Rifle Association, 234
Black, Driver William G., 245
Blackater, C.F., *Gods Without Reason*, 238
Blackburn, Signalman W. Stanley 'Stan', 77, 224, 228, 243
  Mrs (mother), 243
Blitz, 7–8
blood transfusions, 141–2
Bombay, 199, 201
Boon Pong, 140, **141**
Borneo, 155, 171–2, 221, 223–4, 226, 240
Braham, Captain Mark Gordon, 122
Brankassi, *see* Prang Kasi
Brewhouse Theatre, Taunton, 237
Bridge over the River Kwai, *see* Tamarkan [Tha Makham]
Bridge, Signalman Jim, 8, 19, **21**, 122–3, **123**, 175, 221, 243
  Elizabeth (wife), 243
Briggs, Pilot Officer Maurice, 180
British Expeditionary Force (BEF), 7
British Federation of University Women, 237
British United Shoe Machinery Company, 149
Britt, Leo, 157, **159**, **160**, 162–3

Brooke-Popham, Sir Robert, 36
Brown, Lieutenant B. G., officer, Milner's unit, 83
Brown, Lieutenant Sutherland, 8, 21, 49, 60, 238, 243
  Beatrice Winifred (wife), 8, 21, 49
Bukit Timah, 47, 69–71, 82, 92
Bury, Colonel, 8–9
Bygrave, officer, Milner's unit, 83

Cabanatuan, *see* Luzon
Calcutta, 201
Calgary, Canada, 180, 203, 209
Cambridge
  ADC Theatre, 3
  Copper Kettle Café, 3
Cambridge University
  King's College, 3, 129, 147, 151, 162, 214, 220
  Newnham College, 3, 4, 23, 32, 214
  St Catherine's College, 241
  St John's College, 162
Canning, Driver Hugh, 94, **95**, 175, 229, 231, 243
  A. McNicol (sister), 243
  Annie Bateman (wife), 94–5, 175, 243
  Mrs (mother), 175, 243
Cape Town, 16
Carr, Signalman Stephen R., 182–4, **183**, 238, 243
  Mrs T. (mother), 182, 243
Carter, Signalman Walter Henry 'Harry', 9, **50**, 231, 239, 243
  Diane (daughter), 50, 239
  Lilian Frances May (mother), 243
Cassels, W. J., 245
Catterick Camp, 3, 214, 220, 233
Chalker, Jack, PoW artist, **131**, **139**
Changi, 29, 46, 59–62, 69, 77–8, 82, 92, 168, 181, 193
Chindits, 162
Chitham, Miss Mary, *see* Earnshaw, Jack Kenneth Sunderland; Miss Mary Chitham (fiancée)
Chungkai, 83, 122, 125, 130–3, 138–42, 147–51, 157–63, 186, 201, 227, 234
  Theatre Company, 138, 157, 159, **159–60**, 162–3, 196, 200
  theatre productions, *see* theatre, PoW productions
Churchill, Sir Winston, 61

Citizens Advice Bureau, 237
Clipper Air Mail, 18–19, 22–3, 25, 35–6, 39–42, 55, 57, 153, 238
Clough, Arthur Hugh, 61
Colchester, 224
Colombo, 212, 214–5

Dawson, Signalman William 'Billy' Eric, 19, **21**, 175–6, **176**, 231, 243
  William (father), 231, 243
Devals, Archbishop Adrien Pierre, 68
disease & sickness in PoWs, 91, **131**, **139**
  beriberi, 71, 106, 125, 131, 164, 176, 188, 197, 238
  blackwater fever, 188
  cholera, 122–5, 132
  dysentery, 60, 70, 79, 81, 92, 120–2, 125, 131, 137–8, 141, 155, 162, 164, 183, 187, 197, 222, 228, 232, 238
  Japanese river fever, 27
  malaria, 61, 120, 122, 125, 131, 137, 155, 175–7, 188, 197, 227, 233
  malnutrition, 81, 131
  pellagra, 176
  septicaemia, 168, 238
  tropical ulcers, 138–40, **139**, 155, 168, 175, 178, 227
Dishonourable Guest, 174
dossier for War Office, *see* 27 Line Section; dossier of,
Douglas, Driver Gilbert 'Gibby' Black, 55, 124, 136, 144–5, 175, 228–31, 239, 243
  Tina (wife), 55–6, 136, 144–5, 175, 229, 243
Drower, Captain Bill, 188
Dunkirk, 7–9, 239
Dunlop Rubber Company, 149
Dunlop, Colonel Edward 'Weary', 142

Earnshaw, Corporal Jack Kenneth Sunderland, 8, 19, **21**, 46, 117, 175, **179**, 227–8, 232, 239, 243
  Jack (nephew), 239
  Mary Chitham (fiancée), 175, 179, 243
  Verdi Lindley (father), 46, 179, 243
East Surrey Regiment, 2 Company, 245, 246
Eddington, Sergeant, Milner's unit, 93
Eden, Sir Anthony, 144
Eldredge, Professor Sears, 163
elephants, 108, 111
ERA racing team, 150
Ewing, Marjorie (née Walling), 65–6

Farrell, Signalman Henry 'Harry', **117**, 164,
    166, 176, 229, 243
  Jean Eldred (sister), 243
  Mrs J. (mother), 164, 166, 243
Flower, Sibylla Jane, 238
Forester-Walker, officer in Milner's unit, 93
Formosa [Taiwan], 155, 217, 222, 227, 232

Garner, Marjorie, *see* Parker, Driver Ernest
    Bernard; Marjorie (wife)
Garrod, Lieutenant Robert 'Bob', 21, 57–8,
    97, 153, 157–60, **158**, **160**, 176, 211, 238,
    243
  Queenie (wife), 57–8, 97, 99, 153, 176, 211,
    238, 243
Gee, Geoffrey, PoW artist, **160**
George, Lance Sergeant Cyril, 56, 60, 136–7,
    243
  Dorothy Siddons (fiancée), 56, 243
  Mr A. D. (brother), 136–7, 243
Georgetown, Penang, 35
Gilbert, Signalman Clarence Victor 'Jim', 228,
    243
  Mrs E. (mother), 243
Gimson, Lieutenant George Stanley, 176, 245
Glasgow, 8, 9, 26–7, 43, 55–6, 70, 94, 136,
    144–5, 164, 166, 175, 225, 229, 231
  Post Office, 8, 19, 164
Glossop, 8, 19, 115, 122, 125, 166–7, 184–5,
    221–2, 239
Goddard, Signalman Samuel, 232, 238, 243
  Margaret Haw (girlfriend), 243
  Sarah (mother), 243
Goldie, James, 245
Gould, Mrs G., 154
Graham, Driver George Albert 'Judd', 154,
    172, 176, 217, 244
  Agnes (wife), 172, 244
  Ivy (mother), 154, 172, 217, 244
Graham, Lance Corporal Andrew S., **77**, 224,
    226, 228, 230, 244
  Mary (mother), 244
Grant, Driver James 'Jimmy', 125, **126**, 164,
    244
  Miss Austwich (friend), 154
  Robina (mother), 164, 244
Greater Co-Prosperity Sphere, 51
Grierson, Signalman J. A., 57, 106, 129, 137,
    244
  Mary (wife), 57, 129, 137, 154, 244
Group 1 PoWs, 224

Group 2 PoWs, 10, 77, 118, 136, 145–6, 179,
    186
Group 4 PoWs, 118
Gunn, Gunner Alexander, 246

Hanlon, Mrs, *see* Bamford, Signalman William;
    Mrs Hanlon (aunt)
Hann, Lance Corporal C., 82, 229, 244
Hannam, Driver Reginald T., 8, 47, **48**, 71,
    161, 186, 229, 239–40, **240**, 244
  Eileen (wife), 186, 239
  Reg (son), 186, 239
Hardie, Dr Robert, 124–5
Harnham Camp, Salisbury, 7–10, 15, 214
Harrison, Lance Corporal Ernie G., 8, 117,
    176, 217, 227–8, 231–32, 244
  Mrs E. M. (mother), 217, 244
Havelock Road, Singapore, 227
Hedges, Driver Reginald Albert Walter, 9, 45,
    124, **191**, 244
  George and Mrs (parents), 244
hellships, Japanese, 117, 148, 152–6, 173, 239,
    240
  Hofuku Maru, 148, 152–4, 156, 172, 174–5,
    177, 184, 221, 239
  Osaka Maru, 148, 217, 227
Hepworth, Joe, 149, 241
Hewitt, Private William 'Muffin', 246
Hindato Camp, 120
Hirohito, Emperor of Japan, 121, 141, 147, 193
Hiroshima, 184, 193, 195
Hobson, Signalman George, 8, 125, 167, 184,
    185, 221, 239, 244
  Michael Taylor (great-nephew), 184, 239
  Ruth (wife), 166, 167, 184–5, **185**, 239, 244
Holmes, Driver Leonard E., 117, 244
  W. G. (brother or sister), 244
Holmes, Signalman Reginald S., 8, 19, **21**, 47,
    48, 51, 239, 244
Hounslow, 171, 174
Hunt, Sergeant Gordon Leonard, **61**, 181, 225,
    239–40, **240**, 244
  Bertha E. (mother), 181–2, 225, 244
  Mr Watson (brother-in-law), 225

Imperial War Museum, 130
Indian National Army, 61
Inglefield, Gibby, 162
Irvine, Miss, see McNicholl, Lance Corporal
    Daniel; Ebeth Irvine [?Irving] (girlfriend),
    154

Jackson, Corporal Lewis, 19, **21**, **78**, 244
 Eva States (fiancée), 244
 Mrs E. (mother), 244
Japanese Government, 75, 155
Japanese High Command, 141, 147
Jardine, Driver J. C. 'Big Jock', 117–18, **118**,
 228, 230–2, 244
 Annie (mother), 244
 Isla (daughter), **118**
 Isobel 'Bella' (wife), 244
Java, 59, 63, 77–9, 168, 172, 221, 225–6
Jennings, Company Sergeant Major Edward,
 246
Jennings, Signalman Reginald Edmund, 125,
 126, 176–7, 184, 232, 244
 Rose (mother), 176–7, 184, 244
Johnston, Lance Corporal Charles, 8, 177, 229,
 231–2, **231**, 244
 Williamina 'Ina' (wife), 177, 244
Jones, Driver Douglas Henry 'Jeny', 177, 228,
 244
 Annie (mother), 244
 Beatrice Dawson (aunt), 244

Kanchanaburi, 82, 149, 186–8, 190, 238
Kandler, Reuben, 178
 Richard (son), 178
Kanyu, 120, 125
Kelantan
 British Advisor, 5, 40, 45
 His Highness, The Sultan of, 5, 45
Kempeitai, 51, 61, 187–8
Kennedy, L, 154, 229
Kenny, Miss, 154
Kew, *see* National Archives, The
Kidd, George, 45
King's College, Cambridge, *see* Cambridge
 University; King's College
King's College, Taunton, 237
Kingston-on-Thames, 191
Kinsaiyok, 120
Kirkman, Maurice, 128, 200
Kirkpatrick, Captain Scott McMurray 'Kirk',
 246
Kittwood, Signalman William, **177**, 231, 244
 E. [?J.] Ellison (aunt), 244
 M. Hardy (cousin), 244
Knee, Signalman Charlie, 78, 228, 232, 244
Kongsi, 148–51, 233, 240–241
Konkuita, 130
Kota Bharu, Kelantan, 5, 34, 38, 40, 221
Kota Tinggi, 19, 92, 119

Kranji, **240**
 Memorial, 239
Kuala, SS, 49
Kwai Mae Klaung, 79, 82, 186
Kwai Noi, 79, 106, 119, 163

Labuan Memorial, 239
Lamont, Signalman Alex, 246
Lanarkshire Yeomanry 155 company, 246
Lane, Mrs Alice, *see* Newton, Signalman Arthur
 H.; Alice Lane (grandmother)
Larne Football Club, 170
Liberal Party, 237
liberation questionnaires, *see* National Archives,
 The
Light Anti Aircraft Battery, 49/48th A troop,
 245
Liverpool Docks, 15–16, 212, 216, 221, 239
Lockerbie, 129, 137
Lovell, Signalman Dennis S., 8, 77, 217, 228,
 231, 244
 Rose (mother), 244
Lucas, Dickie, 158–9, **158**, 163
Luzon, 174, 178, 182, 185, 221, 239
Lyons, Driver John Henry, 10, 19, **21**, **77**, 228,
 230, 244
 Mr (father), **230**
 Olwyn (wife), 230, 244

MacArthur, Private James Neil, 246
MacDonald, Captain, 178
mail, PoW Far East, 67, 134, 145
Malaya Command Signals, 10, 19, 44, 59, 118,
 232
Malaya Patriotic Fund, 5
Malayan Civil Service, 3, 5
Manchester, 167–8, 170, 204, 223, 226–8
Manila, 217, 227–8, 232
Manttan, Terry, 188, 238
Markowitz, Dr Jacob, 138–41
Marlborough College, 3, 61
McCarthy, Signalman Daniel 'Mac', 74–5, **75**,
 95, 124, 244
 Edith (mother), 57, 74–5, 95, 244
 Evelyn Almer [?], 244
McDonald, Driver Neil George, 177, 230–1,
 230, 244
 Margaret Cardno (wife), **230**, 244
McElduff, Miss, *see* McNicholl, Lance Corporal
 Daniel: Miss McElduff (friend)

McNicholl, Lance Corporal Daniel, 82–3, **83**, 228, 230, 232, 244
  Ebeth Irvine [?Irving] (girlfriend), 154
  Miss McElduff (friend), 154
  Rose (mother), 244
McNicol, Signalman Alex, 246
McOstrich, Lieutenant Colonel, 120
McWhirter, Corporal Robert 'Bobby' C., 82, 124, 228, 230, 232, 239, 244
  Sheila McColm (fiancée), 244
MI10 (Technical Intelligence), 237
Milner, Lieutenant Colonel Selby, 78, 82, 84, 91, 93, 106–7, 111, 117, 120–5, 188
Ministry of Supply, 99
Minshull, Signalman C. Andrew 'Andy', 8, 221, 244
Moffatt, Jonathan, 238
Moffatt, Miss, 154
Monaghan, Signalman Hugh, 246
Montgomery, Field Marshal, 46
Morris, Signalman Hugh B., 244
Mountbatten, Lord Louis, 202
Murray, Signalman George Archibald Brown, 246
Murrell, Signalman Ronald M., 8, 117, 125, 217, 228, 231–2, 244
  Mrs M.E. (mother), 217, 244

N Party, Changi to Thailand, 78
Nagasaki,184, 193, 195
Nairn, Signalman H., 26–7, 43, 245
  Ellen (wife), 27, 39, 43, 245
Nakhon Nayok, xiii, 188, 190, 196–7, 207, 238
Nam Chon Yai Camp, *see* 211 kilo Camp [Nam Chon Yai]
Nanking, 29
National Archives, The, 82, 238
National Children's Home, 171
News Chronicle, 213
Newton, Signalman Arthur H., 77, 171–2, 223–4, 228, 245
  Alice Lane (grandmother), 171–2, 224–5, 245
  Gay Webb (friend), 245
Noguchi, Captain, 121–3, 188, 195
Nong Pladuk, 79, 106, 130, 227
Nottingham, 149, 218, 225

O'Dea, Miss, 154
O'Donnel, Signalman H. P., 77, 245
O'Neill, Corporal James 'Sally', 246
Orduña, SS, 212, 214–16
Orontes, SS, 16

Osaka PoW Camp, 171
Ossett, 149

Pallard, Joyce, *see* Tomkinson, Signalman David Lloyd; Joyce Pallard (fiancée)
pantuns, Malay poems, 17, 119
Pargeter, Lieutenant Colonel, 47
Parit Sulong, 45
Parker, Driver Ernest Bernard, 8, **9**, 115, 117, 177, 221–2, **222**, 228, 232, 239, 245
  Marjorie (wife), 115, 221–2, **222**, 239, 245
Paterson, Yvonne (née Koster), 65, 213, 215
Pawson, Sergeant Eric W., 15, 221, 228, 232, 245
Peacock, Major Basil, Royal Artillery, 163
Pearl Harbor, 33–4, 37, 62
Penang, 3, 16, 21, 35
pensions, 58
Percival, Lieutenant-General Arthur, 36, 49, 61
Perret, John, 149, 233, 240–1
  Dorothy (wife), 241
Perry, R. G., 154
Perth, Australia, 46
Peters, Signalman S., 246
Philippines, 240
Philips Electronics Company, 241
Phipps, Mrs, 154
Pike, Driver W., 245
Plane, Driver John 'Jack', **177**, 245
  Elizabeth E. (mother), 245
Plymouth, 7
Pompong, 49
Portsmouth, 7–8, 171, 224
Post Office, 40, 68, 75, 134, 143, 166
  British Postmaster General, 64, 67, 129
  Post and Telegraph Co, Malaya, 19, 30–1, 46–7, 60
Postma, Joop, 157, **158**
Potter, Signalman Thomas, 118, 171, 173–8, 181–4, 225, 228, 239, 245
  Mrs G. M. (wife), 171, 174–5, 245
Povey, Signalman 'Nobby', 94, 245
  Hilda (wife), 94, 245
  Katie L. Norris (sister), 245
Prang Kasi, 120, 161
Prentis, Roger Elvey, 17–8, **18**, 49, 63–4, 73, 102, 116, 193, 201
  Joyce 'Joy', 17–8, **18**, 49, 64, 98, 102, 201
Preston, 152–3
Prince of Wales, HMS, 34, 62
Prisoner List, The, 178

Puddletown, 9–10, 15
Pye Ltd, 241

RAMC, *see* Royal Army Medical Corps (RAMC)
Randle, Signalman Horace, 78, 152, 245
    Vera (wife), 152, 245
Rangoon, 199–201, 211–12, 213–14, 231, 233
RAPWI, *see* Repatriation of Allied Prisoners of War and Internees (RAPWI)
RASC, *see* Royal Army Service Corps (RASC)
RCOS, *see* Royal Corps of Signals (RCOS)
Reckie, Captain, 164
Red Cross, 57, 65, 73, 137, 140, **169**, 172, 195, 224, 228
    American Red Cross, 208
    journal, *Far East*, 153, **219**
    Thai Red Cross, 176
Renfrew, Sergeant Arthur, 246
Repatriation of Allied Prisoners of War and Internees (RAPWI), 221
Repulse, HMS, 34, 62
Riley, Signalman Walter Geoffrey 'Geoff', 173–4, 239
    Stephen J. (son), 174, 239
Rintin Camp, 120
Roberts, Miss, 154
Robinson, Miss, 154
Rogers, Mr, War Office, 172, 174–5, 182–4, 193
Rose Hill School, 128, 200
Royal Army Medical Corps (RAMC), 122, 124, 138
Royal Army Ordnance Corps (RAOC), 246
Royal Army Service Corps (RASC), 157, 239, 245
Royal Artillery, 163, 245, 246
Royal Corps of Signals (RCOS), 3, 8, 27, 46, 57, 75, 114, 135, 152, 155, 164, 171, 175, 179, 182, 223, 243–6
    10 Line Section, 8
    27 Line Section (RCOS), *see* under number 27 above
    39 Line Section, 8
    4th North Midland Signals, 8
    5th A/A Group (M) Signal Unit, 174
    M. Section 1 Company 11th Division, 228
    No. 1 Company, 8, 70
    Royal Signals Association, 43, 97, 154, 170
    Royal Signals Museum, xiii
    Royal Signals Records, 43, 55, 57, 75, 115, 129

Royal Engineers, 46, 59
Royal Military College, Shrivenham, 237
Russell, Signalman Leonard Charles, 118, 170, 177, 217–18, **218**, 225, 228, 245
    May (wife), 170, 177, 218

S'Pore, *see* Singapore
Sagano, Renichi, Japanese engineer & photographer, **110**
Saigon Camp, 231
Sampson, Lance Corporal Peter, **56**, 82, 225–6, 229, 231, 238, 245
    Helen (wife), 226, 245
    Margaret (mother), 56, 226, 245
San Francisco, 134, 143–4, 146, 169, 181, 193, 201–202, 204–206, 208, 210, 220
Sandakan PoW Camp, 171–2, 223–4
Scott, Colonel, 78
Scott, Major, 234
Selarang Incident, 69
Shaw, Driver Percy 'Pip, Perce', 19, **21**, 204, 245
    Mrs E. (mother), 19, 204, 245
Shrivenham, *see* Royal Military College, Shrivenham
Signals Association, *see* Royal Corps of Signals; Royal Signals Association
Sinclair, Signalman David, 228, 232, 245
    Annie (mother), 245
    Ernest (brother), 245
Singapore, 5, 17–19, 29, 34–6, 38, 40, 46, 50, 57–59, 62, 65, 68–9, 72, 77, 79, 87, 94, 132, 148, 193, 225–6, 228, 230, 239
    Fall of, 37, 49–51, 55, 57, 63, 68, 88, 115, 154, 239
    Town, 7, 17–18, **18**, 29, 34, 46–9, 57, 59, 68, 78, 227
Smijth-Windham, Helen, 65, 103–104, 137
    Colonel William 'Smidge' (husband), 65, 103, 137
Smith, Sergeant, RCOS, *Hofuku Maru* survivor, 175, 178, 184
    wife, 175, 178
Southampton, 7, 8, 227
Southern Command Signals, 10
Special Reserves, Scotland, 8–9
speedo, 121–2, 183, 221
Sri Akar, Tengku, 6
Stephenson, Patrick H., 149–50, **150**, 157, 233, 240–1
Stettin [Szczecin], 99

Stewart, Corporal James, **81**, 82, 166, 231, 239, 245
  William (father), 166, 245
Stewart, Lance Corporal James Albert, 164–6, **166**, 175, 246
  James (father), 164, **166**, 175
Stockport, 228
Stockton, 244
Straits Volunteer Force, 246
Stranraer, 166, 229
Subic Bay Memorial, 240
Suddaby, Roderick, 130
Suez, 215–16
Sumatra, 59, 155
surgery, *see* Markowitz, Dr Jacob
Swinton, Lieutenant Colonel, 77

Taiwan, *see* Formosa [Taiwan]
Takanoon, Tarkanun, *see* Tha Khanun
Takilen, *see* Tha Kilen
Tamarkan [Tha Makham], 82, 106, 125, 175, 177, 186
Tamuang, 82
Tarsao [Tha Sao], 120, 125
Taunton Thespians, 237
Taylor, Gunner James 'Jim', 246
Taylor, Michael, *see* Hobson, Signalman George; Michael Taylor (great-nephew)
Taylor, Signalman John 'Jack' A. 'Cowboy Ted', 19, **21**, 56, 229, 231, 245
  Jessie W. (wife), 56, 231, 245
TBRC, *see* Thailand-Burma Railway Centre (TBRC)
Telegraph, The Daily, 67, 202
tenko, 82, 84, 121, 187
Territorial Army (TA), 8
Tett, David, 58
Tha Khanun, 79, 120, 122–5, 136, 161, 168
Tha Kilen, 93, 106, 222, 238
Tha Makham, *see* Tamarkan [Tha Makham]
Thailand-Burma Railway Centre (TBRC), 110, 141, 188
Thanbyuzayet, 79
theatre, PoW productions
  'Café Colette Show', 159
  'Cinderella', 162–3, 200
  'Hay Fever', 157, 159, 200
  'King's Carols', 162
  'Lichten Op', **158**
  'Love Thais', **161**
  'Major Barbara', 200
  'Night Must Fall', 159, **160**
  'Outward Bound', 163, 200
  'Wonder Bar', 157, **159**
Thomas, Sir Shenton, 36
Three Pagodas Pass, 79, 106
Tilbury Docks, 219
Times, The, 206, 210, 213
Tobruk, 46
Tomkinson, Signalman David Lloyd, 77, 168, 223, 245
  Joyce Pallard (fiancée), 168, 245
  Mr and Mrs F. (parents), 168, 223, 245
Toosey, Lieutenant Colonel, 186
Tootal, John Walton's Bleach-works, 167
Toyama Camp, 227
troopships, 15, 16, 92, 200–201, 212, 214-16, 239, see also hellships, Japanese
Tunbridge Wells, 128

United States Air Force (USAF), 190, 199

Vienna, 237

Wakeling, Signalman C. 'Ginger', 82, 224–5, 245
  Kate (mother), 224–5, 245
Walls, Lance Corporal John J. 'Scotty/Jock', 8, **165**, 176–7, 229, 232, 245
  Ellen (wife), 177, 245
  Jean Irvine (sister), 245
Walstow, Signalman A. E., 118, 245
Walton-on-Thames, 94
Wampo Viaduct, 106–111, **107**, **109**, **110**, 111, 118–20
Wang Lan, 82, 84, 91
Wang Pho, *see* Wampo Viaduct
war crimes, 187–8
War Office, 55–8, 64, 88, 97, 129, 137, 145, 152–6, 164–72, 174–6, 181–4, 193, 222–4
Watson, *see* Hunt, Sergeant Gordon Leonard; Mr Watson (brother-in-law)
Wavell, General, 46, 62
Wensleydale Heifer, The, 3, 210, 220
White, Lance Corporal William 'Jock', RASC, 239
  Joanne McQuillan (granddaughter), 239
Whitton, Driver Lawrence 'Larry/Lol', 19, **21**, 118, 170–71, **170**, 177, 226–8, 232, 239, 245
  Mr and Mrs M. E. Robinson (parents), 226–7, 245
  Olive (wife), 170–71, 177, 226–7, 245

Wilder, Signalman William, PoW artist, **109**
Wilson, Signalman Charlie 'Chuck', 19, **21**, **124**, 245
    Mrs (mother), 245
Wire, Royal Signals Magazine, 23
Women's Institute, 237
Wood, Christine, 239, see also Parker, Driver Ernest Bernard

Woodend, Driver J. Alf 'Dabber', 118, 177, 227–8, 245
    Mrs A. (mother), 245
Wye, Kent, 22, 26, 30–31, 41, 45, 66–7, 96–7, 103, 200–201, 234

Yokohama, 227
Youth Centre (YMCA), Taunton, 237